LEGITIMACY AND COMPLIANCE
IN CRIMINAL JUSTICE

Ques   tice
syste   the
essent   ness
of cri   s of
legiti   nce
remai   erto
negle   the
effect   t be
enha

T   r of
conn   s of
crimi   bate
that c   ving
toget   ing,
anti-s   ing,
impri   cory
and c   ime
contr

T   s to
comp   ness
and l   be
invalu   inal
justic   tice
practi

Adar   for
Crim   and
Justic   ject
and P   ces
and Ljusticand c

Anthea Hucklesby is Reader in Criminal Justice and Deputy
for Criminal Justice, University of Leeds. Her research interests
criminal justice process and its treatment of suspects, defendants and offenders.

LEGITIMACY AND COMPLIANCE IN CRIMINAL JUSTICE

*Edited by Adam Crawford and
Anthea Hucklesby*

Routledge
Taylor & Francis Group

NEW YORK AND LONDON

First published 2013
by Routledge
2 Park Square, Milton Park, Abingdon, Oxon, OX14 4RN

Simultaneously published in the USA and Canada
by Routledge
711 Third Avenue, New York, NY 10017

Routledge is an imprint of the Taylor & Francis Group, an informa business

British Library Cataloguing in Publication Data
A catalogue record for this book is available from the British Library

Library of Congress Cataloging in Publication Data
Legitimacy and Compliance in criminal justice/edited by Adam Crawford
    and Anthea Hucklesby.—1st ed.
    p. cm.
    Includes bibliographical references and index.
    1. Criminal justice, Administration of. 2. Compliance. I. Crawford,
    Adam.
    II. Hucklesby, Anthea.
    HV7419.C66 2012
    364.068'1—dc23   2011050780

ISBN: 978-0-415-67155-2 (hbk)
ISBN: 978-0-415-67156-9 (pbk)
ISBN: 978-0-203-11399-8 (ebk)

Typeset in Bembo by
Florence Production Ltd, Stoodleigh, Devon

CONTENTS

LIST OF ILLUSTRATIONS

Figures

Tables

NOTES ON CONTRIBUTORS

Ben Bradford is a Career Development Fellow in Criminology at the Faculty of Law, University of Oxford. He was formerly a LSE Fellow at the Methodology Institute, London School of Economics. His research applies issues of trust and legitimacy to the police and other criminal justice institutions.

Valerie Braithwaite is a Professor in the Regulatory Institutions Network in the School of Regulation, Justice and Diplomacy at the Australian National University, Canberra, where she studies psychological processes in regulation and governance.

Adam Crawford is Professor of Criminology and Criminal Justice at the Centre for Criminal Justice Studies, University of Leeds and Director of the Security and Justice Research Group of the Building Sustainable Societies Transformation Project at the University of Leeds.

Mike Hough is Director of the Institute for Criminal Policy Research. Mike has published on a range of criminological topics including probation work, youth justice, policing, crime prevention and community safety, anti-social behaviour, probation and drugs. He was the President of the British Society of Criminology (2008–2011).

Anthea Hucklesby is Reader in Criminal Justice at the Centre for Criminal Justice Studies, University of Leeds. Her research focuses on criminal justice responses to suspects, defendants and offenders. Her recent work has included empirical studies of electronic monitoring, bail support schemes and pre-charge bail.

Jonathan Jackson is a Senior Lecturer in Research Methodology at the Methodology Institute and member of the Mannheim Centre for Criminology at the LSE. Jon would like to thank Cambridge's Institute of Criminology and New York University's Department of Psychology for hosting him during the period in which he was working on this chapter.

Doreen McBarnet is Professor of Socio-Legal Studies at the University of Oxford. She is a member of the Centre for Socio-Legal Studies and Fellow of Wolfson College, Oxford. From 2008 to 2010 she was a Visiting Professor at Edinburgh Law School.

Fergus McNeill is Professor of Criminology and Social Work at the University of Glasgow. Prior to becoming an academic in 1998, Fergus worked for a number of years in residential drug rehabilitation and as a criminal justice social worker.

Katherine Murray is a PhD research student at the University of Edinburgh, studying trust and confidence in the police in Scotland. Her work focuses on public perceptions of procedural fairness, reporting crime, policing ethics and Human Rights in policing.

Mike Nellis is Emeritus Professor of Criminal and Community Justice at the Law School at the University of Strathclyde. He has written widely on the work of the Probation Service, including its relationship with voluntary organisations, and on alternatives to prison, particularly electronic monitoring.

Gwen Robinson is Reader in Criminal Justice in the Centre for Criminological Research at the University of Sheffield. Her research focuses on offender rehabilitation and management, community sanctions/penalties and restorative justice.

Sonja Snacken is Professor of Criminology, Penology and Sociology of Law in the Faculty of Law and Criminology at the Vrije Universiteit Brussel, Belgium. During the academic year 2010–2011 she held a Straus Fellowship at the Institute for Advanced Study of Law and Justice at New York University.

Tom Tyler is Professor of Psychology in the Department of Psychology at New York University. He also holds a Professorship in New York University's School of Law.

ACKNOWLEDGEMENTS

We would like to thank all the contributors for their work and their forbearance in the realisation of this project. We are grateful to our colleagues at the Centre for Criminal Justice Studies at the University of Leeds for their kind assistance in hosting the conference out of which this collection originally arose, especially Sam Lewis and Stuart Lister who both assisted significantly in the organisation of the event. We would also like to acknowledge the generous financial support of the School of Law at the University of Leeds which enabled us to bring together such a gathering of prominent international scholars. Many thanks to Julia Willan and Nicola Hartley for their patience and their support in bringing this collection to fruition.

INTRODUCTION

Compliance and legitimacy in criminal justice

Adam Crawford and Anthea Hucklesby

> Force is a physical power; I do not see how its effects could produce morality. To yield to force is an act of necessity, not of will; it is at best an act of prudence. In what sense can it be a moral duty? . . . If force compels obedience, there is no need to invoke a duty to obey, and if force ceases to compel obedience, there is no longer any obligation . . . Surely it must be admitted, then, that might does not make right, and that the duty of obedience is owed only to legitimate powers.
>
> (Rousseau 1968: 52–3)

Legitimacy lies at the heart of all forms of government. As Jean-Jacques Rousseau implied, legitimate authority is different from mere force or coercion. For him (1968: 49), the 'social contract' itself provides (and was explicitly advanced as providing) an answer to the fundamental question of how to render legitimate both power and constraint; the 'chains' that bind 'peoples born free'. At first sight one might assume, from Rousseau, that criminal justice and policing, as elements in the coercive arm of the state, demand little further legitimation, as their legitimacy derives, at least in large part, from the very fact that they act in response to perceived, actual or anticipated breaches of the social contract. Nevertheless, as both key elements of state authority and central symbols of sovereign power, institutions of crime control are fundamentally part of a broader moral enterprise designed to influence human behaviour through more than compulsion. They constitute institutions of political authority that seek to govern through broad public consent. Furthermore, their efficacy and effectiveness demand conferred consent by those individuals who are subjected to systems of power. Legitimate social arrangements will generate commitments to compliance, where levels of trust and confidence exist in both systems of authority and those that operate them. As such, the legitimacy demands with regard to policing and criminal justice are especially great, precisely because: first, coercion is evident and, second, the potential consequences for constraints upon individual liberty are frequently more significant in crime control than other areas of public policy. Like other forms of authority and power, systems of crime control seek to generate commitments to compliance and cooperation. In this, judgements about the legitimacy of legal authorities – people and systems – are crucial to why people obey the law and comply with decisions taken. Tyler (2006) identifies two forms of legitimacy in this context. First, personal legitimacy resides in the competency and honesty of legal authorities. Second, institutional legitimacy exists where the role of legal authorities entitles them to make decisions which ought to be deferred to, complied with and obeyed. According to Tyler and Huo (2002; and Tyler in this volume), the relationship between the legitimacy of legal authorities and personal experiences resides in judgements that the agents of the legal authority have treated them with respect and in a procedurally just manner. Experiencing the law and legal authorities as legitimate has positive implications for compliance.

Whilst criminal justice is ultimately bound up with coercive power, force and compulsion – the policing of, and decisions over, citizens – these rely inherently upon a considerable degree of 'quasi-voluntary compliance' on the part of citizens. As many of the contributions to this collection of essays seek to demonstrate, such consent is not purely self-interested or instrumental but also has a normative base, strongly linked to perceptions of legitimacy. It is important because the coercive powers of criminal justice officials and police officers are themselves limited and only used as an option of last resort. Most human interactions occur in the 'shadow of the law' (Mnookin and Kornhauser 1979) rather than through its machinations. The police invariably rely upon citizens – even as 'potential suspects' – assisting the police with their enquiries, courts' rulings depend upon offenders fulfilling their sentence (be it payment of fines, compensation or community-based penalties) and prisons could not operate if offenders did not conform to the prison regime most of the time. Furthermore, tax authorities rely most of the time on people paying their taxes in conformity with the prevailing rules. It is only if compliance breaks down that there is recourse to coercive legal powers and sanctions. Consequently, criminal justice professionals routinely anticipate and work upon the assumption that the citizenry as a whole will generally observe directions given; they will comply. Police, in particular, depend on the authority that police officers can invoke, rather than the coercive force that they can deploy (if the contingencies demand so doing). Given the limits of coercive power, authorities must depend upon 'consensual' deference to their decisions by most of the people they interact with most of the time. Ultimately, conformity and deference to authority are necessary and prevailing assumptions. As such, legal systems are heavily dependent upon voluntary or quasi-voluntary compliance and cooperation. As Tyler notes:

> Authorities need to have people take the obligation to obey the law onto themselves and act voluntarily on that perceived obligation . . . Hence, efforts to understand the effective exercise of legal authority inevitably lead to a concern with the attitudes towards authorities that exist in the general

population, rather than to an exploration of the coercive resources available to legal authorities.

(1998: 272)

Legitimacy, as Weber (1978) noted, constitutes important moral glue that informs people's internal motivational systems and guides their behaviour. Legitimacy speaks to, and derives from, intrinsic motivations which foster self-regulation. It encourages the internalisation of social norms and values. As such, people are not only self-interested but also moral agents, who as active decision-makers are 'co-operative and obedient on grounds of legitimacy as well as reasons of prudence and advantage' (Beetham 1991: 27).

This book arose out of an international colloquium held at the Centre for Criminal Justice Studies in the University of Leeds on 25–26 June 2009 under the title 'Legitimacy and Compliance in Criminal Justice'. It was generously sponsored by the University of Leeds, Law School's strategic development fund. This allowed us to invite an impressive cast of key international scholars to participate in the initial deliberations and for many of them to work up their reflections and thoughts into the current essays in this collection. Early drafts of all the chapters published here were first presented and discussed at the conference. On behalf of all the contributors, we would like to thank all those who attended the colloquium and contributed to the various deliberations and discussions over the two days, in particular: Catherine Appleton, Tony Bottoms, Valerie Braithwaite, Philip Hadfield, Mike Hough, Jon Jackson, Susanne Karstedt, Sam Lewis, Stuart Lister, Doreen McBarnet, Fergus McNeill, Andy Myhill, Mike Nellis, Paul Quinton, Gwen Robinson, Joanna Shapland, Clare Sims, Sonja Snacken, Richard Sparks, Peter Traynor, Tom Tyler, Clive Walker and David Wall. We are grateful to our colleagues at the Centre for Criminal Justice Studies in the Law School at the University of Leeds for their assistance in the organisation and hosting of the initial conference.

The aim of the original symposium and this volume of resultant essays was to explore a number of connected themes relating to compliance, legitimacy and trust in different areas of criminal justice and regulation, and in doing so to draw together contributions from leading scholars in the fields of criminology, psychology and socio-legal studies in an inter-disciplinary dialogue and debate. Collectively, the essays attempt to consider conceptual and normative, as well as descriptive and empirical themes and questions. The prescience and timeliness of such a careful conceptual reflection upon the related themes of compliance and legitimacy, which inform this book, has been heightened by the confluence of a number of wider policy shifts and intellectual debates over recent years. First, the emergent acknowledgement of the limited capacity of the sovereign nation-state to act as the sole guarantor of order and monopoly of coercive force (Garland 2001) and the ineffectiveness of institutions of criminal justice to meet their own explicit aims of rehabilitation, reform and prevention have prompted both legitimacy deficits and the quest for alternative modes of regulation and crime control. Consequently, we have seen a growing interest in plural forms of regulation, both within but also beyond the role of formal law and the nation-state. Developments in regulation have opened up possibilities for multiple sites and modes of regulation of conduct through non-state, as well as state, auspices, operating through networks and hybrid alliances. These have raised new opportunities for, and questions about, the exercise of power, control and compliance, as well as the legitimacy of the sources of authority. They have also prompted questions about the effectiveness, responsiveness and coherence of diverse systems of regulation. Second, there has been a growing body of research-informed knowledge about alternative, and perhaps more subtle, ways in which governments, public, quasi-public and private authorities can and might influence personal behaviour and the role of technology and design therein. New opportunities for modes of regulation and controls are being fostered by technological advances and novel architectural (in its broadest sense) arrangements. The study of individual behaviour and personal responsibility has been stimulated by considerable theoretical insights from sociology, social psychology and behavioural economics in particular. Third, there has been a growing desire on the part of governments to enhance personal responsibility and individual control, emphasising customer sovereignty and consumer satisfaction (responsiveness) in wide-ranging arenas of public policy reform from healthcare through to criminal justice. Fourth, important conceptual insights have been provided by regulatory scholars in the development of notions of 'responsive regulation' and 'procedural justice' with considerable implications for thinking about legitimacy and compliance in criminal justice and public policy more generally. Fifth, there has been a growing emphasis on enforcement particularly in terms of community sentences and licence conditions which have contributed significantly to growing prison populations around the world. This has provided greater impetus to seek alternative ways to bring about compliance within offender and potential offender populations. Finally, there has been a growing awareness and acknowledgement of the social implications of forms of legitimacy for understanding public attitudes and actions.

Consequently, legitimacy and compliance are both deeply implicated in and interconnected with each other in ways that require close conceptual scrutiny and empirical analysis and demand our attention in thinking about ways of better regulating people's behaviour and fostering conformity with prevailing social norms.

Organisation of the chapters

The focus of the first two chapters is on questions of legitimacy in the context of policing. Both chapters argue that a model of crime control based wholly on deterrence is misguided and connect with procedural justice theory to explore its implications for police work. Tom Tyler's chapter highlights the importance of, and basis for, citizen cooperation in effective crime control. Tyler engages with the paradox that whilst objective measures of police performance and professionalism have improved in the US, the public's support for the police has remained 'moderately positive' and stable over the last thirty years. He uses his procedural justice theory to suggest that public support for the police will improve if they view the police as legitimate, that is, fair, respectful and just. Consequently, the police should not only focus on outcomes such as clear up rates but also the ways in which they interact with the public. He argues that each encounter between police and the public should be viewed as a 'teachable moment' whereby the public learns something about the law and legal authorities. Consequently, the police need to regard public assessment about how the police (and other legal authorities) exercise their authority as crucially important, precisely because public experiences and views shape how they behave in interactions with the police. The chapter concludes with a discussion of the ways in which procedural justice values can be embedded in everyday police work.

In the second chapter, Jon Jackson, Ben Bradford, Mike Hough and Katherine Murray explore and test key concepts in 'procedural justice theory', linking these ideas to the relationship between legitimate policing and public commitments to the rule of law. Their focus is on policing in the UK, which they argue can be distinguished from policing in the US or Europe in a number of respects. They argue that this has implications for the way in which procedural justice theory can be applied in the UK, suggesting that distinctions need to be made between police legitimacy, legal legitimacy and self-reported compliance behaviour. Using empirical data, they suggest that police legitimacy is usually linked with greater compliance whilst also pointing out that there are exceptions to the rule. They concur with Tyler that applying procedural justice approaches to policing is likely to pay dividends in terms of increased compliance. However, they also warn that there may be a significant gap between theory and practice and that procedural justice might act as a veil to hide 'business as usual' for the police.

The first two chapters both suggest that the ideas surveyed therein have implications beyond policing to wider institutions of criminal justice. This is taken up by Sonja Snacken in her discussion on 'legitimacy' in the context of penal policies. In her chapter, Snacken examines the distinction between what she calls 'normative' and 'empirical' legitimacy of penal policies in democratic constitutional states. She discusses the tensions that arise between human rights, the rule of law and democracy. She examines a range of examples including the death penalty and prisoners' and victims' rights to demonstrate that the public is less punitive than is often portrayed. Furthermore, she highlights the importance of procedural justice in the opinions of the public and in the expectations of victims of crime. She concludes that governments and politicians would be able to implement less punitive penal policies without compromising political legitimacy.

The next two chapters examine the legitimacy and compliance issues raised by the banking crisis and payment of tax, respectively. The focus of both chapters is on the distinction between compliance and cooperation. They engage with debates about how businesses and individuals react to, and subvert, the legal constraints and regulatory frameworks placed upon them by the authorities. In the first of the chapters, Doreen McBarnet focuses on the nature of the compliance engaged in by big business. She suggests that creative compliance is the dominant culture of big business and those that have the resources to utilise the law to suit their own interests. She uses empirical data to support her argument that big business focuses its efforts on frustrating the purpose of the law whilst technically complying with it using a process which she terms 'legal engineering'. She explores the implications of her arguments for the efficiency of the law, the legitimacy of creative compliance strategies and wider moves towards holding business to account.

Valerie Braithwaite in her chapter uses the example of individuals' responses to requests from tax authorities to examine questions of individual compliance and the legitimacy of the whole tax system. She explores some of the strategies which are used to resist the power of authorities using the concept of motivational postures and suggests possible explanations for the actions of tax payers. She uses empirical findings to demonstrate the complexities involved in gaining the cooperation and not just the compliance of tax payers and why a 'one size fits all' regulatory strategy is likely to fail. She demonstrates why regulation is both a costly and a difficult enterprise in the face of forms of defiance in which people seek to protect their freedom. Understanding and appreciating such strategies is therefore pivotal in designing responsive modes of regulation. She concludes by arguing that forms of regulation that provide opportunities for negotiation, the exchange of views and mutual understanding are more likely to overcome problems of non-cooperation. They provide prospects for building cooperation through meaningful dialogue between those who enforce law and those expected to obey its will, and thus offer better platforms for consent, compliance and legitimacy.

The final four chapters focus on questions of legitimacy and compliance in relation to community sentences and anti-social behaviour interventions. In their chapter, Fergus McNeill and Gwen Robinson note that the role legitimacy plays in community sentences generally and compliance particularly is an important yet neglected aspect of policy and scholarly debates. They suggest that offenders' views of the legitimacy of community sentences are especially important in fostering active engagement with community sentences rather than simply formal compliance. They draw on their dynamic model of compliance (Robinson and McNeill 2008) and introduce the notion of 'liquid legitimacy' to explain how the legitimacy of, and compliance with, community sentences changes over the course of orders and examine how both are built, maintained and eroded during the lifetime of an order. They conclude by suggesting that where sanctions aim to foster change, the skills of practitioners – notably probation officers and social workers – are crucial in bridging the social distance between the 'punished' and those 'punishers'. However, they sound a cautionary note, warning that practitioners' scope for influence is also constrained by the conditions in which they work which can serve to limit the quality and the authenticity of the practitioner's moral performance thus weakening their legitimacy.

Anthea Hucklesby draws on an empirical study of electronically monitored curfew orders to examine offenders' accounts of what influences their decisions to comply and how the working practices of monitoring officers' impact upon compliance. She highlights the complexities in offenders' decisions to comply with many factors influencing their decisions to comply, not all of which have been recognised sufficiently by existing theoretical approaches. She concludes by suggesting that an equally complex set of initiatives are required to improve compliance rates.

In his chapter, Mike Nellis suggests that questions of legitimacy and compliance raised by the introduction of increasingly sophisticated and new forms of techno-corrections have not been sufficiently elucidated or debated. He examines the potential issues – moral and ethical – raised by the use of implants by drawing on historical and contemporary materials and warns against complacency, urging us to actively debate and engage with the potential implications of the 'science fiction' of the future.

In the final chapter, Adam Crawford explores issues of legitimacy and compliance at the boundaries of criminal justice in the context of anti-social behaviour interventions with young people, where crime control interfaces with wider dynamics of public policy – including housing, education and welfare services – and interacts with civil legal interventions and multiple systems of behavioural regulation. He suggests that the novel technologies and tools of control spawned in the name of regulating anti-social behaviour present critical challenges for legitimacy and embody mixed assumptions about motivation and agency that inform possibilities of compliance. These assumptions he argues are particularly salient, yet often in reality decidedly confused, in relation to children and young people who are subject to diverse and inconsistent messages as to their competencies in their transition to adulthood. In line with the insights offered by all the authors in this collection, the chapter seeks to shed some light on the conceptual parameters and empirical issues that pertain to a more rigorous discussion and analysis of how we might understand and think about legitimacy and compliance in, and around, criminal justice.

References

Beetham, D. (1991) *The Legitimation of Power*, London: Macmillan.

Garland, D. (2001) *The Culture of Control*, Oxford: Oxford University Press.

Mnookin, R. H. and Kornhauser, L. (1979) 'Bargaining in the shadow of the law: The case of divorce', *Yale Law Journal*, 88: 950–99.

Robinson, G. and McNeill, F. (2008) 'Exploring the dynamics of compliance with community penalties', *Theoretical Criminology*, 12(4): 431–49.

Rousseau, J.-J. (1968) *The Social Contract* (trans. M. Cranston), London: Penguin Books.

Tyler, T. (1998) 'Trust and democratic governance', in V. Braithwaite and M. Levi (eds) *Trust and Governance*, New York: Russell Sage Foundation, pp. 269–94.

Tyler, T. R. (2006) *Why People Obey the Law,* Princeton: Princeton University Press.

Tyler, T. R. and Huo, Y. J. (2002) *Trust in the Law*, New York: Russell-Sage.

Weber, M. (1978) *Economy and Society* (edited by G. Roth and C. Wittich, first published in English 1968), Berkeley: University of California Press.

1

LEGITIMACY AND COMPLIANCE

The virtues of self-regulation

Tom Tyler

My goal in this chapter is to argue for a new approach to policing. I will focus my comments upon the United States, although I believe they apply more broadly. The 2004 National Academy of Science report on policing (Skogan and Frydl, 2004; Skogan and Meares, 2004) argued that in recent decades the objective quality of policing has improved in the United States. The police are more effective in fighting crime; they are less corrupt; and they are less likely to engage in unprofessional acts such as unlawfully shooting civilians. While there are many ongoing issues involving police performance, in particular in terms of the relationship of the police with minority communities, the overall impression given by the report is of increasingly professional and effective police departments and of more and more sophisticated policing practices. There is indeed a new professionalism in policing and it benefits all of those people, White or non-White, who will have contact with the police.

The paradox of policing in America today

Increases in the objective quality of policing notwithstanding, the other consistent finding of studies of the police is that over the last thirty years public support for the police – often indexed as 'trust and confidence' in the police – has been at best moderately positive. In 2009, the percentage of Americans expressing trust and confidence in the police was at 59 per cent (Sourcebook of Criminal Justice Statistics, no date). Second, that level of trust has been more or less unchanged in recent years. Between 1980 and 2009 it has generally ranged between 50 and 60 per cent.[1]

This discrepancy between the improving level of police performance and generally unchanging levels of public support suggests the need for a focus on the factors that shape public views about the legitimacy of the police. If public trust and confidence in the police is not linked to objective performance, the nature of trust and confidence needs to be addressed as a distinct question in and of itself. The issue is: 'What is the basis of perceived police legitimacy?' Understanding how public views about police legitimacy form and change can provide us with a new framework through which to evaluate policing policies and practices. That framework is the lens of public views on police legitimacy.

Current policing policies and practices reflect a psychological framework of social control referred to as deterrence: the use of or the threat of the use of punishment to motivate behaviour. This model shapes how the police behave in their everyday interactions with the public; it supports policies such as broken windows or zero tolerance policing (Kelling and Cole, 1996; Wilson and Kelling, 1982), and the resultant widespread use of police stops, fines, arrest and incarceration as a law enforcement strategy (Harcourt, 2001; Punch, 2007). By a forceful intrusion into people's lives, the police make it evident that those who break the rules can and will be punished. The use of such proactive high-discretion police street stops is emerging as a key strategy in major city policing efforts to manage crime in urban communities (Alpert *et al.*, 2005; Collins, 2007; Long, 2009).

One question is whether such policies are effective. Research is mixed concerning whether this model is effective, with police officials (Baker, 2009) and some researchers (Kubrin *et al.*, 2010) suggesting that these policies reduce robbery and homocide. The argument outlined here is that punishment – real or threatened – is not generally the best mechanism for policing if the goal of policing is to deter law-breaking (Tyler, 2007, 2008). This is first true both because punishment is not the best way to achieve compliance and because its use undermines willing deference and voluntary cooperation, both of which greatly aid the police in performing their jobs. This is not to say that deterrence is not found to lower the crime rate. Some studies suggest that it does (Nagin, 1998). However, those studies typically find at best a weak connection between the risk of punishment and rule breaking (MacCoun, 1993).

Further, the quality of police performance in fighting crime is not found to be the most important factor motivating public cooperation with the police (Sunshine and Tyler, 2003; Tyler and Fagan, 2008). Indicators of the rate of crime, personal fear of crime victimisation and/or police performance in fighting crime have, at best, a weak connection to public willingness to work with the police by reporting crime or participating in collective actions like community meetings and neighbourhood watch.

Over the last twenty years, research has shown that people obey the law and cooperate with legal authorities primarily if and when they view those legal authorities as legitimate (Tyler, 2006b). That legitimacy, in turn, is a product of how the police treat people and make decisions when they are exercising their regulatory authority. Fairness in decision making, that is, neutral and non-discriminatory behaviour, and fair interpersonal treatment are the key to securing cooperation. This message means that in this arena doing what is right (acting ethically) and doing what works converge. Realising that the fairness of police behaviour, not the fear of police force and the threat of punishment, drives public actions has dramatic implications for a range of policing policies, policies such as racial profiling and zero tolerance policing.

The framework of policing needs to be reconceptualised to focus upon how policing policies and practices impact upon public views about police legitimacy. The police need to select, train and reward officers with an eye to ensuring that police encounters with the public build legitimacy, a focus that leads to concerns about the quality of people's experiences not just their outcomes. Even legally trivial interactions, that is, situations in which a person is not arrested or incarcerated, can have a strong influence on people's views about the police.

This argument further suggests that we need to measure police legitimacy when evaluating the police and policing practices, and not just pay attention to arrest or clearance rates. This argument involves accountability to the public. It suggests that accountability includes focusing on how the public evaluates the police and then building policies and practices that reflect this public conception of justice and accountability. And studies of the public suggest clearly that the public holds the police to account for delivering justice (Tyler and Huo, 2002).

Legitimacy as an issue

How is perceived legitimacy assessed? A simple approach used in national surveys is the already mentioned 'trust and confidence' index, which asks people to express confidence in the police as an institution or in the ability of the police to protect citizens against crime and to otherwise do their jobs well.

As defined by scholars, legitimacy is typically argued to involve two core issues (Tyler, 2006a, 2006b). First, legitimacy involves the belief that police officers are trustworthy, honest and concerned about the well-being of the people they deal with. It is this aspect of legitimacy that is often described as 'trust and confidence' in the police and measured on national surveys to reflect legitimacy.

Second, legitimacy involves the belief that police authority ought to be accepted and people should voluntarily defer to police decisions and directives. As Skogan and Frydl suggest 'Legitimacy is a property that a rule or an authority has when others feel obligated to voluntarily defer to that rule or authority. In other words, a legitimate authority is one that is regarded by people as entitled to have its decisions and rules accepted and followed by others' (Skogan and Frydl, 2004: 297). From this perspective, the police are legitimate if people defer to their decisions and follow their directives (also see Tyler, 2007, 2008).

To address the question of the legitimacy of the police and policing practices among members of the public, there is a need to think about policing in a new way. This requires a focus on the influence of police policies and practices on the views that the public has about police legitimacy. In particular, there is a need to focus on the views of the minority community (Tyler, 2001).

How do people evaluate police practices?

From a legitimacy perspective every encounter that the public has with the police, the courts and the law should be treated as a socialising experience that builds or undermines legitimacy. Each contact is a 'teachable moment' in which people learn about the law and legal authorities. To understand the consequences of personal experiences for views about police legitimacy, it is important to consider what it is about their own personal experiences that the public considers when reacting to encounters with police officers.

People often assume that the primary issue to people dealing with legal authorities is their outcome, that is, if people receive a ticket they are upset, if not they are happy. But, what does research indicate about how people evaluate their personal experiences with the police? Fortunately, there are a number of research studies that explore personal experiences with the police (see Belvedere *et al.*, 2005; Bradford *et al.*, 2009; Gau and Brunson, 2009; Hinds, 2007, 2009; Mastrofski *et al.*, 1996; Reisig and Chandek, 2001; Sunshine and Tyler, 2003; Tyler and Huo, 2002; Tyler and Fagan, 2008). These studies suggest a different conclusion. They show that the primary issue shaping people's reactions to personal encounters with the police is whether or not the police exercise their authority in fair ways, something referred to as procedural fairness.[2]

Procedural fairness involves two issues. First, the fairness of decision-making, that is, whether the police are neutral, unbiased, and consistent in their application of rules and provide people with opportunities to explain their point of view about what the issues are and how they should be handled. Second, whether the police treat people fairly (i.e. are courteous toward people, are respectful of people and their rights) and trustworthy (i.e., they explain the reasons for their actions in ways that communicate a concern for the people with whom they are dealing). Overall, there are four procedural elements: voice, neutrality, respect and trust.

Studies consistently find that these procedural judgements have a stronger influence upon people's reactions to the police than do the outcomes of their experiences. People who feel fairly treated are more likely to view the police as legitimate and more willing to defer to their decisions and directives (Lind and Tyler, 1988; Tyler, 2003; Tyler and Lind, 2001).

This body of research can be illustrated using a study of police–citizen encounters in Oakland and Los Angeles (Tyler and Huo, 2002). In this study, 1,656 residents were interviewed about recent experiences with the police and/or the courts. This discussion will focus on those who dealt with the police, which is 85 per cent of those interviewed.[3] The question of concern is why people voluntarily deferred to decisions made by police officers, accepting those decisions willingly and feeling they should obey them. In the study, people were interviewed about several aspects of their experience: the favourability and fairness of the outcome; the fairness of police decision-making; the fairness of police treatment; and their willingness to accept the decisions made by police officers.

What shapes willingness to accept police directives during police stops?[4] In this study, people were somewhat more willing to accept police decisions that were favourable or that had fair outcomes.[5] However, they were more strongly influenced by procedural fairness. This includes whether or not they evaluated police decision-making to be fair and/or whether or not they evaluated the police as treating them fairly. In other words, the key issue shaping acceptance was the manner in which the police exercised their authority, not the favourability of the outcome. And, in particular, people paid attention to whether the police treated them fairly, with a secondary influence of whether or not they made decisions fairly.

What does this mean in practical terms? To get a sense, we can divide those stopped by the police into four groups along two dimensions: outcome favourability and quality of treatment.[6] The results of this analysis are shown in Table 1.1. They indicate that people are about 15 per cent more willing to accept decisions that are favourable, compared to those that are unfavourable. However, people are about 70 per cent more willing to accept decisions when they received fair treatment as opposed to when they receive unfair treatment, a difference found irrespective of whether the outcome was good or bad. Hence, while both factors matter, quality of treatment dominates people's reactions to personal encounters with the police.

This study further shows that procedural fairness is central to the reactions of people of all the ethnicities studied – White, African American, and Hispanic – to their personal experiences with the police.[7] Although minor differences in issues of concern between ethnic groups can be identified, the overall finding is that people of all groups want basically the same thing – procedural fairness – when dealing with the police (Tyler, 2005).

These findings are typical of this literature (Tyler, 2006a, 2006b, 2009). There is an especially strong influence of quality of interpersonal treatment upon people's reactions to their personal experiences with the police (Tyler and Huo, 2002). This includes influences of whether people feel treated with dignity and respect; whether they feel their rights are acknowledged; whether they believe that the authorities care about their needs and concerns; and whether they feel that they have had a chance to explain their situation/make their arguments to an authority who considers them when deciding what to do.

TABLE 1.1 Willingness to voluntarily accept decisions made by the police

Police stops (n = 521) DV = willingness to defer to the police	Outcome is	
	Favourable	Unfavourable
Treated fairly	87% (155)	73% (172)
Treated unfairly	15% (103)	3% (91)

Beyond the issue of regulation is the role of the police in problem solving. Tyler and Huo (2002) found that the primary reason that the police dealt with members of the public is that they responded to a call for service. While we might initially imagine that such calls would lead to more favourable interactions, their study found that the proportion of interactions that resulted in negative outcomes (in this case failures to solve the problem as opposed to receiving a ticket) was about the same with both types of encounter – approximately 30 per cent in each case. Hence, the same issue, in this case managing disappointment over failures to solve problems or manage disputes, occurs in the case of calls.

The issue of unmet expectations links into the insatiable demand for policing services. Public policing is essentially a free service for those who call upon the police, so there is potentially an infinite demand for police services. Unfortunately, too much demand upon limited resources leads to performance failures. And this problem has grown steadily as the public has increasingly seen the police as managing an expanding and broadening list of problems, ranging from incivilities to medical problems, all funnelled through readily available emergency services.

How can such expectations be managed? The findings of Tyler and Huo (2002) provide a suggestion. That study also includes interviews with people who dealt with the police because they called them. Here we can consider what influences satisfaction with the way the call was managed by the police.[8] Again, we might imagine that such satisfaction would reflect the outcome, that is, whether the problem was favourably resolved. However, this is not the case, as is shown by the analysis in Table 1.2. Just as with regulatory encounters, the primary issue shaping satisfaction was the quality of the interpersonal treatment that people experienced when dealing with the police.

And, more broadly the message is that the key issue to people is procedural fairness, that is, how they are treated and how decisions are made, not the outcome when they deal with the police. This is also true when the general views of people in the community are considered. However, at the institutional level, people focus upon both the quality of decision-making and the quality of treatment and weight these two aspects of procedural fairness more equally. There is something about disrespect that is especially central to personal experiences.

TABLE 1.2 Satisfaction following requests for police help

Calls to the police (n = 896) DV = Satisfaction	Outcome is	
	Favourable	Unfavourable
Treated fairly	98% (408)	65% (303)
Treated unfairly	19% (16)	5% (93)

Why is it important to care how people end up feeling about the police? Success in policing efforts depends upon gaining supportive public behaviour. This includes the already discussed deference to police orders. In fact, police researchers have noted that skill in 'handling the rebellious, the disgruntled, and the hard to manage' in ways that lead to compliance is the litmus test of the quality of a street officer's performance (Mastrofski *et al.*, 1996: 272). Based upon observational data, Mastrofski *et al.* estimate that the general public noncompliance rate when dealing with the police is around 22 per cent. As was noted in the last section, the nature of such public behaviour – whether people react to police orders with deference or defiance – depends upon how members of the public perceive the police and interpret police behaviour. If people evaluate police policies and practices as procedurally fair, they view the police as legitimate and accept their decisions.

More broadly, public judgements about police practices matter because the legal system relies upon widespread voluntary public compliance with the law and cooperation in police efforts to fight crime. Other studies suggest that such general compliance and cooperation is linked to overall assessments of the procedural fairness of policing policies and practices through the role of such judgements in shaping people's views about the legitimacy of the police (Sunshine and Tyler, 2003; Tyler and Fagan, 2008). Justice leads to legitimacy, which promotes compliance and cooperation. Hence, it is also important that those members of the public who have little or no personal contact with the police and the courts believe that those authorities generally exercise their authority through fair procedures.

Race and policing

In addition to the low general level of public confidence in the police, there has been a large and persistent racial gap in confidence. In 2000, a national Gallup poll suggested that White people were 27 per cent more likely to express confidence in the police (Gallup Polls, www.gallup.com), while a 2009 national United States Department of Justice survey reported that White people were 26 per cent more likely to express confidence in the police (Sourcebook of Criminal Justice Statistics, no date). Similarly a 2007 Pew Research Center study[9] suggested that White people are 29 per cent more likely to have confidence that the local police will enforce the law; 29 per cent are more likely to say that the police will not use excessive force; and 30 per cent are more likely to say that the police will treat all races equally.

Because of this clear evidence of racial differences in trust and confidence in the police any new approach to policing needs to address issues of race and policing. The interaction between Harvard Professor Henry Lewis Gates and Cambridge Police Sergeant James Crowley in July of 2009 has been suggested to have provided a teachable moment concerning race and policing in America.[10] This teachable moment should be about police practices in general, not just those directed toward the minority community. But given the high levels of mistrust within the minority community, it is a necessary focus of any discussion about policing.

The encounter between Gates and Crowley involved a misunderstanding in which Sergeant Crowley suspected that Gates might be a burglar, while Gates was actually entering his own home. Gates reacted with anger and was arrested. It has encouraged a great deal of public discussion because it touched on a wide variety of newsworthy issues related to race and policing. For the same reasons it provides an opportunity to address those issues, in a nation that Attorney General Eric Holder has characterized as being 'cowards' when it comes to discussing race-related topics.[11] But, as with any teachable moment, the key question is: 'What is the lesson to be learned?' The lesson is broader than just one of race relations, although they are central to the Gates incident. The message is that America's policing model for dealing with the people in all communities and of all ethnicities needs to change.

Immigration

A parallel area of increasing policing activity is immigration, that is, dealing with people who are both minority group members and often in the United States illegally. Here the same concerns exist but there has not been research in this area (Cornelius and Salehyan, 2007). Certainly the earlier work on Hispanics that was mentioned suggests that, like other ethnic groups, Hispanics are strongly affected by the procedural fairness they experience when dealing with the police (Tyler and Huo, 2002). This provides a framework through which to evaluate legal policies toward immigrants. For example, the use of local police forces to enforce immigration laws can be considered from the perspective of whether such laws undermine police legitimacy and make it more difficult for the local police to get cooperation from immigrant communities.

Dealing with minority group members or illegal immigrants does not require a distinct policing strategy. Rather, research suggests that everyone, White or minority, shares similar concerns. Everyone would like to receive fair treatment and to have decisions made through fair procedures. And, when they receive fairness, both White and minority group members of the community respond by deferring to and cooperating with the police, the courts, and the law.

Changing police practices

Can the police implement changes and develop practices that lead them to be viewed as fairer? The answer is clearly yes. First, many of the changes in police procedure needed are simple and easy to implement. They involve learning to provide people with opportunities for explanation before decisions are made, explaining how decisions are being made, allowing people mechanisms for complaint, and in particular treating people with courtesy and respect. These changes are inexpensive. Certainly in comparison to the costs of putting more officers on the streets or buying new technologies, these programmes would be low cost. Hence, these low-cost high-impact changes are a smart use of limited policing funds.

From a policy change perspective, the crucial question is why the police would want to implement these changes. Two assumptions are obstacles to change. First, the belief that the situations the police face are dangerous and that they are safer if they project force and dominate people and situations. While the argument that projecting force leads to safety is widely held, research does not support it (McCluskey, 2003). On the contrary, when the police react to perceived threats by displaying force, it often leads to escalations of conflict, while treating people with respect and explaining decisions lowers hostility and minimises conflict.

A second assumption is that projecting force, threatening to or making arrests, putting people in jail or prison are the best strategy of crime control. Research shows that, on the contrary, high legitimacy is more strongly linked to low rates of criminal behaviour than is creating a greater fear of being caught and punished by the police or the courts (Sunshine and Tyler, 2003; Tyler, 2006a; Tyler and Fagan, 2008). Further, studies demonstrate that the type of community cooperation that flows from high police legitimacy is important to efforts to control crime (Sampson *et al.*, 1997).

As has been noted, research findings raise doubts about both of these assumptions. A multi-pronged strategy for addressing them seems indicated. First, the counter intuitive research findings need to be reinforced through further studies, with a particular eye to finding results that will be compelling to the police. The belief that the projection of force protects officers and controls crime is central to the dominance of this model in policing strategies in America.

There are multiple aspects to any strategy for changing policing. The overall goal is to build police legitimacy by enacting policing procedures that the public views as procedurally fair.

The organizational culture of police departments is shaped by the values articulated by their leaders (Tyler *et al.*, 2007). This tone must, of necessity, involve attention to issues of crime control and citizen/officer safety. But it can also be about a broader set of issues that include the importance of building legitimacy through fair policing practices. Tone from the top needs to emphasise that the police should be professionals who are respected and who act to reassure and help the public to feel comfortable and safe as well as to enforce laws.

Further, leaders can articulate the benefits of building public support, benefits which include not only help in fighting crime and greater officer safety, but also general support for policing and for the community. People are more likely to come to and revisit communities in which they feel that they will be well treated by the representatives of government they are most likely to encounter – the police. This benefits communities economically because people more willingly come to them to work, to shop, as tourists and for entertainment and sporting events. Hence the police play a central role in creating the ambiance that makes a community inviting and desirable to the general public.

Leaders can further communicate that while the resort to force will always have a role in policing, that role should be as a last resort, with the police viewed as 'reluctant warriors'. This concept is not a new one. On the contrary, Sir Robert

Peel, who established the first police force in England in 1829, is famous for his nine principles of policing. The sixth principle is that 'Police should use physical force to the extent necessary to secure observance of the law or to restore order only when the exercise of persuasion, advice, and warning is insufficient.'[12]

To implement change, police training needs to emphasise the importance of framing policing actions when dealing with the public in terms of procedural fairness since building legitimacy is a goal of policing. While recent research findings point to the importance of citizen cooperation in effective crime control, traditional models of policing are built upon a compliance-based approach to dealing with people in the community. That approach leads officers to seek to dominate people and situations using the threat of force and punishment. Officers need to be trained in new approaches and the value of these approaches to their mission of crime control needs to be emphasised. This training should lead officers to frame every interaction as an opportunity to build or undermine legitimacy through quality treatment.

While training is important, police departments can also promote changes in policing by designing new operational guidelines. For example, it can become a part of police procedure for officers to carry and give to people a statement of police principles and procedures for filing complaints. This statement, which officers can both read to people and give them as a written brochure, should indicate that they have a right to have the reasons for the stop explained, to tell their side of the story before decisions are made, to have the laws and rules explained to them, to appeal decisions they disagree with, and to complain about unfair treatment.

Police reward structures also need to be reshaped so that building legitimacy in the community is viewed as a goal of equal importance to crime control. Police officer behaviour responds to the directives of the leadership, and tone from the top is crucial to communicating the need for a new approach to policing. If officers believe that their opportunities for advancement, their compensation, and the respect that they will have in the eyes of their leadership are linked to their ability to create legitimacy and motivate cooperation, then they are more likely to engage in procedurally just behaviour when on the street.

When thinking about reward structures in police departments, it is important to think beyond material rewards. Studies of work organisations suggest that the impact of material rewards generally flows through their role in signalling management respect for employees and their contributions to the workplace (Tyler and Blader, 2000). Employees, whether police officers or for-profit employees, want to know that they and their efforts are valued by their superiors (Tyler and Blader, 2000). Studies of police organisations suggest that one of the best ways to communicate respect to officers is to treat them with the same fairness that has already been outlined. When officers feel respected, they are more likely to follow workplace policies when they are out on the street (Tyler et al., 2007). And officer respect is built upon working in an environment in which they are treated fairly through fair decision-making procedures and fair interpersonal treatment.

In the case of policing practices on the street, the key point is that changes can be made that are easy to implement and not costly. However, officers need to be trained in these new approaches and they need to believe that adopting a new style of policing will be recognised by their superiors. Being able to reward the police in this new way requires the collection of new data on police legitimacy, both among those who have had personal experiences with the police and in the community more generally.

For most police departments, the crime rate is the only quantitative information that is available for benchmarking performance. If commanders had information on the impact of policing practices on legitimacy, that impact could also be considered in making decisions about whom to reward, promote, or reassign. Providing counterbalancing information on how policies and practices shape public views on police legitimacy would allow police leaders to reward performance that impacts on the legitimacy of the police in the community.

What do the police gain? First, they have a more efficient and viable strategy for managing public order. This better strategy is linked to capturing the cooperation of the public in all communities, White or minority. Second, they gain a safer and less hostile working environment. And, given political realities, emphasising gains to the police is central to changing police culture. Without police 'buy in' it is difficult to motivate changes in police behaviour. There needs to be a change in what the police want to do. Just as with the public, seeking to compel change through lawsuits and consent decrees is not particularly effective because the police then seek ways to avoid accountability. For example, the NYPD sought to avoid the study of racial profiling in their street stops by resisting providing information about who they stopped on the street to researchers (Fagan et al., 2009).

Currently the police focus on sanctions and force, which has two negative consequences. First, it undermines their ability to secure cooperation through legitimacy. Threat becomes the central focus on interactions with the public and the role of other values fades. Second, a force orientation undermines the relationship between the police and people in the community (Collins, 2007; Delgado, 2008). This is undesirable because the police want willing cooperation from the public.

It is possible to imagine two alternative dynamic models. The first begins with sanctions, which undermine the role of legitimacy and produce a need for the ever greater use of sanctions to secure compliance. This requires a larger police force and more prisons, and these requirements continue to grow as community compliance and cooperation diminishes. The police are gradually transformed into an occupying force, rather than partners with the community. Conversely, we can focus on legitimacy and build cooperation based upon legitimacy by emphasising procedurally just policing. This allows the role of sanctions to diminish and builds community cooperation. Over time, fewer police and prisons are needed and resources can be redirected to education and job creation, which lead to further reductions in the rate of crime.

One immediate reaction to the suggestion for change is to suggest that both models be enacted at the same time. The difficulty with this approach is that strategies involving force projection and securing compliance via threats undermines a legitimacy-based approach. First, when the police are primarily associated with threats and punishment, this undermines positive feelings about the police. Those feelings are central to building cooperation. Further, a sanction focus crowds out the role of values in shaping public behaviour by defining the relationship between people and the law as one of risk of apprehension and punishment, not as a link based upon shared values and civic virtue. Hence, it is difficult to build legitimacy within the current framework of policing (Tyler, 2007, 2008).

Identifying points of contact

Efforts to improve policing require identifying major points of citizen contact with the police and the courts.[13] We then need to evaluate these points of contact in terms of their impact upon public views. A focus on the content of experiences provides a basis for designing these experiences to create and enhance legitimacy and cooperation. The key point is to recognise that every contact socialises people because it communicates information about the legitimacy of the law and legal authorities. This is true both of personal encounters and of indirect experiences that occur when people learn about police behaviour from friends, family or the media.

The underlying assumption of this approach is that the quality of treatment and the quality of decision-making are distinct from the favourability or unfavourability of the outcome. Tyler and Huo (2002) illustrate this finding. In their study of police–citizen encounters, they found that the correlation between outcome favourability and quality of treatment was $r = 0.25$, while the correlation for quality of decision-making was $r = 0.28$. This suggests that there is considerable separation between these issues in everyday interactions with the police. Of course, the bulk of these interactions were everyday encounters, so we can still ask what the limits of this effect are. Further, we do not address the issue of repeated interactions. For example, with racial profiling one typical grievance is that minority males 16–25 believe they are stopped repeatedly by the police. These interactions, however experienced, may lead to the wider perception of being targeted as a group and through it to the broader belief that one and/or one's racial group are the victims of social injustice (see Tyler and Wakslak, 2004).

Personal contacts are especially important because the widespread use of police street stops involving minority adolescent and young adult males is emerging as a key strategy of urban police departments in their efforts to manage crime in major cities. There have recently been expansions in the use of street stops, as well as the use of fines, arrests; and incarceration by the police. For example, in New York City, the number of street stops went up 500 per cent from 2003 to 2007, although the crime rate was stable during this period (Fagan *et al.*, 2009). Such tactics are not unique to New York City and are also being used in other urban areas; for example, in Baltimore (Collins, 2007) and Chicago (Harcourt, 2001).

Recent anecdotal reports about police stops suggest that they have a negative impact especially in the minority community (Collins, 2007; Delgado, 2008; Taylor, 2006). The police are criticised because 'day after day, the cops continue harassing and degrading these innocent New Yorkers' and 'the people getting stopped and frisked are mostly young, and most of them are black or brown and poor' (Herbert, 2010). These comments about street stops parallel similar ongoing criticisms of the practice of racial profiling in motorist stops. The general suspicion that the police stop minorities disproportionally while driving has led to the expression 'being arrested for driving while Black'.

More generally, we need to understand that all types of experience, but especially those in childhood and adolescence, impact on values and behaviour. Contacts during this period both shape adolescent criminal behaviour (Fagan and Tyler, 2005) and are the precursors of adult anti-social behaviour (Lahey *et al.*, 2003; Rutter *et al.*, 1998). Contacts that are direct and those that are indirect (i.e., information about others) combine to create an overall assessment of the police, which then influences how people behave. The key question is identifying both which types of experiences and, with them, which aspects of those experiences, create or undermine values such as legitimacy.

Children and adolescents, in particular, are consumers in a marketplace of ideas, with parents, teachers, gangs and the media all trying to communicate a particular message about the police, the courts and the law (Fagan and Piquero, 2007; Fagan and Tyler, 2005). The views of the young are shaped by many factors, including family influences, schooling, peer groups and interactions with the police. Since adolescence, in particular, is a period in which adult orientations toward the law are formed, as well as a time in which considerable criminal activity occurs, understanding these pre-adult precursors of adult attitudes is crucial. While some evidence links adolescent procedural fairness and legitimacy judgements to criminal activity, further work on this issue is needed (Fagan and Tyler, 2005).

And, of course, studies need to explore the transition on views into adult attitudes and behaviours, all with particular reference to those groups in which legitimacy has been a particular concern of the police, that is, minorities. Those growing up in America, particularly in the minority community, experience conflicting pressures about the internalisation of the values that shape their behaviour toward the police. There are alternative values available – for example, through gang membership – and there may be community pressures against cooperation (anti-snitching norms are one example). Understanding how these messages shape legitimacy will provide the basis for strategies of effective law enforcement through legitimacy-based cooperation (Tyler, 2009).

The courts

While this essay has focused upon issues of policing, research on procedural fairness began in the context of studies of why people defer to decisions made by judges and other judicial authorities; for example, mediators (Lind and Tyler, 1988). That research suggests that people are very sensitive to how judicial authorities exercise their legal authority (Lind and Tyler, 1988; Thibaut and Walker, 1975). The most direct evidence of this sensitivity to procedural fairness comes from interviews with people who have been personally involved with the courts (Tyler and Huo, 2002).[14] Irrespective of why they are in court, people's reactions are most strongly shaped by whether they think they have received a fair 'day in court', in the sense that their concerns have been addressed through a just process (Tyler and Huo, 2002). The idea that people might be more interested in how their case is handled than they are in whether or not they win often strikes people as counterintuitive and 'wrong-headed'. Yet it is the consistent finding of numerous studies conducted over the last several decades.

Studies show that people use procedural fairness criteria to evaluate their experiences, and that they particularly focus on comparisons of their experiences to their views about appropriate ways for authorities to act when making decisions about how to resolve legal problems (Tyler and Huo, 2002). Of course, this concern about receiving a fair procedure does not mean that people do not care about the outcome of their case. They do care if they receive a favourable or fair outcome and no one is happy if they feel that they have received an unfavourable or an unfair outcome. However, studies consistently find that procedural fairness judgements are more central to people's willingness to accept the outcome of court cases than are outcome judgements (Tyler and Huo, 2002). And, this is true both with cases handled through formal trials and informal processes such as mediation. People recognise that in a dispute not everyone can receive the outcome they want or feel they deserve. Hence, they focus upon whether decisions about outcomes are made in fair ways. A fair process leads to an acceptable outcome.

What makes a process fair in the eyes of the members of the public? Four factors dominate evaluations of procedural fairness. First, people want to have an opportunity to state their case to legal authorities. They are interested in having a forum in which they can tell their story, that is, they want to have a voice.

Second, people react to evidence that the authorities with whom they are dealing are neutral. This involves making decisions based upon consistently applied legal principles and the facts of the case, not their personal opinions and biases. Transparency or openness about how decisions are being made facilitates the belief that decision-making procedures are neutral.

Third, people are sensitive to whether they are treated with dignity and politeness, and to whether their rights as citizens are respected. The issue of interpersonal treatment consistently emerges as a key factor in reactions to dealings with legal authorities. People believe that they are entitled to treatment with respect and react very negatively to dismissive or demeaning interpersonal treatment.

Finally, people focus on cues that communicate information about the intentions and character of the legal authorities with whom they are dealing. People react favourably to the judgement that the authorities with whom they are dealing are benevolent and caring, and are sincerely trying to do what is best for the people with whom they are dealing. Authorities communicate this type of concern when they listen to people's accounts and explain or justify their actions in ways that show an awareness of and concern about people's needs and concerns.

Further a recent study of the California state courts indicates that general public evaluations of the courts are dominated by procedural concerns (Rottman, 2005). Studies of general public views about the courts also reflect this procedural focus (Tyler, 2001). And, as is true with the police, the concerns of the White and minority communities are similar.

When people are dealing with a particular legal authority, they focus on whether they think that person is trustworthy and caring. They try to discern whether that person is concerned about their situation and is sincerely trying to do 'what is right' in the situation. Trust, in other words, is a key issue in personal experiences with judges and other court personnel. If people are not personally involved in a court case, but are generally rating their trust and confidence in the courts, they focus more on issues of neutrality, that is, whether they believe that judges are honest, make their decisions based upon the facts, and consistently apply the principles of law to everyone. In either situation, however, it is process-based evaluations that are central to people's reactions to the courts.

What is particularly striking about procedural fairness judgements is that they shape the reactions of those who are on the losing side of cases. If the person who does not receive an outcome that they think is favourable or fair feels that the outcome was arrived at in a fair way, they are more likely to accept it. And, studies conducted over time show that people continue to adhere to decisions arrived at fairly over time, suggesting that their acceptance of those decisions is genuine and not simply the result of fear or coercion (see Tyler, 2009). Further, people who experience procedural fairness in court rate the courts and court personnel more favourably, indicating higher levels of trust and confidence in the courts and the court system.

As noted above, these same procedural fairness judgements are also a key factor in the evaluations made by the general public of the courts as institutions. The findings of the recent California study of the courts are typical of studies of trust and confidence in the courts. For example, consider a national survey of public trust and confidence in state courts (Tyler, 2001). This study shows that public evaluations of state courts are based upon evaluations of the fairness of court procedures. In particular, people were sensitive to whether the courts protected their rights and to whether they thought that judges were honest. While these procedural fairness judgements were the most important factor shaping trust and confidence in the courts, those interviews were also sensitive to whether the courts treated the members of different groups equally, as well as to other structural issues about the courts. But, their primary basis for evaluation was the procedural fairness judgements noted.

What is especially striking about both the results of studies of personal experiences with the courts and the studies involving general evaluations of the courts (Tyler, 2008) is that these results are true irrespective of the ethnicity or race of the person involved, or of their economic or social status. Procedural fairness concerns are central to people's reactions to the court, irrespective of who the people are. Since ethnicity and economic status often shape people's views about what constitutes a fair outcome, it is especially striking that there is a general willingness to defer to fair procedures. And, there is also general agreement about what constitutes a fair procedure. The four elements outlined – participation, neutrality, treatment with dignity and respect, and trust in authorities – generally shape reactions to the courts irrespective of the type of person involved. The use of just procedures is, therefore, an ideal way to bridge differences in backgrounds among those who are disputing in court.

These findings have implications for the design of the courts. In particular, they suggest the value of building public trust and confidence by designing court procedures which lead the people who personally deal with the courts to have positive experiences. Based upon the recent California survey, efforts should concentrate on traffic, family and juvenile courts, where dissatisfaction is currently high (Rottman, 2005). And they should be directed at all of those members of the community who deal with the legal system, since the same survey indicates that jury duty, or serving as a witness, also educates people about the legal system.

This discussion began by noting a paradox in policing: improved performance without greater legitimacy. This situation in the courts is similar in that the courts are concerned about public views because of evidence that the public does not hold the courts in generally high regard. For example, the Sourcebook of Criminal Justice Statistics (no date) indicates that in 2007 a national sample of Americans found that 46 per cent of Americans gave local judges high or very high ratings for 'honesty and ethical standards'. This was lower than the rating of a similar national sample in 1999 in which 53 per cent gave local judges high or very high ratings for 'honesty and ethical standards'.

For this and other reasons,[15] court administrators have recently focused on designing court systems along the lines of procedural fairness so that they can build the trust and confidence of the public (Burke and Leben, 2008; Rottman, 2005, 2007, 2008). The California Courts, for example, have an initiative which involves creating 'Procedural fairness in the California Courts'. This initiative was inspired by independent research conducted by the California Courts which confirms the research findings already outlined in the context of people's experiences with the court system (Rottman, 2005). The initiative responds to a set of issues in the courts, including the increasing diversity of the population of California, increases in pro se representation, and public distrust of the courts. Its focus is on making every experience with the courts – as a litigant, a juror, etc. – one that contributes to building the legitimacy of the courts.

Conclusion

This is an ideal moment to consider transforming policing. If we put into place policies that encourage an approach to communities, particularly the minority community, in which public views are central, we are addressing the concerns of both the minority and the majority population. We can build upon that approach through adopting policing styles that motivate voluntary acceptance and willing cooperation on the part of the public.

The Gates–Crowley encounter has been referred to as a teachable moment about race and policing in America. And, Attorney General Holder has more generally noted the need for more dialogue among Americans on issues related to race. If this is a teachable moment, what is the lesson? One important lesson is that research consistently suggests that White people and minorities want the same thing from the police: fair treatment. Minorities are, however, more likely to say that they have not historically and do not now receive fair treatment. This perceived unfairness leads to lower legitimacy ratings, less deference to the law among minorities and lower levels of cooperation with the police. However, it is not important to distinguish between minority group concerns and the concerns of the White majority since those concerns are very similar.[16] Instead, we can broadly address public concerns.

Addressing public concerns involves reframing the way we think about the goals of policing. The police need to view public judgements about how they are exercising their authority when policing as a key concern. They need to focus upon how people evaluate the police and police actions. Why? Because public views shape how people behave in reaction to the police.

Finally, the arguments we are making have broader application. They are, first, true of people's dealings with the courts and other governmental agencies. More broadly, they speak to issues of incarceration and corrections.[17] The policies and practices of all these aspects of the legal system – policing, the courts, corrections – are built upon the same model that underlies America's strategies of regulation and that we are arguing is ineffective at best and counterproductive as worst. But, such a model can be supplemented with an approach that focuses upon legitimacy. That model we argue avoids many of the negatives of a sanction-based approach and has the virtue of building voluntary deference and cooperation among members of the public.

References

Alpert, G. P., MacDonald, J. M. and Dunham, R. G. (2005) 'Police suspicion and discretionary decision making during citizen stops', *Criminology*, 43: 407–34.

Baker, A. (2009) 'New York on track for fewest homicides on record', *New York Times*, December 29 .

Belvedere, K., Worrall. J. L. and Tibbetts, S. G. (2005) 'Explaining suspect resistance in police-citizen encounters', *Criminal Justice Review* 30(1): 30–44.

Bonta, J. and Gandreau, P. (1990) 'Reexamining the cruel and unusual punishment of prison life', *Law and Human Behavior*, 14: 347–66.

Bottoms, A. E. (1999) 'Interpersonal violence and social order in prisons', in M. Tonry and J. Petersilia (eds) *Crime and Justice: An Annual Review*, 26, Chicago: University of Chicago Press, pp. 437–513.

Bradford, B., Jackson, J. and Stanko, E. A. (2009) 'Contact and confidence: Revisiting the impact of public encounters with the police', *Policing and Society*, 19: 20–46.

Bukstel, L. and Kilmann, P. (1980) 'Psycological effects of imprisonment on confined individuals', *Psychological Bulletin*, 88: 469–93.

Burke, K. and Leben, S. (2008) 'Procedural fairness: A key ingredient in public satisfaction', *Court Review*, 44: 4–25.

Collins, R. (2007) 'Strolling while poor: How broken-windows policing created a new crime in Baltimore', *Georgetown Journal on Poverty Law and Policy*, 14: 419–39.

Cornelius, W. A. and Salehyan, I. (2007) 'Does border enforcement deter unauthorized immigration? The case of Mexican migration to the United States of America', *Regulation and Governance* 1: 139–53.

Davis, R. C., Henderson, N J. and Cheryachukin, Y. (2004) *Assessing Police-Public Contacts in Seattle*. New York: Vera Institute of Justice.

Delgado, R. (2008) 'Law enforcement in subordinated communities: Innovation and response', *Michigan Law Review* 106: 1193–212.

Fagan, J. and Piquero, A. R. (2007) 'Rational choice and developmental influences on recidivism among adolescent felony offenders', *Journal of Empirical Legal Studies*, 4(4): 715–48.

Fagan, J. and Tyler, T. R. (2005) 'Legal socialization of children and adolescents', *Social Justice Research*, 18(3): 217–42.

Fagan, J., Geller, A., Davies, G. and West, V. (2009) 'Street stops and broken windows revisited: The demography and logic of proactive policing in a safe and changing city', in S. K. Rice and M. D. White (eds) *Race, ethnicity, and policing*. NYU Press.

Franke, D., Bierie, D. and MacKenzie, D. L. (2010) 'Legitimacy in corrections', *Criminology and Public Policy*, 9: 89–118.

Gau, J. M. and Brunson, R. K. (2009) 'Procedural justice and order maintenance policing: A study of inner-city young men's perceptions of police legitimacy', *Justice Quarterly*, 1–25.

Gray, J. (2007) 'Fair decision making and legitimacy: the effects of treatment on compliance and outcome satisfaction in a sample of incarcerated males', unpublished doctoral dissertation. Carbondale: University of Souther Illinois.

Harcourt, B. (2001) *Illusion of Order: The false promise of broken windows policing*. Cambridge, MA: Harvard University Press.

Herbert, B. (2010) 'Watching certain people', *New York Times*, March 2.

Hinds, L. (2007) 'Building police-youth relationships: The importance of procedural justice', *Youth Justice* 7(3): 195–209.

—— (2009) 'Youth, police legitimacy and informal contact', *Journal of Police and Criminal Psychology*, 24: 10–21.

Holder, E. (2009) 'Remarks prepared for delivery by AG Eric Holder at the Department of Justice African American History Month Program', February 18.

Kelling, G. and Cole, C. (1996) *Fixing Broken Windows*. New York: Free Press.

Kubrin, C. E., Messner, S. F., Deane, G., McGeever, K. and Stucky, T. D. (2010) 'Proactive policing and robbery rates across U.S. Cities', *Criminology*, 48: 57–97.

Lahey, B. B., Moffitt, T. E. and Caspi, A. (2003) *Causes of Conduct Disorder and Juvenile Delinquency*. New York: Guilford.

Lind, E. A. and Tyler, T. R. (1988) *The Social Psychology of Procedural Justice*. New York: Plenum.

Long, C. (2009) 'Police stop more than one million people on street', *Seattle Times*, October 8.

MacCoun, R. J. (1993) 'Drugs and the law', *Psychological Bulletin*, 113: 497–512.

Mastrofski, S. D., Snipes, J. B. and Supina, A. E. (1996) 'Compliance on demand: The public's responses to specific police requests', *Journal of Crime and Delinquency*, 33: 269–305.

McCluskey, J. D. (2003) *Police Requests for Compliance: Coercive and procedural just tactics*. New York: LFB Scholarly Publishing.

Nagin, D. S. (1998) 'Criminal deterrence research at the outset of the twenty-first century', in M. Tonry (ed.) *Crime and Justice*, Vol. 23. Chicago: University of Chicago Press, pp. 1–42.

Petersilia, J. (2003) *When Prisoners Come Home: Parole and prisoner reentry*. Oxford: Oxford University Press.

Punch, M. (2007) *Zero Tolerance Policing*. Bristol: Policy Press.

Reisig, M. D. and Chandek, M. S. (2001) 'The effects of expectancy disconfirmation on outcome satisfaction in police-citizen encounters', *Policing: An International Journal of Police Strategies and Management*, 24(1): 88–99.

Rottman, D. B. (2005) *Trust and Confidence in the California Courts*. San Francisco: Office of the California Courts.

—— (2007) 'Adhere to procedural fairness in the justice system', *Criminology and Public Policy*, 6: 835–42.

—— (2008) 'Procedural fairness as a court reform agenda', *Court Review*, 44: 32–5.

Rutter, M., Giller, H. and Hagell, A. (1998) *Antisocial Behavior by Young People*. Cambridge: Cambridge University Press.

Sampson, R. J., Raudenbush, S. W. and Earls, F. (1997) 'Neighborhoods and violent crime: A multilevel study of collective efficacy', *Science*, 277: 918–24.

Skogan, W. G. and Frydl, K. (eds) (2004) *Fairness and Effectiveness in Policing: The evidence*. Washington, DC: The National Academies Press.

Skogan, W. G. and Meares, T. (2004) 'Lawful policing', *The Annals of the American Academy of Political and Social Science*, 593: 66–83.

Sourcebook of Criminal Justice Statistics online (no date) *Sourcebook of Criminal Justice Statistics online* Washington, DC: US Bureau of Justice Statistics. www.albany.edu/sourcebook.

Sparks, R., Bottom, A. and Hay, W. (1996) *Prisons and the Problem of Order*. Oxford: Clarendon.

Sunshine, J. and Tyler, T. R. (2003) 'The role of procedural justice and legitimacy in shaping public support for policing', *Law and Society Review*, 37(3): 555–89.

Taylor, R. B. (2006) 'Incivilities reduction policing, zero tolerance, and the retreat from coproduction: weak foundations and strong pressures', in D. Weisburd and A. A. Braga (eds) *Police Innovation: Contrasting perspectives*. Cambridge: Cambridge University Press, pp. 98–114.

Thibaut, J. and Walker, L. (1975) *Procedural Justice*, Hillsdale, NJ: Erlbaum.

Travis, J. (2000) *But They All Come Home: Rethinking prisoner reentry*. Washington, DC: Urban Institute.

Tyler, T. R. (2001) 'Public trust and confidence in legal authorities: What do majority and minority group members want from law and legal institutions?' *Behavioral Sciences and the Law*, 19: 215–35.

—— (2003) 'Procedural justice, legitimacy, and the effective rule of law', in M. Tonry (ed.) *Crime and Justice: A review of research*, Vol. 30. Chicago: University of Chicago Press, pp. 431–505.

—— (2005) 'Policing in Black and White: Ethnic group differences in trust and confidence in the police', *Police Quarterly*, 8: 322–42.

—— (2006a) 'Legitimacy and legitimation', *Annual Review of Psychology*, 57: 375–400.

—— (2006b) *Why People Obey the Law*. Princeton: Princeton University Press.

—— (2007) *Psychology and the Design of Legal Institutions*. Nijmegen, the Netherlands: Wolf Legal Publishers.

—— (2008) 'Psychology and institutional design', *Review of Law and Economics*, Symposium issue on 'Law and Social Norms', 4(3): 801–87.

—— (2009) 'Legitimacy and criminal justice: The benefits of self-regulation', *Ohio State Journal of Criminal Law*, 7(1): 307–59.

Tyler, T. R. and Blader, S. L. (2000) *Cooperation in Groups*. Philadelphia: Psychology Press.

Tyler, T. R. and Fagan, J. (2008) 'Legitimacy and cooperation: Why do people help the police fight crime in their communities?' *Ohio State Journal of Criminal Law*, 6: 231–75.

Tyler, T. R. and Huo, Y. J. (2002) *Trust in the Law*. New York: Russell-Sage.

Tyler, T. R., and Lind, E. A. (2001) 'Procedural justice', in J. Sanders and V. L. Hamilton (eds) *Handbook of Justice Research in Law*. New York: Plenum, pp. 65–92.

Tyler, T. R. and Wakslak, C. (2004) 'Profiling and the legitimacy of the police: Procedural justice, attributions of motive, and the acceptance of social authority', *Criminology*, 42: 13–42.

Tyler, T. R., Callahan, P. and Frost, J. (2007) 'Armed, and dangerous(?): Can self-regulatory approaches shape rule adherence among agents of social control', *Law and Society Review*, 41(2): 457–92.

Weitzer, R. and Tuch, S. A. (2006) *Race and Policing in America: Conflict and reform*. Cambridge: Cambridge University Press.

Wilson, J. Q. and Kelling, G. L. (1982) 'Broken windows', *Atlantic Monthly*, March, 29–38.

Notes

1 It could be argued that high trust and confidence slowly moved from around 50 per cent to 60 per cent of the American public over this time period. It is difficult to unambiguously show this because the public opinion polls available at different time periods were conducted by different groups and vary in methodology and wording. However, a cautious statement would be that trust and confidence, if it is increasing, is doing so very slowly.

2 The literature on procedures uses the terms 'procedural fairness' and 'procedural justice' interchangeably. This discussion will use the term 'procedural fairness'.

3 This discussion focuses upon situations in which people deal with the police because the police stop them on the street or in a car. However, people also contact the police for help. In either type of situation, outcomes are negative about 30 per cent of the time. This study found no differences between the basis of people's reactions to these two types of encounters with the police. The study also examined experiences with the courts and again found no difference in the basis of people's reactions to their experiences with the courts.

4 The discussion in this essay distinguishes between police motorist stops and street stops. However, this study only asked people if they were stopped and did not consider which of the two possible situations was involved.

5 The beta coefficient for outcome favourability was 0.12. The beta coefficient for quality of decision-making was 0.17, and the beta coefficient for quality of interpersonal treatment was 0.59. These numbers come from a regression analysis in which three factors – outcome favourability/fairness, quality of decision-making, and quality of treatment – were used to explain the willingness to accept decisions. In such an analysis, the beta weights reflect the relative contribution of each variable to that explanation distinct from the influence of the other factors in the regression.

6 As noted above, quality of treatment is one of two aspects of procedural fairness. The other is quality of decision-making. In this study, quality of treatment emerged as the more important of these two aspects of procedural fairness.

7 Among White people the beta weights were: outcome favourability (0.21); outcome fairness (0.12); procedural fairness (0.67). Among African Americans the beta weights were: outcome favourability (0.13); outcome fairness (0.04); procedural fairness (0.75). Among Hispanics the beta weights were: outcome favourability (0.04); outcome fairness (0.17); procedural fairness (0.66). Also see Davis, Henderson and Cheryachukin (2004); Weitzer and Tuch (2006).

8 Satisfaction was measured using two items: 'How good a job did the police do?' and 'How satisfied were you with what the police did?'

9 Pew Research Center for the People and the Press, www.pewresearch.org.

10 This encounter occurred when the sergeant answered a call about a possible burglary. He confronted an African-American man who, as it turned out, was breaking into his own home having forgotten his key. This event led to the exchange of angry remarks and, in the end, the arrest of the homeowner. Because the homeowner was a very prominent Harvard professor and since he was in fact in his own home, this incident became a flash point for discussions of race relations in contemporary America.

11 Holder, E. (February 18, 2009). Remarks prepared for delivery by AG Eric Holder at the Department of Justice African American History Month Program, 1/18/2009.

12 Further, and consistent with the argument made here, Peel notes that 'The ability of the police to perform their duties is dependent upon public approval of police actions (Principle 2)' and 'The police must secure the willing cooperation of the public in voluntary observance of the law to be able to secure and maintain the respect of the public (Principle 3).'

13 While people are influenced by contact with both the police and the courts, people are generally more likely to deal with the police.

14 As with the police, people go to court about a wide variety of types of disputes and problems. And, they can be in court because they have come to the courts for help or in response to a complaint against them by someone else.

15 There are a variety of reasons that the courts are concerned about public views. The people who come to court have an increasingly diverse social background, and pro se representation is more widespread so judges are more likely to be directly dealing with litigants whose background is different than their own. As a consequence, there is a general interest in understanding 'what people want' from the courts.

16 One way in which these concerns can be distinguished is in terms of the objective reality of the situation of the White and minority communities. In normative terms, the minority community may, in fact, suffer higher levels of discrimination in the outcomes they receive in society and/or from the police. If procedural justice leads to high levels of satisfaction without addressing these objective grievances, we also need to be sensitive to the ethical issues raised by that disjuncture.

17 See Bonta and Gandreau, 1990; Bottoms, 1999; Bukstel and Kilmann, 1980; Franke et al., 2010; Gray, 2007; Petersilia, 2003; Sparks et al., 1996; Travis, 2000 for recent discussions of corrections.

2

COMPLIANCE WITH THE LAW AND POLICING BY CONSENT

Notes on police and legal legitimacy

Jonathan Jackson, Ben Bradford,
Mike Hough and Katherine Murray

Introduction

Ideas ebb and flow. In the 1970s and 1980s, both police leaders and academics routinely appealed to concepts of policing by consent and police legitimacy (cf. Reiner, 2010). In Britain in the 1990s, these ideas were submerged under a wave of crude managerialism from which we are only now emerging (Hough, 2007). Recent years have seen a resurgence of interest in ensuring that the public (a) find the police trustworthy, (b) think the police are a legitimate authority, and (c) believe it is morally just to both obey the law and cooperate with legal institutions.

This chapter analyses key concepts in 'procedural justice theory' (Tyler, 2006a, 2006b, 2008; Tyler *et al.*, 2010; Schulhofer *et al.*, 2010), which we hope will prove useful in thinking about the links between crime-control policies and public commitment to the rule of law. Considering the institutional context within which members of the general public comply (or do not comply) with the law, we focus on the distinction between instrumental and normative motivations for compliance (Tyler, 2011). Building upon some preliminary analyses of a representative sample survey of England and Wales (Hough *et al.*, 2010), we provide some empirical support for the ideas that we present.

Compliance and crime control models

Penal and criminal policy has always reflected tensions between simple, or even simplistic, models of crime control and ones that have more texture and depth. The key features of the simple 'crime control' models are that:

- people are rational–economic calculators in deciding whether to break the law;
- a deterrent threat is the main weapon in the armoury of criminal justice;

- offenders – and thus crime rates – are responsive primarily to the risk of punishment, which can vary on dimensions of certainty, severity and celerity;
- increasing the severity of sentencing, and extending the reach of enforcement strategies, are therefore seen as sensible responses to crime;
- offender's rights tend to be seen as a constraint on effective crime control.

Questions about why people break the law tend – not inevitably, but because of the political climate in which policy is developed – to yield answers framed within the boundaries of simple crime control models. They imply approaches to crime control that are designed to secure *instrumental compliance*, where people's reasons for law-breaking are based on self-interested calculation. Such compliance will be secured by the presence of formal or informal mechanisms of social control and the existence of severe sanctions for wrong-doers (Nagin, 1998; Kahan, 1999).

But deterrence is only a small piece of the puzzle (Pratt *et al.*, 2006; Bottoms, 2001). More subtle models of crime control recognise that formal criminal justice is only one of many systems of social control, most of which have a significant normative dimension. Individuals comply with the law for reasons other than an instrumental calculation of benefits and risks of offending. Most people obey most laws most of the time because it is the 'right thing to do'. In this regard, genetics, socialisation, psychological development, moral reasoning, community context, social norms and networks may all help sustain the routine compliance that is 'ingrained in everyday life' (Robinson and McNeill, 2008: 436).

In these pages, we focus on the role of institutions in encouraging citizens to comply with the law (Tyler, 2003). From a psychological perspective, the legitimacy of the law is the belief that laws are personally binding and the corresponding obligation to obey (Tyler, 2006a). When people believe that rules are binding in their 'existential, present lives' (Sampson and Bartusch, 1998: 786), they feel a duty to abide by the rules put in place by authorities. This is regardless of the morality of a given act (Kelman and Hamilton, 1989; Tyler, 2006b). Granting legitimacy to authorities such as the police and courts cedes them the right to define what constitutes proper behaviour. Holding the system of rules to be legitimate overrides specific questions concerning the morality of particular rules.

Context and moral reasoning

Many motivations to obey the law may be deeply embedded, even subconscious. But the decision to break the law must always comprise a choice at some level on the part of those involved. Locating individuals in the potentially criminogenic contexts within which they act, Situational Action Theory (SAT, see, Wikström, 2004, 2006; Wikström *et al.*, 2010) helps us flesh out the way in which individual decisions are related to the morally binding nature of the law. SAT sees intentional criminal acts as a subset of a wider universe of moral rule-breaking acts: 'An act of crime is to intentionally break a prescription for behaviour stated in the law' (Wikström, 2006: 2). For a person to commit a crime in a given situation, they must first perceive the criminal act to be an option; they then make a judgement about that option; and finally they must choose to act based on that judgement (Wikström, 2006).

Whether an actor sees crime as an option is central to SAT. If – and only if – he or she perceives committing a crime to be a possibility, then a (moral) judgement is made based on this perception. The possibilities of action are evaluated against moral rules and principles: 'is doing this right or wrong?' If a judgement is made that committing the crime is a desirable option or morally ambivalent, or simply a 'neutral' act, the individual must finally choose to act. This choice will be influenced by their personal characteristics such as self-control and their general framework of values, as well as external contingencies such as the level of informal social control evident in the situation, or the probability of getting caught by agents of formal social control.

It is by influencing the decision-making processes described by Wikström that institutions may reasonably be able to encourage public compliance with the law. Instrumentally oriented crime-control models would concentrate efforts at the end of the process. Forced compliance and deterrence work to dissuade would-be offenders who have already decided to commit a crime. Social control mechanisms and credible risks of sanction hope to persuade individuals that a criminal act, while otherwise desirable, is not worth the risk. To achieve this, agents of criminal justice must send out strong signals to would-be offenders of strength, effectiveness, force, detection and justice. They seek to deter those who would otherwise choose to commit a criminal act.

Institutional legitimacy and procedural justice

But a different approach 'intervenes' earlier in the process. According to procedural justice models of legitimacy and compliance (Tyler, 2008), institutional configurations can influence moral decision-making processes in more socially and economically advantageous ways. When people believe it is morally just to obey the law – that is, that the law has the right to dictate appropriate and personally binding behaviour – then so long as they know that a particular act is illegal, the immorality of the act becomes a given. A different sort of morality 'kicks in'. Believing that it is the right thing to do to respect legal rules closes down the possibility of seeing crime as an option: obeying the law becomes routinised, backed up by feelings of obligation and normative motivation. In as much as such orientations are embedded in the routines of everyday life, one does not need to think about the morality of the specific act or the likelihood of getting caught.

Focusing on the normative dimensions in people's orientation to the law, procedural justice models recognise the interplay between formal and informal systems of social control. Normative compliance with the law occurs when people feel a moral or ethical obligation or commitment. If people willingly offer their obedience to systems of authority that command legitimacy, then questions about the nature of the legitimacy of authority figures (such as the police) and the 'drivers' of institutional legitimacy become of central policy importance.

A growing body of largely US research shows an association between the experience or perception of the procedural fairness of the criminal justice system and perceived legitimacy of the institution in question. Legitimacy is, in turn, correlated with greater public respect for the law and stronger felt obligation to obey the law (Tyler and Huo, 2002; Sunshine and Tyler, 2003b; Tyler, 2003; Tyler, 2007). On the basis of various surveys of the public, Tyler has demonstrated that public perceptions of the *fairness* of the justice system are more significant in shaping its legitimacy than perceptions of its *effectiveness*. Existing when the policed regard the authorities as having earned an entitlement to command, legitimacy is formed most importantly via interpersonal interaction, particularly through the experience of procedural justice. Tyler's findings suggest that procedural justice – that is, fair and respectful treatment that 'follows the rules' – is more important to people than obtaining outcomes that they regard either as fair or favourable to themselves. It is the quality of treatment received that is more important in encounters with the police than the objective outcome.

In explaining why the legitimacy of the police shapes compliance, Tyler (2006a, 2008) draws upon the work of Kelman and Hamilton (1989). Fundamentally relational, legitimacy is the right to command others, the authorisation of authorities (by subordinates) of the right to dictate appropriate behaviour, and the subsequent obligation to follow those directives or rules. As Kelman and Hamilton (1989: 54–5) put it:

> A person holds authority only over, or with respect to, another person. Thus, authority refers to a role relationship between two sets of actors within a social unit: the authority holders (or 'authorities') on the one hand and the subordinates or ordinary members on the other . . . Since authority is a relationship, the role of each of the two parties is defined with reference to the role of the other: The role of authorities entitles them to make certain demands on citizens, and the role of citizens obligates them to accede to these demands.

Tyler's empirical focus is on police legitimacy, that is, the authority of police officers and its corollary – the duty to obey instructions from officers. Police legitimacy resides most importantly in the belief that it is (morally) correct in and of itself to obey officers' instructions. Obviating the need for judgements and choices about the content of those instructions, one follows a police directive whether or not one agrees with it. Assuming that police legitimacy translates into legal legitimacy, Tyler then links police legitimacy to compliance: people obey laws out of a respect for law and a more general duty to obey legal authorities. Contrasting instrumental and normative models of compliance, Tyler argues that normative compliance is economically more viable – and is more stable over time – than instrumental compliance, which in the US context at least carries a growingly unaffordable social and fiscal cost.[1]

Tyler's work also addresses the interactions between officials and the public. The procedural justice model positions a perceived duty to obey officers as the core component of police legitimacy, at least as this finds expression in the public mind. If the police powerfully represent the law, then the link between obligation to obey the police and obligation to obey the law is unproblematic. The police are powerful representatives of the law so to feel obligation to obey the police is also to feel obligated to obey the law.

Moral alignment and a broader definition of police legitimacy

In a departure from Tyler's work, we distinguish in our study between legal and police legitimacy (cf. Murphy et al., 2009).[2] By examining links between police legitimacy, legal legitimacy and self-reported compliance behaviour, we can tease out the separate roles that each might play. In the sense that it is morally just to obey law, legal legitimacy is the belief that laws are binding, irrespective of whether one agrees with their moral content.[3] In the US, the 'police' and 'law' may be so closely aligned that to obey one is necessarily to obey the other. But in Britain, the link between police and law may be weaker. The nature and strength of the police 'brand' in Britain may be such that policing can be, and often is seen as, an end in itself, rather than as simply a component in the process of law. British policing may be as much about the maintenance of order as it has been about enforcing the law (Reiner, 2010; Emsley, 1996). A narrowly legalistic approach to policing – concerned, for example, with the rigid application of equal sanctions to equivalent offences – may be actively unpopular among many members of the public, who might prefer to see policing applied in more subtle ways, reinforcing existing social structures and relationships without immediate recourse to the 'heavy hand of the law' (Girling et al., 2000; Wells, 2008). The roots of this phenomena can be traced back to the foundational myths of the Metropolitan police, which paint the police officer as a uniformed citizen mediating between people and state rather than enforcing the will of the state (the law) on the people.

But we also consider the utility of expanding the definition of police legitimacy. According to Beetham (1991), people confer legitimacy on institutions not simply because the latter adhere to standards of good behaviour (that we may extend to acting fairly, which then generates authority), but also because they regard the institutions as representing particular normative and ethical frameworks (see Tankebe, 2010). Conferring legitimacy on an institution – that is, granting it the right to exist, the right to determine authority, and the right to exert power – is a stance or act based on the expression of shared values: a sense of 'moral alignment'. Obligation to obey is not uniquely constitutive of the legitimacy of legal authorities. It is part of a set of ideas, beliefs and behaviours that individuals exhibit in relation to those authorities that combine to establish (or negate) their legitimacy.

Police legitimacy may flow not simply from factors such as its procedural fairness (and general trust and confidence), nor instantiated only in obedience as prerogative, but be partly based in the belief that the police broadly share one's moral values (cf. Tankebe, 2009: 1280–1). *A sense of shared moral values and subsequent group identity may be part of the conferred right of the police to possess the right to govern.* To say that legitimacy is both (a) obligation to obey police directives and (b) moral alignment with the police is not to say that the police must enforce laws that all citizens agree with if they are to be considered legitimate. Instead, by demonstrating 'moral authority' (through procedural justice and defending and representing community values), the police can embody in more general terms a shared sense of right and wrong and a commitment to the rule of law. This does not require them to be moralists, or to demonstrate moral superiority. But it does require them to negotiate order in a way that maximises consent.

Why, then, might a sense of moral alignment between police and people be an important component of police legitimacy in Britain? One answer lies in the history of policing in the UK that is quite distinct from that of the US and mainland Europe. Consider Tonry's (2007: 4) thoughts on why the procedural justice and legitimacy literature developed almost entirely in the US context:

> My guess that the answer centers on the United States' distinctive constitutional scheme premised on notions of limited power of government and entrenched rights of citizens, compared with the étatist traditions of Europe, including Britain and most of the rest of the world. Concepts of vested substantive rights against the state and procedural protections against state intrusion were probably predicates to the development of a theory of procedural justice and a research agenda aiming to understand the effects of alternative ways of implementing procedural protections. This American hegemony will not last because these differences between the United States and Europe are eroding. Within Europe, the application of the European Declaration of Human Rights and the decisions of the European Court of Human Rights are creating stronger substantive rights and procedural protections.

The Metropolitan Police Force for London was established in 1829 by Robert Peel and it is commonplace to refer to his principles of policing operation, which speak to issues of policing by consent and accountability. While doubts exist as to the primary source (Lentz and Chaires, 2007),[4] the spirit and theme of the principles are important. Phrases such as 'The police are the public and the public are the police' and 'The ability of the police to perform their duties is dependent upon public approval of police actions' (e.g., Reith, 1952: 154) call for a close social connection between what were then 'subjects of the crown' and the police. They allude to a belief that the police should be a source of moral authority that stems from being *of the community*, where the community is primarily defined as the imagined (Anderson, 1991) community of Great Britain (i.e., the nation).

Officers typify and symbolically defend the norms and values not necessarily just of the immediate community but also of the superordinate national community. As time passed, many individuals may have come to accept the influence of the police, in order to maintain a self-defining relationship with this symbol of order and 'Britishness' (Loader and Mulcahy, 2003; Jackson and Sunshine, 2007).

In the British context, a history of policing by consent may have left citizens with closer social bonds with the police than in the US. This raises the possibility that identification is to some degree based on a sense of shared moral values, grounded in the social and cultural significance of the police in Britain, as a widely held symbol of order and defender of community values. Demands from authorities may call upon commitments from subordinates that are, in part, related to the relationship that individuals have to the group. Activating a sense that the roles defined by the legitimate power relationship are personally meaningful to the individuals involved, central here may be identification with the norms, goals and values of the police that are partly constitutive of the legitimacy of the authority (cf. Turner, 2005).

An important human motivation is the desire to act in accord with one's values about what is morally right and wrong. For example, Tyler and Blader (2005) found that employees in a management setting were motivated by the assessment that their work organisation acts in ways that are consistent with their own moral values (see also de Cremer et al., 2010). It follows that when people feel aligned with the moral values of an authority in a group setting, they will act in ways that support the group that the authority represents: moral alignment activates a group-based morality. Triggering the ethical motivations that lead people to adhere to group rules, moral norms become particularly strong guidelines for individual behaviour. First, identifying with an authority transforms our motives from the individuals to the group. Second, enacting shared moral values may also be an important way of receiving or maintaining in-group respect and acceptance (Pagliaro et al., 2011).

This expanded definition of legitimacy suggests that the British police can employ different processes and instruments of influence depending on the authority relationship that an individual has with the police. If people base the authority relationship on the fear of punishment, then demonstrations of deterrence and power will be most effective. If people base it on compliance with rules and authority, then social influence and demonstrations of authority will be critical. If people base it on common moral values, then demonstrations of shared purpose will be key. And if social identification and connected identities are based upon shared normative and ethical grounds, we can begin to address the familiar issues that surround notions of legitimacy as pure obligation. A legitimacy that suppresses individual's moral judgement of the character of the police directives flattens normativity, minimising the active role citizens can play in judging those that govern them. If most people are concerned about justice and morality, then legitimacy is given a sounder normative basis. Legitimacy is not just a dull compulsion to obey (cf. Tankebe, 2010).

Preliminary analysis of data from a representative sample of England and Wales

The National Policing Improvement Agency (NPIA) fielded questions on public trust and police legitimacy in a representative sample-survey of England and Wales, allowing us to test a series of hypotheses that link trust in the police to perceived legitimacy and to self-reported compliance. While many of the elements shown in the models will be familiar from extant studies based on procedural justice theory (Reisig *et al.*, 2007; Sunshine and Tyler, 2003b; Tyler and Fagan, 2008; Tyler and Huo, 2002; Murphy *et al.*, 2009), distinguishing between police legitimacy and legal legitimacy is a relatively novel addition to such models (although see Murphy *et al.*, 2009), as is a differentiation between everyday crime and a type of offending that may be particularly calculative – and thus separate from common views of the law.

What follows is an outline of some of the preliminary findings from the NPIA survey (see also Hough *et al.*, 2010), the full findings will be reported in due course.[5] Our data come from face-to-face interviews in respondents' homes using Computer Assisted Personal Interviewing, with a response rate of 62 per cent yielding an analytical sample of 7,434 respondents aged 16 and over (although we draw in this article on data from the sub-sample (n = 937) of respondents who were asked the procedural justice questions). Because it is likely that self-report measures of personal morality and compliance behaviour are affected by bias associated with social desirability, we made provision for questions relating to those two concepts to be completed via Computer Assisted Self-Interviewing, where responses are entered directly into the computer (out of sight of the interviewer).

Consider, first, the distinction between instrumental and normative compliance. The instrumental model predicts that people comply with the law because the police present a powerful risk of sanction and punishment. An instrumental route to compliance traces paths from individuals believing that the police are effective in their job (that the police are good at catching criminals, preventing crime, dealing with victims, and so forth) to believing that the risk of getting caught is high (if one were to shoplift, buy stolen goods, vandalise public property, illegally dispose of rubbish, or commit a traffic offence) and from there to complying with the law (the same acts).[6]

Figure 2.1 summarises the first set of results, estimated using structural equation modelling.[7] Police legitimacy is here represented by a single latent variable construct measured by a series of questions about obligation to obey (e.g., agree/disagree: 'You should do what the police tell you, even if you disagree') and a series of questions about moral alignment (e.g., agree/disagree: 'The police in this area usually act in ways that are consistent with my own ideas about what is right and wrong'). While trust in police effectiveness[8] predicts people's perceptions of the risk of being caught (if they were to commit an 'everyday crime'), the perceived risk of sanction is not a significant factor in predicting the odds of falling into the 'occasionally committing a crime' group. The NPIA data do not offer empirical support for a

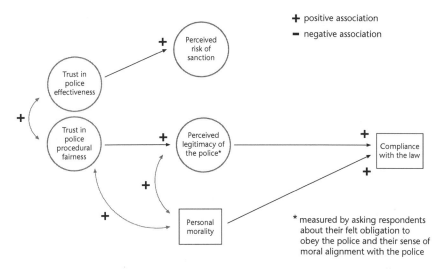

FIGURE 2.1 A procedural justice model of compliance

simple deterrence-based model of crime control – at least within the limits of observational data and the modelling of self-reports views, beliefs, calculations and behaviours. This combines with prior evidence (Pratt *et al.*, 2006) to suggest that deterrence is not an effective route to securing compliance.

Second, trust in the police is a strong predictor of perceived legitimacy (Figure 2.1). Combining with a good deal of experimental and observational work (e.g., Tyler and Huo, 2002), this suggests that trust in procedural fairness fosters in people feelings of motive-based trust in (and shared group membership with) the authority concerned – that both it and they are 'on the same side'. According to Tyler and Lind's relational model of procedural justice (Tyler and Lind, 1992), the manner in which people – as members of social groups – are treated by those in authority communicates information to them about their status within those groups. When police provide individuals with appropriate status information (through fair procedures), they are more likely to feel a sense of obligation to the police and an alignment with the ethical and moral framework they believe the police to embody. That is, they are more likely to perceive the police to be legitimate. Third, police legitimacy is a powerful predictor of compliance, even holding constant personal morality (cf. Robinson and Darley, 1995) thus replicating Tyler (2006b).

But what happens when we disentangle moral alignment and obligation to obey? Recall our earlier distinction between duty to obey and moral alignment. Figure 2.2 summarises the findings of a model that divides the legitimacy of the police into two: moral alignment and obligation. What emerges is striking. While moral alignment is an important predictor of compliance, obligation to obey is not. This does not mean that legitimacy should not include a felt obligation to obey the police. Rather, insofar as legitimacy shapes compliance behaviour, it is the moral

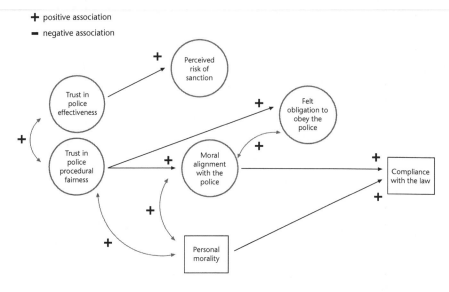

FIGURE 2.2 Differentiating between obligation to obey and moral alignment

alignment and identification that seems to encourage individuals to act in line with the law (crucially, conditioning on their beliefs about the specific morality of the act and the situational dynamics of deterrence and punishment).

Some form of duty to obey may still be important however. Consider the distinction between obligation to obey police officers and obligation to obey the law itself. Perceived obligation to obey the law may offer a more proximate and more directly measurable path from police legitimacy to compliance with the law. Figure 2.3 summarises the findings of the model that includes legal legitimacy (using a scale of legal cynicism, e.g., agree/disagree: 'Laws are made to be broken' and 'It's ok to do anything you want as long as you don't harm anyone'). We find that legal cynicism, police legitimacy and personal morality each explain variation in compliance.

Tracing paths from left to right, the model suggests that when individuals perceive police to be acting unfairly and unjustly, this will damage their assessment of police legitimacy, which may encourage an impression that their community (or society) lacks moral cohesion, and subsequently damage their sense of obligation towards their society and its rules. Procedurally unfair treatment may foster among those on the receiving end a growing sense of 'legal cynicism', which is the sense that 'laws or rules are not considered binding in the existential, present lives of respondents' and the 'ratification of acting in ways that are "outside" of laws and social norms' (Sampson and Bartusch, 1998: 786). Procedurally unjust behaviour may communicate powerful messages about the behaviour of important group representatives: the extent to which they adhere to the rules laid down for their behaviour.

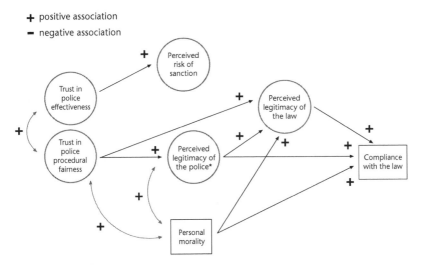

+ positive association
− negative association

* measured by asking respondents about their felt obligation to obey the police and their sense of moral alignment with the police

FIGURE 2.3 Introducing legitimacy of the law into the model

The police are the most visible agent of social control – the most high-profile institution in a justice system that is empowered to define right and wrong behaviour. If they abuse their powers and wield their authority in unfair ways, this not only damages people's sense of obligation to obey their directives (their authority in the normal sense of the word), but it also affects public perceptions of their moral authority. Because the police are powerfully linked to the law (even if the two are not synonymous), unfairness may undermine the moral right of the law to dictate appropriate behaviour. Put another way, if the police are seen to act in ways outside of social norms – which dictate that such authorities should treat the people they serve with fairness and dignity – this then generates a powerful cynicism: 'if the police can behave however they please, and ignore the rules, so can I'.

It seems probable that legal cynicism will arise as a response not simply to *perceived* police failings, or to the failings of individual officers, but to instances (and more likely long series of instances) of institutional indifference, neglect and injustice. Research from the United States consistently finds that legal cynicism is higher in areas that are policed less well – sometimes barely policed at all, in the proper sense of the word – and is highly correlated with neighbourhood structural conditions that would appear to predict negative, neglectful and/or confrontational police behaviours, such as high levels of concentrated poverty and high proportions of young people (Kirk and Papachristos, 2011).

To suggest that legal cynicism *causes* non-compliance would, however, be excessive. Legal cynicism, where it exists, is likely to be a rather diffuse set of feelings, emotions and oppositional stances that operates at both the individual and the collective level. Kirk and Papachristos (2011) draw on Goffman's notion of cultural frames to suggest that legal cynicism becomes a way of seeing the world that opens up or broadens the possibility of criminal acts, while in no way determining that they will occur. At the same time, a cultural frame that includes – even revolves around – legal cynicism occludes or precludes other acts, most pertinently in relation to cooperating with legal authorities such as the police. Kirk and Papachristos show that high levels of legal cynicism in an area predict higher murder rates, and suggest this is in part because such cynicism creates a space in which 'self-help' violence (Black, 1983) is seen as a viable option in response to slights or threats that in other contexts would be solved by recourse to formal agents of social control.

Seen in these terms, legal cynicism may be one mechanism that broadens the range of (criminal) possibilities perceived by individuals in criminogenic situations. Police behaviours that generate legal cynicism may trigger changes in the decision-making processes envisaged by SAT. Conversely, if this is a two-way process, and if the experience of procedural fairness (for example) is linked to lower legal cynicism, then a different cultural frame may emerge that shuts down the possibilities for criminal acts, while also opening up the potential for engagement and cooperation with police.

The special case of unpopular laws

While police legitimacy might be linked to greater compliance in the aggregate, what of the special case of laws that are unpopular or, perhaps more importantly, do not attract very widespread censure (at least as it relates to the moral character of the law)? Traffic policing has long been known to be a problematic area for police–public relations (Girling *et al.*, 2000; Wells, 2008). It does not seem too controversial to say that a major reason for this is that many people do not think current road legislation is correctly formulated, that it is over-harshly enforced, and that it does not apply to them and serves as a distraction from the things the police 'should really be doing'.

The link between morality and law may in such cases be severely attenuated. Conversely, the risk of sanction may become a more important predictor of compliance. Testing the model, which is shown in Figure 2.4, we explore the possibility that the relationship between police legitimacy, legal cynicism and compliance with traffic laws is different to that described in the more general models shown in Figures 2.1, 2.2 and 2.3.[9] Strikingly, the link between legitimacy and compliance is not in evidence, with no significant path running from either aspect of police legitimacy to compliance (net of other predictors in the model). Rather, in this model, compliance is associated with personal morality and to a lesser but still significant extent with perceived risk of sanction. This suggests that people comply with traffic laws most importantly because they think it is wrong to commit traffic offences. They are also more likely to comply when they think they will be caught if they do not (again with the usual caveats about observational data and modelling self-reports).

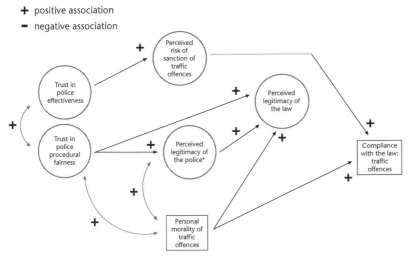

+ positive association

− negative association

* measured by asking respondents about their felt obligation to obey the police and their sense of moral alignment with the police

FIGURE 2.4 The special case of traffic offences

The lack of a significant association between legal cynicism and compliance is notable. Surely a feeling that 'laws are made to be broken' will be linked to a greater propensity to commit traffic violations? This unexpected finding may serve to underline just how differently many people think about traffic compared with other laws. When formulating their answers to the survey questions used to measure legal cynicism, respondents may do so with little notion that traffic offences fall into the general category of 'the law'. Equally, traffic offences may be so distant from other laws in people's minds that their responses to them are influenced by institutional context in ways quite different to the general picture (most notably in the current setting by perceptions of the risk of sanction).

Instrumental fairness, human rights and the legitimacy of the police

In an over-simplified discourse about crime control, as we see in the UK, the rationale for improving 'confidence in justice' is that greater consumer satisfaction on the part of the 'law-abiding majority' will secure their cooperation with the authorities. When citizens report crimes, act as witnesses and so forth, this enhances the deterrent effectiveness of the system. By contrast, a procedural justice perspective directs attention to 'confidence building' amongst those parts of the population whose commitment to the rule of law is more tentative. The primary purpose is to secure compliance first, and cooperation second. It also alludes to the fact that the 'law-abiding majority' also commit crime, and that in any case they too care more about fair procedure than effectiveness narrowly defined. All available evidence suggests that fostering trust and legitimacy via fair and decent treatment would pay dividends across the population.

There is, however, a problem. For all that procedural justice holds out the possibility of achieving two desirable ends at once (a better relationship between police and public based on notions of fairness and greater compliance with the law) it also contains a danger. Compliance might be 'bought' by an empty fairness based not on voice, respect and dignity, but implemented in a purely instrumental fashion, intended only to make people *feel* that they have been fairly treated. After all, almost all the evidence we have that procedural justice 'works' is based on public perceptions of police and policing, not on objective measures of actual police behaviour. Ultimately, perhaps, the risk is that procedural fairness might be free-floating and cynical: not tied to any ethical or normative principles but channelled by circumstance and exigency, used as a tool by authorities to extract compliance from a systematically misled public.

MacCoun describes this risk as 'the dark side of procedural justice'. He suggests that we should extend the analytical focus from the beliefs of citizens to the substance of decision-making, for instance, we might ask '[h]ow are procedures selected, how are they represented to citizens, and when are they deployed' (2005: 193). Here we return to the normative justifiability of power. In an echo of Beetham (1991), Buchanan states that 'an entity has political legitimacy if and only if it is morally justified in wielding political power' (2002: 689). Buchanan cites criteria that must be met to claim legitimacy, namely a minimum standard of democracy, adherence to procedural justice and 'processes, policies, and actions [that] respect the most basic human rights' (2002: 703). Taking the example of human rights, we can begin to map out how empirical understandings of policing and fairness might be tied to a set of external referents that harness the free-floating aspects of procedural justice theory.

Human rights refer to a fundamental set of rights and freedoms – for example, equality, dignity and respect – which assert the moral value of human life in its own right. In the UK, the Human Rights Act 1998 has entrenched the European Convention on Human Rights in domestic law. Whilst all policing in the UK must be undertaken in accordance with the strictures of the HR (as Sanders and Young, 2008: 283 note), the difficulty in applying a human rights framework to policing is that the formulations are either vague – for example, 'to be treated fairly and without discrimination' – or conditional. Making the 'right' policing choice is further exacerbated by conflicting priorities and objectives that are not equally achievable (Sanders and Young, 2008). Indeed, it is doubtful that *any* policing principle can entirely escape the difficulties and contestations of applied policing. Rather, the key task is to set out a 'philosophical standpoint' (ibid.: 284) that is broadly perceived to be legitimate (taking empirical values as our guide). We can use this to inform proportionate policing. In short, we need to establish a moral compass that allows the police to balance means and ends and 'do the right things, for the right reasons' (Neyroud and Beckley [2001: 37], cited in Neyroud, 2008: 669).

For all that the possibility of 'instrumental fairness' is, and should be, a concern underlying any efforts toward implementing procedural justice policing policies (policies that, realistically, will be sold to practitioners on the promise they hold regarding fairly instrumental ends in terms of cooperation and compliance), we might take some reassurance from the relevance of Beetham's notion of legitimacy to policing in the UK. The public can and do make nuanced judgements about the police – how they act, whether they are fair, whether they operate according to a shared moral framework. These are, by and large, congruent with normative conceptions of legitimacy derived by police or legal scholars. Indeed, one of the strengths of Beetham's approach is that it blurs the line between lay and specialist accounts and allows for the fact that 'ordinary' people may hold the authorities that govern them to account in similar ways to those developed within the academy.

Equally, just as a human rights approach offers procedural justice theory an external normative referent (Murray, 2010), normative conceptions of legitimacy can be used to tie empirical police legitimacy – of the type described above – to standards that derive from moral, legal or political philosophy. To do this, it is necessary to take a step back from Beetham, to draw a distinction between concepts of legitimacy and conceptions of legitimacy (see Hinsch, 2008, for an overview). Concepts of legitimacy tell us what it means to say something is legitimate. Two distinctions are often made. First is the empirical concept of the social sciences. Second is the normative concept of political philosophy. The empirical concept goes back to Weber (1948), for whom legitimacy denoted the approval or sincere recognition of a norm, law or social institution. This is, in essence, the concept we have applied so far in this chapter: the rule of law is legitimate when people see the legal system and authorities as providing an appropriate standard of conduct that must be complied with (crucially, compliance arises not because of external sanctions but because it is seen to be the correct standard). As Hinsch (2008: 40) states: 'Since no political regime or social order could persist without a fairly high level of unenforced compliance with its rule, the empirical understanding of legitimacy naturally occupies a central place in explanatory theories of social order.'

The empirical understanding of legitimacy raises a set of questions about the ability of a criminal justice system to command legitimacy in the eyes of the public – whether the *policed* see the *police* as legitimate. These questions are open and empirical. Leaving aside whether that system actually meets any given set of objective (or ethical/normative) criteria, they turn our attention to surveys and qualitative methods of research. Such questions give us insight into public attitudes, values, behaviours and beliefs, we can develop a descriptive account of legitimacy. One result of this process is that a system is said to be legitimate when the public grant it legitimacy. An observer sitting outside the system might find a particular arrangement unjust and unacceptable, but they must nevertheless conclude that it is legitimate when those governed believe it to be so. *Under this concept, to say something is legitimate is to make a factual claim about the subjective state of mind of particular individuals that belong to one political society.*

By contrast, within political philosophy, political systems tend to be understood in the normative sense whereby a set of objective criterion are laid out that must be met in order to secure legitimacy; for example, Locke's treatises on government and writings on Human Rights (1989 [1689]), Rousseau on democracy and democratic approval (1988 [1762]), Bentham's utilitarianism (1987 [1843]), J. S. Mills on liberty (1998 [1869]), Rawls on justice (2001, 2005) and Miller on social justice (1991). Take for example, the presence of a democratic system of election, adherence by both rulers and the governed to the rule of law and the absence of endemic corruption. Experts can, for instance, judge the Zimbabwean justice system to lack legitimacy, since by any objective standard it is corrupt and lacks public accountability. Assessments of this sort also involve subjective judgements, of course, about the nature of the 'good or just society'. Intriguingly, it is possible to have a system of governance that commands high levels of perceived legitimacy from the governed whilst also, paradoxically, failing to meet the criteria of legitimacy that political philosophers would generally accept. Examples are to be found in many totalitarian and revolutionary regimes in their early phases.

A normative concept of legitimacy sets out 'objective' criteria, according to which an authority or institution is legitimate, not because of the subjective state of mind of those it governs, but because the arrangement meets certain substantive requirements (usually requirements of justice and rationality). In addition, any normative conception of legitimacy has to describe why meeting these criteria confers authority on norms, institutions, or persons. Why do the criteria generate morally binding rules? Empirical legitimacy means stating that people believe an arrangement to be right and just. *Normative legitimacy means substantive recognition that the truth (or validity) of these arrangements is right and just.*

In sum, application of the human rights framework to procedural justice theory can be seen as a special case of a more general process through which empirical understandings of public attitudes and orientations towards the police are held up against normative conceptions of what policing is and should be about. As suggested by the brief discussion of Beetham's notion of legitimacy above, there may often be considerable overlap between the two. We should not assume public notions of fairness, trust and morality to be deficient when compared with allegedly more 'sophisticated' viewpoints. But without recourse to normative accounts developed separately to lay understandings, our models of legitimacy and compliance will remain both free-floating – tied simply to perceptions – and at least implicitly goal-directed. That is, we risk compliance *as an outcome* becoming the only real goal, whereas what should be at stake is the mutually reinforcing development of public compliance in conjunction with equally desirable developments in police practice that are, in many respects, ends in themselves.

References

Anderson, B. R. (1991) *Imagined Communities: Reflections on the Origin and Spread of Nationalism*. London: Verso.

Beetham, D. (1991) *The Legitimation of Power*. Basingstoke: Palgrave Macmillan.

Bentham, J. (1987[1843]) 'Anarchical fallacies' in E. Craig (ed.) *Nonsense upon Stilts*. London: Taylor & Francis.

Black, D. (1983) 'Crime as social control', *American Sociological Review*, 48: 34–45.

Bottoms, A. E. (2001) 'Compliance and community penalties', in T. Bottoms, L. Gelsthorpe and S. Rex (eds) *Community Penalties*. Cullompton: Willan Publishing, pp. 87–116.

Buchanan, A. (2002) 'Political legitimacy and democracy', *Ethics*, 112(4): 689–719.

de Cremer, D., van Dijke, M. and Mayer, D. (2010) 'Cooperating when "You" and "I" are treated fairly: The moderating role of leader prototypicality', *Journal of Applied Psychology*, 95(6): 1121–33.

Emsley, C. (1996) *The English Police: A Political and Social History*. Harlow: Pearson Education Limited.

Girling, E., Loader, I. and Sparks, R. (2000) *Crime and Social Change in Middle England*. London: Routledge.

Hains, S. C., Hogg, M. A., and Duck, J. M. (1997) 'Self-categorization and leadership: Effects of group prototypicality and leader stereotypicality', *Personality and Social Psychology Bulletin*, 23: 1087–100.

Hinsch, W. (2008) 'Legitimacy and justice: A conceptual and functional distinction', in Kuhnelt, J. (ed.) *Political Legitimation without Morality?* London: Springer, pp. 39–52.

Hogg, M. A. (2001) 'A social identity theory of leadership', *Personality and Social Psychology Review*, 5: 184–200.

Hough, M. (2007) 'Policing, new public management and legitimacy' in T. R. Tyler (ed.) *Legitimacy and Criminal Justice*. New York: Russell Sage Foundation, pp. 63–83.

Hough, M., Jackson, J., Bradford, B., Myhill, A. and Quinton, P. (2010) 'Procedural justice, trust and institutional legitimacy', *Policing: A Journal of Policy and Practice*, 4(3): 203–10.

Jackson, J. and Bradford, B. (2010) 'What is trust and confidence in the police?', *Policing: A Journal of Policy and Practice*, 4(3): 241–48.

Jackson, J. and Sunshine, J. (2007) 'Public confidence in policing: A neo-Durkheimian perspective', *British Journal of Criminology*, 47(2): 214–33.

Jackson, J., Bradford, B., Hough, M., Kuha, J., Stares, S. R., Widdop, S., Fitzgerald, R., Yordanova, M. and Galev, T. (2011). 'Developing European indicators of trust in justice', *European Journal of Criminology*, 8(4): 267–285.

Kahan, D. (1999) 'The secret ambition of deterrence', *Harvard Law Review*, 113: 413–500.

Kelman, H. C. and Hamilton, V. L. (1989) *Crimes of Obedience*. New Haven: Yale.

Kirk, D. S. and Papachristos, A. V. (2011) 'Cultural mechanisms and the persistence of neighborhood violence', *American Journal of Sociology*, 116(4): 1190–233.

Lentz, S. A. and Chaires, R. H. (2007) 'The invention of Peel's principles: A study of policing "textbook" history', *Journal of Criminal Justice*, 35: 69–79.

Loader, I. and Mulcahy, A. (2003) *Policing and the Condition of England*. Oxford: Oxford University Press.

Locke, J. (1989 [1689]) *Two Treatises of Government*, Richard Aschcraft (ed.). London: Routledge.

MacCoun, R. J. (2005) 'Voice, control and belonging: The double-edge sword of procedural fairness', *Annual Review of Law and Social Science*, 1: 171–201.

McAdams, R. and Nadler, J. (2008) 'Coordinating in the shadow of the law: Two contextualized tests of the focal point theory of legal compliance', *Law and Society Review*, 42: 865–98.

Miller, D. (1991) *Principles of Social Justice*. Cambridge, MA: Harvard University Press.

Mills, J.S. (1998 [1869]) *On Liberty and Other Essays*, J. Grey (ed.). Oxford: Oxford University Press.

Mnookin, R. H. and Kornhauser, L. (1979) 'Bargaining in the shadow of the law: The case of divorce', *Yale Law Journal*, 88: 950–99.

Murphy, K., Tyler, T. R. and Curtis, A. (2009) 'Nurturing regulatory compliance: Is procedural justice effective when people question the legitimacy of the law?' *Regulation and Governance*, 3: 1–26.

Murray, K. H. (2010) 'Police legitimacy and policing public protest', University of Edinburgh School of Law Working Paper No. 2010/36. Available at SSRN: http://ssrn.com/abstract=1709401.

Nagin, D. S. (1998) 'Criminal deterrence research at the outset of the 21st century', in M. Tonry (ed.) *Crime and Justice*, vol. 23. Chicago: University of Chicago Press, pp. 1–42.

Neyroud, P. (2008) 'Policing and ethics', in T. Newburn (ed.) *Handbook of Policing*. Cullompton: Willan Publishing, pp. 666–92.

Neyroud, P. and Beckley A. (2001) *Policing, Ethics and Human Rights*. Cullompton: Willan Publishing.

Pagliaro, S., Ellemers, N. and Barreto, M. (2011) 'Sharing moral values: Anticipated ingroup respect as a determinant of adherence to morality-based (but not competence-based) group norms', *Personality and Social Psychology Bulletin*, 37(8): 1117–29.

Paternoster, R., Brame, R., Bachman, R. and Sherman, L. W. (1997) 'Do fair procedures matter? The effect of procedural justice on spouse assault', *Law and Society Review*, 31: 163–204.

Pratt, T. C., Cullen, F. C., Blevins, K. R., Daigle, L. E. and Madsen, T. D. (2006) 'The empirical status of deterrence theory: A meta-analysis', in Cullen *et al.* (eds) *Taking Stock: The Status of Criminological Theory*. New Brunswick, NJ: Transaction Publishers, pp. 367–95.

Rawls, J. (2001) *Justice as Fairness: A Restatement* (2nd rev. edn). Cambridge, MA: Harvard University Press.

—— (2005 [1971]) *A Theory of Justice*. Cambridge, MA: Harvard University Press.

Reiner, R. (2010) *The Politics of the Police* (4th edn). Oxford: Oxford University Press.

Reisig, M., Bratton, J. and Gertz, M. G. (2007) 'The construct validity and refinement of process-based policing measures', *Criminal Justice and Behavior*, 34: 1005–28.

Reith, C. (1952) *The Blind Eye of History: A Study of the Origins of the Present Police Era*. London: Faber and Faber.

Robinson, G. and McNeill, F. (2008) 'Exploring the dynamics of compliance with community penalties', *Theoretical Criminology*, 12(4): 431–449.

Robinson, P. H. and Darley, J. M. (1995) *Justice, Liability, and Blame: Community Views and the Criminal Law. New Directions in Social Psychology*. Boulder, CO: Westview.

Rousseau, J.-J. (1988 [1762]) *The Basic Political Writings* (trans. A. Cress). Indianapolis, IN: Hackett Publishing Company.

Sampson, R. J. and Bartusch, D. J. (1998) 'Legal Cynicism and (Subcultural?) Tolerance of Deviance: The neighborhood context of racial differences', *Law and Society Review*, 32: 777–804.

Sanders, A. and Young, R. (2008) 'Police powers', in T. Newburn (ed.) *Handbook of Policing*. Cullompton: Willan Publishing, pp. 281–312.

Schulhofer, S. J., Tyler, T. R. and Huq, A. Z. (2010) 'American policing at a crossroads', NYU School of Law, Public Law Research Paper No. 10–55. Available at SSRN: http://ssrn.com/abstract=1663819.

Stoutland, S. E. (2001) 'The multiple dimensions of trust in resident/police relations in Boston', *Journal of Research in Crime and Delinquency*, 38: 226–56.

Sunshine, J. and Tyler, T. R. (2003a) 'Moral solidarity, identification with the community, and the importance of procedural justice: The police as prototypical representatives of a group's moral values', *Social Psychology Quarterly*, 66(2): 153–65.

—— (2003b) 'The role of procedural justice and legitimacy in public support for policing', *Law and Society Review*, 37(3): 513–48.

Tankebe, J. (2009) 'Public cooperation with the police in Ghana: Does procedural fairness matter?', *Criminology*, 47(4): 1265–93.

—— (2010) 'Legitimation and resistance: Police reform in the (un)making', in L. K. Cheliotis (ed.) *Roots, Rites and Sites of Resistance: The Banality of Good*. Basingstoke: Palgrave Macmillan.

Tonry, M. (2007) 'Foreword', in T. R. Tyler (ed.) *Legitimacy and Criminal Justice: International Perspectives*. New York: Russell Sage Foundation, pp. 3–8.

Turner, J. C. (2005) 'Explaining the nature of power: A three-process theory', *European Journal of Social Psychology*, 35: 1–22.

Tyler, T. R. (2003) 'Procedural justice, legitimacy, and the effective rule of law', in M. Tonry (ed.), *Crime and Justice: A Review of Research*, vol. 30. Chicago: University of Chicago Press, pp. 431–505.

—— (2006a) 'Legitimacy and legitimation', *Annual Review of Psychology*, 57: 375–400.

—— (2006b) *Why People Obey the Law* (2nd edn). Princeton: Princeton University Press.

—— (ed.) (2007) *Legitimacy and Criminal Justice: International Perspectives*. New York: Russell Sage Foundation.

—— (2008) 'Psychology and institutional design', *Review of Law and Economics* (symposium issue on Law and Social Norms), 4(3): 801–87.

—— (2011) *Why People Cooperate: The Role of Social Motivations*. Princeton: Princeton University Press.

Tyler, T. R. and Blader, S. L. (2005) 'Can businesses effectively regulate employee conduct?: The antecedents of rule-following in work settings', *Academy of Management Journal* 48(6): 1143–58.

Tyler, T. R. and Fagan, J. (2008) 'Why do people cooperate with the police?', *Ohio Journal of Criminal Law*, 6: 231–75.

Tyler, T. R. and Huo, Y. J. (2002) *Trust in THE Law: Encouraging public cooperation with the police and courts*. New York: Russell Sage Foundation.

Tyler, T. R., and Lind, E. A. (1992) 'A relational model of authority in groups', *Advances in Experimental Social Psychology*, 25: 115–91.

Tyler, T. R., Schulhofer, S. J. and Huq, A. Z. (2010) 'Legitimacy and deterrence effects in counterterrorism policing: A study of Muslim Americans', *Law and Society Review*, 44(2): 365–402.

Weber, M. (1948) *From Max Weber: Essays in Sociology* (trans. H. Gerth and C. W. Mills). London: Rouledge and Kegan Paul.

Wells, H. (2008) 'The techno-fix versus the fair cop: Procedural (in)justice and automated speed limit enforcement', *British Journal of Criminology* 48(6): 498–817.

Wikström, P.-O. H. (2004) 'Crime as alternative: Towards a cross-level situational action theory of crime causation', in J. McCord (ed.) *Beyond Empiricism: Institutions and Intentions in the Study of Crime, Advances in Criminological Theory, Vol. 13*. New Brunswick, NJ: Transaction Publishing, pp. 1–37.

—— (2006) 'Individuals, settings and acts of crime: Situational mechanisms and the explanation of crime', in P.-O. H. Wikström and R. Sampson (eds) *The Explanation of Crime: Context, Mechanisms and Development*. Cambridge: Cambridge University Press, pp. 61–107.

Wikström, P.-O. H., Ceccato, V., Hardie, B. and Treiber, K. (2010) 'Activity fields and the dynamics of crime: Advancing knowledge about the role of the environment in crime causation', *Journal of Quantitative Criminology*, 26(1): 55–87.

Notes

1 The case for such an approach will be strengthened, of course, as the need to reduce public expenditure becomes ever more pressing in the years ahead.

2 In a series of three studies, Murphy *et al.* (2009) measured the legitimacy of tax laws (study 1) in terms of the perceived morality of tax dodging (we would call this 'perceived morality of the offence'); the legitimacy of welfare laws (study 2) in terms of whether individuals questioned the legitimacy of the welfare system, whether the laws were consistent with the views of Australians and whether the system worked well; and moral alignment with the laws that police officers enforce (study 3). They found that for people who questioned the legitimacy of the law, procedural justice (in study 3 this was the belief that the police are trustworthy to be fair and treat individuals with dignity and respect) was a stronger predictor of compliance and cooperation than for those who did not question the legitimacy of the law. People who question the legitimacy of the law may thus be more powerfully affected by the experience of procedural justice because of a greater social distance between such individuals and the authorities who enforce the law (assuming that procedural justice decreases social distance and that people who grant legitimacy to the law feel relatively little social distance to legal authorities). We not only make a distinction between police and legal legitimacy, but we also treat the morality of specific offences as separate to both forms of legitimacy. We define legal legitimacy as the presence or absence of legal cynicism, that is, a more general sense that laws are psychologically binding.

3 Low perceived legal legitimacy is a cynicism about the law: a sense that one does not need to comply with the law simply because *it's the law*. At its extreme, legal cynicism is active antagonism and personal validation of deviant behaviour (Sampson and Bartusch, 1998).

4 Lentz and Chaires (2007) suggest that these principles may be somewhat the 'invention' of twentieth-century textbooks.

5 See, also, Jackson *et al.* (2011) for details of the development of similar measures of trust, legitimacy, compliance and cooperation.

6 We used latent class analysis to combine answers to these five questions into one dichotomous variable, since the manifest variables were categorical and since we assumed the underlying latent variable to be categorical. A two-class model was tested using Full Information Maximum Likelihood estimation in LatentGold 4.0 (which includes all available information in the estimation procedure). The model allocated 93 per cent of the sample into class one (very unlikely to report having shoplifted, bought stolen goods, vandalised public property, illegally disposed of rubbish, or committed a traffic offence) and 7 per cent of the sample into class two (likely to admit having occasionally committed one or more of the everyday crimes). A dichotomous variable was then derived that identified the modal category, thus categorising each respondent as either 'compliant' or 'occasionally uncompliant'. The data were then exported to MPlus 5.2 for the proceeding statistical analysis.

7 Using MPlus 5.2. We should make three technical notes. First, we treated the latent variable indicators as categorical variables. Second, we dichotomised the measures of

compliance and personal morality using latent class modelling, before entering the derived variables into subsequent structural equation modelling (the final analysis combines linear and logistic regression). Third, all absent structural paths were not statistically significant. The full report of the study will emerge in due course.

8 For thoughts on the meaning and measurement of trust in the police, see Stoutland, 2001; Tyler and Huo, 2002; Jackson and Bradford, 2010; and Jackson et al., 2011.

9 McAdams and Nadler (2008: 892–3) argue that traffic laws may have a 'focal effect' on coordination that then generates widespread public compliance. Consider a driver approaching a red light. He or she stops not just because of the risk of punishment, the morality of the action, or the legitimacy of the law. He or she stops also because he or she fears an accident would otherwise occur. The presence of a red light means that other drivers will expect that he or she will stop. Traffic laws draw collective attention to help individuals coordinate their behaviour. Put another way: 'the law can provide a framework for understanding and predicting what others are likely to do. The shadow cast by law in these situations helps people predict not what a court is likely to do (Mnookin and Kornhauser 1979) but rather what other people who are also aware of the law are likely to do' (p. 867).

3

LEGITIMACY OF PENAL POLICIES

Punishment between normative and empirical legitimacy

Sonja Snacken

Introduction

Discussions on 'legitimacy' of penal policies often focus exclusively on (lack of) popular support as measured by public opinion polling. This chapter wants to draw a distinction between 'normative' and 'empirical' legitimacy of penal policies in democratic constitutional states. It analyses the tensions that arise between the three core characteristics of such states from a normative point of view – human rights, rule of law and democracy – and their implications for penal policies. Empirical legitimacy refers to the perception of the legitimacy of penal policies by different actors: politicians, members of the public, offenders, victims and professionals. In line with the normative argument, this chapter looks into some empirical results concerning the legitimacy of penal policies for politicians, members of the public and victims. It concludes by transforming the empirical findings concerning legitimacy into normative arguments for a reduced punitiveness in penal policies.

'Normative' legitimacy of penal policies

The 'normative' aspect of legitimacy refers to the legal theoretical requirements for policies to be legitimate in relation to the fundamental characteristics of democratic constitutional states: human rights, rule of law and democracy.[1]

Normative legitimacy: human rights, rule of law and democracy

The protection of *human rights* is at the very core of the political construct of a democratic constitutional state. Human rights express the recognition of the power of the individual, drawing the limits and frontiers of the power of the state and of state intervention. In principle, the state is not allowed to encroach upon or to interfere with these rights ('negative' state obligations). They work as a shield or a bulwark, protect individuals against excessive steering of their lives and entitle individuals to freely and autonomously determine their lives and choices and to participate in the political system (De Hert and Gutwirth, 2004). Besides these 'negative' obligations, it has increasingly been argued – for example, by the European Court of Human Rights (ECtHR) – that states also have 'positive' obligations to actively protect the human rights of individuals by taking the 'necessary' or 'reasonable and suitable' measures (Akandji-Kombe, 2007: 6; Sudre, 2005).

The *rule of law* ('constitutionalism') guarantees that a democracy is also a *Rechtsstaat*. It expresses the idea of '*government by law, not by men*': our societies are governed by rational and impersonal laws and not by arbitrary and/or emotional commands of humans. It limits the power of government through a system of imposed weighing, checking and balancing powers and subjects government and other state powers to a set of restricting constitutional rules and mechanisms. The rule of law hence provides for the principle of legality of government: public authorities are bound by their own rules and can only exercise their powers in accordance with the law. It implies that government is *accountable* and that its actions must be controllable, and thus transparent.

Democracy recognises the people's sovereignty or self-determination and the principles of democratic representation. The only valid justification of power must be sought in the citizens' consent or will. This crucial link is expressed through the different variations upon the theme of the social contract (Beccaria, Locke, Rousseau). However, social contract theories can legitimise very different forms of government: from a minimal liberal state (in the line of Locke and Beccaria) to a more republican nation (in the line of Rousseau and Kant). This might help to understand differences not only between respectively Anglo-Saxon and Continental-European legal systems (Garapon and Papadopoulos, 2003), but also between more 'populist' or more 'constitutional' interpretations of 'democracy', which have important consequences for discussions on the 'legitimacy' of penal policies.

Indeed, tensions may occur between these three basic elements; for example, when increased feelings of insecurity and fear of crime lead a majority of the citizens to prioritise crime control over respect for human rights and the rule of law. A democratic constitutional state aims at guaranteeing both and simultaneously a high level of individual freedom *and* a social order in which such freedom is made possible and guaranteed (Gutwirth, 1998; De Hert and Gutwirth, 2004). Human rights are traditionally seen as a bulwark against criminalisation and over-penalisation, as the punitive system of criminal law cuts very deep into the freedom of the citizens. Criminal law should therefore be minimal and marginal and must meet a number of strict constitutional and human rights-related conditions and standards. National constitutional courts and international human rights courts, such as the ECtHR, play an essential role in setting these conditions and standards. Punishment is probably the most interfering intervention by state authorities into the lives, fundamental rights and freedoms of suspects or convicted offenders, such as the right to life (in the case of death penalty), to freedom (in the case of imprisonment), to private and family life (in the case of most sanctions and measures imposed, including in the community), etc. From this point of view, punishment should always be problematic and restricted. But criminal law and punishment are also defended as instruments of crime control and enhanced security. Criminality infringes the social order and (often) the individual rights of victims. Increased feelings of insecurity and fear of crime may lead to popular demands for more punitive policies, based on a belief in their deterrent and incapacitative effects. And while modern criminal law, as part of public law, deals with offences as breaches of the social order and emphasises the need for protection of the fundamental rights of suspects against the penal power of the state, the increased emphasis on the (human) rights and interests of victims has led to criticisms of their marginal position in criminal procedures and sometimes to demands for increased participation in or influence on decision-making. Penal policies are developed and decided within these tensions. And it is within these tensions that more 'constitutional' or more 'populist' interpretations of 'democracy' may lead to different penal policies.

'Populism' refers to an unmediated direct link between politicians and the public (Blommaert *et al.*, 2004: 10). It is characterised by hostility to representative politics, authoritarianism, anti-elitism and mistrust of expert opinion (Taggart, 2000). 'Populist' penal policies are generally more punitive because politicians assume that this is what 'the public' wants ('populist punitiveness': Bottoms, 1995). They pursue electoral results, independent of their real effects on the general interest. Such 'populist' democracies may, however, easily result in a 'tyranny of the majority' (de Tocqueville, 1835/1956), as they emphasise the importance of the will of the majority over the rights and interests of minorities. I have argued elsewhere that this approach endangers the very concept of democracy (Snacken, 2010). Two examples. First, if this majority were to decide to exterminate an unpopular minority, that genocide would still be a crime against humanity, it would not become legitimate because it was decided by a majority. Second, the Third Reich was not a democracy because Hitler was elected in a democratic election; it was a totalitarian state because it flouted the most fundamental human rights of some (unpopular) minorities such as Jews, Free Masons, homosexuals and gypsies. Democracies therefore do not aim at the protection of the interests of a majority, but pursue the *general interest*. The rule of law or *Rechtsstaat* is not limited to the majority but is applicable to all persons subjected to state power. And that includes offenders and prisoners.

In the case of penal policies, where tensions arise between crime control and human rights, 'populist' democracies are equally at risk of flouting the most basic guarantees offered by human rights principles and the rule of law to all citizens,[2] including such unpopular minorities as offenders or prisoners. The descriptions of the developments in penal policies in the US and the UK over the last thirty years seem to illustrate such an approach. Changing sensibilities in the public (Garland, 2001) and/or a more populist approach by politicians (Tonry, 2004; Zimring and

Johnson, 2006) have led to penal policies which are no longer based on a balance between social order and human rights of all citizens, but on the political interpretations of supposed punitive expectations of victims and the general public, and which are hence no longer governed by the rational rule of law but by emotional discourse and expressive justice.

'Constitutional' democracies on the contrary are characterised by an equal importance of the three core elements: human rights, rule of law and democracy. Human rights and the rule of law are hence not dependent on the will of the majority or of a whimsical 'public opinion'. 'Legitimate' penal policies must then aim at the protection of the human rights of all citizens, including unpopular minorities such as offenders. The European policies towards the death penalty and the case law of the European Court of Human Rights (ECtHR) on the treatment of offenders and prisoners illustrate this second approach.

Normative legitimacy of penal policies: a European perspective

Abolition of the death penalty

The abolition of the death penalty in Europe is the result of a clear abolitionist policy, developed by both the Council of Europe and the European Union (EU) over recent years, and primarily based on defining the death penalty as a fundamental human rights violation (Council of Europe, 2001: 12–13). While the death penalty was allowed for by article 2 of the European Convention of Human Rights (ECHR), which came into force in 1950, its gradual abolition was fostered by Protocol 6 (1980) to the ECHR, which proposed abolition in peacetime, and Protocol 13 (2002), which imposed total abolition, including in wartime. When central and eastern European countries wanted to join the Council of Europe (and eventually the EU) in the 1990s, conditions for joining were the ratification of the ECHR and the acceptance of the individual complaint procedure before the ECtHR, the ratification of the European Convention for the Prevention of Torture and Inhuman and Degrading Treatment or Punishment (ECPT), and an immediate moratorium on executions and the obligation to abolish death penalty within two years. This indicates that at the political level, allegiance to human rights protection and abolition of the death penalty were seen as essential values in a 'European identity' and preconditions for acquiring 'European' membership, independent of public attitudes towards these issues (Snacken, 2006). At the level of the European Union, the prohibition of death penalty is similarly found under Title 1 on 'Dignity' of the EU Charter of Fundamental Rights (2000), where art. II-2 on 'Right to life' states: 'No one shall be condemned to the death penalty, or executed.' The death penalty is contrary to human dignity and therefore unacceptable, full stop. No discussion on the effectiveness of the penalty or reference to its legitimacy based on the support from public opinion, as in *Roper v. Simmons* (543 US 551 2005) before the US Supreme Court (Hood and Hoyle, 2008). This has allowed the ECtHR to declare in the case of *Öcalan v. Turkey*

(12 March 2003), that in view of the general abolition of the death penalty in Europe, this form of punishment is now regarded as unacceptable and as inhuman and degrading treatment contrary to art. 3 ECHR.

Increased protection of the fundamental human rights of offenders and prisoners

Over the last thirty years, and more specifically in the last ten years, the ECtHR has strengthened its protection of offenders and prisoners against violations of their fundamental human rights (for a more extensive analysis, see van Zyl Smit and Snacken, 2009).

With regard to the absolute prohibition of *torture and inhuman and degrading treatment* (art. 3 ECHR), its case law used to be fairly restricted, due to the fact that the Court would only consider wilful acts to constitute a violation of art. 3, thus excluding prison conditions such as overcrowding. Moreover, the Court accepts that 'all punishment has an inherent element of suffering or humiliation', and therefore requires a certain threshold to be reached before constituting a violation of art. 3. The case law on prison conditions has, however, been reversed since 2001 (*Dougoz v. Greece*, 6 March 2001, concerning prison overcrowding), and has since been confirmed for other examples of 'impoverished regimes' (*Alver v. Estonia*, 8 November 2005). This reversal is testimony to the increased influence by the European Committee for the Prevention of Torture (CPT), which through its visits of places of detention all over Europe fulfils the role of 'fact finding instrument' for the Court. Restrictions on penal excess have also been imposed by the Court in cases concerning arbitrary strip searches in a special security unit (*Van der Ven v. the Netherlands*, 4 February 2003) or the disproportionate use of solitary confinement for a violent and uncooperative prisoner (*Matthew v. the Netherlands*, 29 September 2005). Its jurisprudence on high security units and solitary confinement clearly indicates that forms of total isolation as imposed in some 'supermax' prisons or units in the US would be considered inhuman and degrading treatment in Europe (*Messina v. Italy*, 28 September 2000; *Ramirez Sanchez v. France*, 4 July 2006), as were death rows (*Soering v. UK*, 7 July 1989). With regard to torture, the Court has explicitly reinforced its protection of suspects and prisoners, explaining in *Selmouni v. France* (28 July 1999, § 101) that

> It takes the view that the increasingly high standard being required in the area of the protection of human rights and fundamental liberties corres- pondingly and inevitably requires greater firmness in assessing breaches of the fundamental values of democratic societies.

Other fundamental civil and political rights laid down in the ECHR, such as arts. 8–11 which protect the right to family life, freedom of conscience and religion, freedom of expression and freedom of association, are less absolute and can be restricted 'in the interest of national security, public safety or the economic well-being of the country, for the prevention of disorder or crime, for the protection of health or morals, or for the protection of the rights and freedoms of others'. In 1975, the Court abandoned the previously held 'theory of inherent limitations' (*Golder v. UK*, 21 February 1975) and recognised that prisoners retain their fundamental human rights, which may only be restricted if the interference is in accordance with the law, pursues a legitimate aim and is absolutely necessary (proportionate) in a democratic society. While the 'prevention of disorder or crime' and 'the protection of rights of others' have been recognised by the Court as legitimate aims in a democratic society, it has increasingly found restrictions imposed on prisoners by national authorities to be disproportionate. Over the last ten years, major cases have thus reaffirmed prisoners' rights to marry (*Hirst v. UK (no 2)* [GC], 6 October 2005), to found a family (*Dickson v. UK* [GC], 4 December 2007: if necessary through artificial insemination), to maintain parental rights where possible (*Sabou and Pircalab v. Romania*, 28 September 2004), to family visits (*Messina v. Italy (no 2)*, 28 September 2000; *Ostrovar v. Moldova*, 13 September 2005; *Ciorap v. Moldova*, 19 June 2007: without undue restrictions to physical contacts), to correspondence (*Cotlet v. Romania*, 3 March 2003), to freedom of expression (*Yankov v. Bulgaria*, 11 December 2003: including a prisoner's right to write a book highly critical of the penal and the prison system), to vote (*Hirst v. United Kingdom (no 2)* [GC], 6 October 2005: total prohibition is contrary to art. 3 of Protocol 1 to ECHR). These judgements bring prisoners in Europe closer to the concept of 'legal citizens' (Kelk, 2008).

Throughout this case law, the Court often refers to the *protection of fundamental human* rights as one of the most important hallmarks of a *democratic society*. The use of 'public opinion' by (often the UK) government as an argument for punitive policies or restrictions on prisoners' rights has been criticised on several occasions by the Court. In *Stafford v. UK* (GC), 28 May 2002, on parole, the Court stated:

> It is not apparent how public confidence in the system of criminal justice could legitimately require the continued incarceration of a prisoner who had served the term required for punishment for the offence and was no longer a risk to the public.
>
> (§80)

Equally, in *Hirst v. United Kingdom (no 2)* [GC] 6 October 2005, on the right to vote for sentenced prisoners, the Court emphasised:

> Nor is there any place under the Convention, where tolerance and broadmindedness are the acknowledged hallmarks of democratic society, for automatic disenfranchisement based purely on what might offend public opinion.
>
> (§70)

This obviously illustrates a 'constitutional' interpretation of 'democracy', where fundamental human rights and freedoms must be protected independent of what might offend public opinion. Even national legislation, 'democratically' voted in national parliaments, has in some instances been found to violate the ECHR for not being in accordance with the 'rule of law'. The Court thus found the censorship of prisoners' letters in several countries to be legal but illegitimate, because the legislation was too vaguely formulated or left too much arbitrary power to prison staff (*Domenchini v. Italy*, 15 November 1996, *Petra v. Romania*, 23 September 1998; *Dankevich v. Ukraine*, 29 April 2003; *Čiapas v. Lithuania*, 16 November 2006, *Frerot v. France*, 12 June 2007).

Interestingly, the Court has also increasingly referred to the importance of 'rehabilitation' or '*reintegration*' as a legitimate aim of imprisonment, thus reinforcing a prisoner's right to family life (*Dickson v. UK* [GC], 4 December 2007: if necessary through artificial insemination) and to family visits (*Messina v. Italy (no 2)*, 28 September 2000: even for members of organised crime networks based on family ties). It has emphasised the legitimacy of a policy of progressive social reintegration through temporary release, even for prisoners convicted of serious violent crimes (*Mastromatteo v. Italy*, 24 October 2002 § 72; *Kafkaris v. Cyprus*, 11 April 2006).

This does not mean that the Court disregards the *rights of victims or society* to be protected from serious offenders. In the case of *Mastromatteo v. Italy*, 24 October 2002, where the temporary release resulted in re-offending leading to the loss of life of the victim, the Court reaffirmed that the authorities have a positive obligation, derived from Article 2 of the ECHR, to protect the life of its citizens (§67). This does not mean, however, that the authorities must be able to prevent any potential violence:

> bearing in mind the difficulties involved in policing modern societies, the unpredictability of human conduct and the operational choices which must be made in terms of priorities and resources. . . . A positive obligation will arise, the Court has held, where it has been established that the authorities knew or ought to have known at the time of the existence of a real and immediate risk to the life of an identified individual or individuals from the criminal acts of a third party and that they failed to take measures within the scope of their powers which, judged reasonably, might have been expected to avoid that risk.
>
> (§68)

As all necessary precautions had been taken by the Italian authorities, no such breaches were found by the Court in the case of *Mastromatteo*. However, in the more recent case of *Maiorano v. Italy*, 15 December 2009, a breach of Article 2 was found to result from the authorities' failure to take adequate note of the repeatedly violent behaviour of the prisoner while in prison and the failure of the prosecutor to refer the case back to the Implementation Court when the prisoner breached the conditions of his semi-liberty.

The Court thus can be said to aim for a balance between the rights of offenders and the rights of victims and society. It has made it clear that victims do not have a right to private vengeance or to have an offender prosecuted or sentenced (*Perez v. France*, 12 February 2004). But in some cases it has stated that member states must apply criminal law, prosecution and penal sentencing in order to combat impunity of offenders, to protect the human rights of victims of crime by their fellow citizens or by the state and to retain credibility with the public (see De Hert et al., 2007). This has raised the question as to whether human rights are a new motor for criminalisation and punitiveness in Europe. Françoise Tulkens, judge in the ECtHR, argues, however, that this is only used in cases concerning the most serious breaches of the most fundamental rights protected by the Convention, such as the right to life (art. 2) and the prohibition of torture and inhuman and degrading treatment (art. 3), and refers mainly to the risk of self-proclaimed impunity of state authorities. She agrees though that the preventive and deterrent effects of criminal law and punishment are overestimated by the Court due to insufficient knowledge of relevant criminological evidence to the contrary (Tulkens, 2012).

Penal policies: choice and length of sanctions

The Court has been more reluctant to interfere in penal policies concerning the choice and the length of sanctions imposed, except for some extreme examples.

Thus, judicial corporal punishment was found to be contrary to art. 3 (*Tyrer v. UK*, 25 April 1978), but life imprisonment is not, if imposed for very serious offences (*Sawoniuk v. UK*, 29 May 2001). 'Life without parole' though would 'raise an issue under art. 3', both for juveniles (*V. v. UK* [GC], 16 December 1999) and for adults (*Kafkaris v. Cyprus* [GC], 12 February 2008). Although there has been no conclusive case yet, the Court declares in *Kafkaris* that art. 3 requires 'that a life sentence is *de jure* and *de facto* reducible' (ibid.: § 98).

As far as imprisonment is concerned, art. 5 §1 ECHR guarantees the right to freedom and security, but also provides for lawful forms of deprivation of liberty: imprisonment after conviction by a competent court (§1a), to secure a legal obligation (§1b), remand custody (§1c), detention of a minor for educational supervision or remand custody (§1d), detention of persons with infectious diseases, of unsound mind, drug addicts or vagrants (§1e), detention of illegal aliens in order to prevent unauthorised entry into the country or with a view to deportation or extradition (§1f). Art. 5 thus protects individuals against undue or arbitrary restrictions of their liberty. The right to liberty is the norm, restrictions are the exceptions and must meet strict requirements of legality, legitimacy and proportionality. 'Arbitrary and disproportionate' punishment is therefore contrary to article 5 of the ECHR (*Winterwerp v. the Netherlands*, 24 October 1979). In order to be legitimate there must be a relation between the aim and the place and regime of the detention (*Ashingdane v. UK* 28, May 1985; *Bouamar v. Belgium*, 27 June 1988; *Aerts v. Belgium*, 30 July 1998). Grossly disproportionate sentences could amount to inhuman punishment contrary to art. 3, but this would depend on the sex, age and state of health of the prisoner (*Ireland v. UK*, 1978; *A v. UK*, 1999). They could also conflict with articles 8 to 11 ECHR (van Zyl Smit and Ashworth, 2004).

Nevertheless, the fact that the detention must be legitimate does not necessarily mean that the sentence must be appropriate, as the ECtHR has stated that art. 5 §1 does not allow it to control the appropriateness of a sentence imposed by a trial judge (*Weeks v. United Kingdom*, 2 March 1987 § 50). In its recent case law, the Court explicitly accepts the principle of *deprivation of liberty as a measure of last resort* (*Saadi v. UK*, 29 January 2008 § 70; reiterated in *Rusu v. Austria*, 2 October 2008 (final judgement 2 January 2009) § 58). However, it distinguishes between the different grounds for detention under art. 5, using less strict criteria of arbitrariness and proportionality for sentences to imprisonment under art. 5 §1 (a) (*Saadi v. UK*, 29 January 2008 §71) and remand custody under §1 (c) (*Bouchet v. France*, 20 March 2001), than for art. 5 §1 (b), (d), (e) and (f) (*Saadi v. UK*, 29 January 2008 § 71). Although this view can be understood considering the large variation in penal trends and levels in Europe,[3] I have argued elsewhere that it is illogical for the Court to apply a stricter subsidiarity and proportionality principle to sanctions imposed under arts 8 to 11 than under art. 5 (Snacken, 2006; van Zyl Smit and Snacken, 2009). Under arts 8 to 11, the Court requires the choice between different types of punishment or measures to be the result of a balancing of their relative severity with regard to interference with fundamental rights and requires States '*to minimise, as far as possible, the interference with these rights, by trying to find alternative solutions and by generally seeking to achieve their aims in the least onerous way as regards human rights*' (*Hatton and others v. United Kingdom*, 2 October 2001 §87).[4] But this balancing is not required by the Court when deciding on penal sanctions or measures under art. 5 §1 (*Bouchet v. France*, 20 March 2001). This is strange, as imprisonment is the most severe interference with the rights and freedoms of suspects and convicts by state authorities in Europe. This is not altered by the evolution of the case law of the ECtHR concerning prisoners' rights. Deprivation of liberty remains a severe restriction of 'normal' life and inevitably hampers the full enjoyment of other rights and freedoms, such as private and family life, association and expression. Research has consistently shown that most detrimental effects of imprisonment increase with the length of the detention (van Zyl Smit and Snacken, 2009: 47–54). Other penalties, such as fines or community sanctions and measures, may also restrict rights and freedoms, but are usually less invasive than imprisonment. Applying the principle of proportionality, as interpreted for arts 8 to 11, to imprisonment would then mean that, throughout the processes of criminalisation, prosecution, sentencing and implementation of sentences, only the least invasive decision could be considered legitimate and proportionate. In every sentencing or early release case, the choice of sanction should be the object of a debate, in which it is up to the prosecutor to demonstrate that a prison sentence is necessary. It should no longer be up to the offenders to prove that they still 'deserve' a non-custodial sanction, as is often the case now. The ECtHR could then evaluate the procedures to decide whether such a balancing exercise had taken place and whether, substantively, it had led to the imposition of the least invasive sanction or measure as regards human rights.

The argument for subsidiarity of imprisonment compared to other, less intrusive forms of punishment, is further reinforced by the Court's argument that deprivation of liberty always entails an 'inherent form of humiliation'. The Court has never defined this 'inherent element'. Based on the definition by a Flemish philosopher of human dignity as 'the recognition of the individual and social identity, and the possibility to choose, decide and act autonomously' (Apostel, 1993), I have argued that all forms of deprivation of liberty fundamentally infringe upon the human dignity of the prisoner. No matter how many rights may be retained by prisoners, no prison can function without somehow 'mortifying' the individual, altering the social identity of prisoners, and limiting their opportunities to choose, act and decide autonomously. This is hence an argument both in favour of reinforcing prisoners' fundamental rights and freedoms, in order to foster their individual and social identity and autonomy, and thus their human dignity, and in favour of using imprisonment as a last resort (Snacken, 2011; van Zyl Smit and Snacken, 2009: 101).

Empirical legitimacy of penal policies

Empirical legitimacy refers to the perception of the legitimacy of penal policies by different actors: politicians, members of the public, offenders, victims and professionals. It is of course impossible within the scope of this chapter to deal with all the actors involved. In line with the arguments developed above concerning 'normative' legitimacy, I will focus on empirical results concerning the legitimacy of penal policies for politicians, members of the public and victims.

Political legitimacy

The 'political legitimacy' of penal policies refers to how politicians construct and interpret the legitimacy of their policy-making. This will also depend on the political culture in a particular country and on the more 'constitutional' or more 'populist' interpretation of democracy by politicians and the public. Increased levels of punitiveness[5] in the US, the UK and other Anglo-Saxon countries have thus been linked to a changing relationship between political decision-making and 'expert' versus 'public' opinion, characterised by the demise of rational responses by experts and practitioners and an increased influence of tabloids and emotions of the 'public' (Garland, 2001; Tonry, 2004; Brown, 2005; Zimring and Johnson, 2006). Concepts such as 'penal populism' or *'populist punitiveness'* (Bottoms, 1995) refer to more punitive discourses and policies being developed by politicians because they believe this is what the public wants and this will get them re-elected, independent of the real effects of these policies. The nature of this change is the object of much academic debate, as some claim that the public mood towards offenders has changed radically (Garland, 2001: from disadvantaged but deserving poor in the 1970s to unruly youth, sexual predators and incorrigible career criminals in the 1990s), while others claim that attitudes of the public towards criminals have always been negative, and that US politicians turned more populist in order to counter increasing public distrust of government competence and legitimacy, and produced structural changes in sentencing that made punishments even harder (Zimring and Johnson, 2006).

This 'governing through crime' has also been linked to the *globalisation* processes of the economy and the resulting transformations and limitations of the traditional competences of national states. One line of thought links globalisation to the decline of the 'welfare state' and to the emergence of 'insecurity' as a major political topic (Mary, 2003). A worldwide shift of the welfare model towards the model of global capitalist competition is developing, although at different paces and with different depths in the different national states. As economic and social matters increasingly escape national control mechanisms, national states are forced to find a new legitimacy. The ongoing deregulation reduces the state to its repressive functions. Insecurity as a political topic hence becomes more a solution than a problem (Van Campenhoudt, 1999). Several authors see the emergence of 'penal states' or 'security states' as a result of this forced reorientation towards a new legitimacy (Garapon and Salas, 1996; Brants, Mevis and Prakken, 2001; Wacquant, 2004). The USA are described in this analysis as the extreme model of the 'penal state': they never were a 'social state' to start with but rather a 'charity state', and they are imprisoning up to twenty times as many of their citizens as other Western countries. The ongoing dismantling of the 'social states' in western Europe is, however, seen as a risky trend in the same direction towards 'penal states' in Europe (Wacquant, 2004).

However, despite similar economic transformations, public opinion patterns, social developments and crime trends in most Western countries, *punishment trends vary widely* (Tonry, 2001, 2007). This has been linked to different political economies (Cavadino and Dignan, 2006; Lacey, 2008; Pratt, 2008). Prison rates are inversely correlated with welfare investments (Becket and Western, 2001 for the US, Downes and Hansen, 2006 for Europe) and are higher in majoritarian than in consensual democracies (Lappi-Seppälä, 2007, 2008). Lappi-Seppälä's (2007, 2008, 2011) comparative analysis of twenty-five countries (sixteen Western European, three Eastern European, two Baltic countries and four Anglo-Saxon countries outside Europe) shows that more welfare-oriented countries enjoy more public trust (both horizontally between citizens and vertically from citizens in institutions), less fear of crime and more political legitimacy. Lappi-Seppälä (2011) argues that the correlation with lower prison rates could then be explained by the fact that there is less political need for punitive discourse and policy, less populism and more expert-oriented penal policies. The lower prison rates in consensual versus majoritarian democracies could relate to the fact that the former necessitate more political compromises between political parties, hence allow less crisis talk and more moderate and long-term policies. They also appear to be more welfare and more expert oriented. However, other aspects such as the judicial culture and structure (elected versus career judiciary) and media culture and structure (Green, 2007) are also important.

Public legitimacy

'Public legitimacy' refers to how 'the public' perceives the legitimacy of penal policies. Opinion polls have become increasingly important tools in this regard, both for researchers and for policy-makers. Quantitative surveys seem to indicate cross-national agreement that the severity of sanctions imposed by judges is not proportionate to the seriousness of the crimes, that crimes are committed because sanctions are too lenient and that a vast majority of respondents in all countries want harsher punishments. At the same time, these surveys also consistently show that respondents overestimate the seriousness of crime and underestimate the use of imprisonment and that more information on individual circumstances and characteristics of offenders, but also on a variety of possible non-custodial sanctions, leads to less punitive results. Levels of public punitiveness also vary over time and space and with the socioeconomic characteristics of respondents (Roberts and Hough, 2002; Roberts *et al.*, 2003).

How much influence should such results have on penal policies? I have already argued in this chapter that 'public opinion' should not overrule the demands of 'normative' legitimacy with regard to respect for fundamental human rights and the rule of law. But these normative demands do not cover all aspects of penal policies. In order to answer the question, we should distinguish between penal actors who develop overall penal policies and are accountable to the general public, that is, politicians, and others whose independence in individual cases is a fundamental prerequisite of a *Rechtsstaat*, that is, the judiciary.

Surveys coupled to qualitative research in the Netherlands thus show that, although there is a gap in punitiveness between the *judiciary* and the public, this gap does not diminish the legitimacy of the judiciary in the eyes of the public, because other criteria relating to the basic values of justice, fairness and independence are seen as more important (Elffers and De Keijser, 2008). Thus,

TABLE 3.1 Ranking of most important traits of judges

Trait of judge	Ranked among five most important (%)	Most important
Just	92	42
Impartial	82	22
Independent	71	14
Critical	54	2
A good listener	52	4
Law specialist	50	3
Understanding towards victims	40	7
Aware of public opinion	33	3
Punishes severely	22	2
Understanding towards accused	4	0

Source: Elffers and De Keijser (2008: 466)

although 84 per cent of respondents thought that 'sanctions in the Netherlands are too lenient', 73 per cent also agreed that 'in the eyes of the general public sentences will never be harsh enough' and 72 per cent agreed that 'judges should sentence independent from public opinion'. When asked what the five most important attributes for judges were, the results show that sentence severity (22%) and being 'aware of public opinion' (33%) scored much lower than the attributes 'just' (92%), 'impartial' (82%) and 'independent' (71%):

The authors thus conclude that the public is willing to accept a certain gap in punitiveness and that 'the traits that are considered most important by the public are closer to procedural justice than they are to responsive justice' (Elffers and De Keijser, 2008: 466).

Politicians of course are not independent but accountable to the public. There are different methods for politicians to know what 'the public' wants (elections, everyday conversations), but opinion polls concerning crime and punishment have become increasingly important sources of information in many countries. What do – and can – these opinion polls tell us about the public construction of legitimacy of penal policies?

There are of course many different forms and formats of public opinion polls, ranging from the one 'yes or no' question on death penalty or conditional release of prisoners through TV-voting to methodologically highly sophisticated quantitative surveys based on a random sample of respondents. The former will be favoured by populist politicians, who like to present 'the public' (or a majority) as a homogeneous body and to defend a 'politics of simplicity' based on common sense and straightforwardness, reducing the public debate to dualisms and uncompromising political essentialism (Abts, 2004; Blommaert *et al.*, 2004; Verfaillie, 2009, 2012; for an example on TV-voting in Belgium, see Snacken and Verfaillie, 2009). The latter, on the contrary, produce knowledge about how opinions are distributed within a social group or across a society. As already mentioned, they conclude that attitudes towards crime and punishment depend on the information provided, vary over time and space and with the socioeconomic characteristics of respondents. Moreover, people seem to be ambivalent about how we should punish (Stalans, 2002; Roberts and Hough, 2002; Roberts *et al.*, 2003; Roberts and Hough, 2005; Hutton, 2005).

According to Stalans (2002: 16–17), the image of an ambivalent, complex and ambiguous public stems from the various methodologies researchers have mobilised to measure attitudes to punishment. Despite these efforts, Stalans (2002: 20) finds that researchers have barely scratched the surface of public attitudes to punishment, and she suggests that we need to come to a more thorough understanding of information processing and attitude structures.

This image of an ambivalent, complex and ambiguous public also emerges from the *Belgian Justice Barometer*, a quantitative survey based on a random sampling of respondents, which questions attitudes of citizens towards the Belgian justice system (Parmentier *et al.*, 2004). With regard to the penal system, a majority of respondents thus favour both harsher sentences and more non-custodial sanctions, believe in retribution and rehabilitation as important aims of punishment, support juvenile prisons but think that education and employment are the most adequate ways to tackle juvenile delinquency. In order to understand these apparent paradoxes, a qualitative research of public attitudes to crime and punishment is currently being undertaken by Verfaillie (Verfaillie, 2009, 2012; Snacken and Verfaillie, 2009), building on the ethnographic method used by Girling *et al.* (2000). The research focuses on the processes of attitudinal development and on the sources of authority used in these processes. Following a 'critical discourse analysis' perspective, developed by Meert *et al.* (2004), opinions are analysed in terms of situated discourses and behaviour and as 'logically structured paradoxes':

> Opinions are shaped relative to concrete events and occurrences in space and time. People interpret or evaluate these events and occurrences, they categorize the information they receive and structure it hierarchically. Opinions are thus situated, dynamic and complex, they are organized thematically, i.e. related to specific issues, themes and fields. Precisely because opinions are organized thematically, people often seem to be ambivalent or inconsistent from an ideological point of view. . . . In the field of education, people might be Muslim, but send their children to a catholic school. . . . Meert, et. al. (2004) thus find it more useful to describe people's attitudes and opinions as 'logically structured paradoxes': people's statements are consistent with almost microscopically and thematically organized hegemonies (see also Blommaert, 2005).
>
> (Verfaillie, 2012: 234)

This 'thematic' or 'polycentric' consistency is also found by Verfaillie (2012) in his ethnographic research into attitudes towards crime and punishment. Asked to comment on her answers to the *Justice Barometer*, one of the respondents thus explains that she simultaneously 'Distrusts the criminal justice system' and thinks that 'Most decisions by judges are fair, equality is guaranteed.' The apparent paradox is explained by media coverage of procedural games played by defence lawyers in high-profile cases versus her confidence in the professionalism of Belgian judges. She also thinks that 'Sanctions are too lenient' and she is 'Against conditional release of prisoners', but she 'Favours social reintegration of prisoners.' She opposes conditional release because she believes this infringes upon a judge's expert assessment of a case and because this leads to too much uncertainty for prisoners about their possible date of release. But she favours social reintegration because every person should be able to hope for the future. She is therefore convinced that prisoners should be given a fixed sentence and that this term should be used to prepare their return to society.

What are the implications of these qualitative findings for the use of opinion polls in assessing the legitimacy of penal policies?

I would agree with Verfaillie (2012) that one of the important findings seems to be that answers are never given *in abstracto*, but always refer to concrete situations, people and events. Answers to survey questions hence cannot be understood apart from the context in which they are produced. Yet, surveys will almost inevitably reduce people's narratives in terms of the categories provided in the survey. The answers may then be misinterpreted by politicians and scholars. For instance, the above-mentioned opinion that prisoners should serve the full length of their sentence would probably be defined as a punitive one, although the reasoning behind the opinion – favouring social reintegration while guaranteeing legal certainty to prisoners – is not. Similarly, the opposition to conditional release seems at first sight in contradiction with the favouring of social reintegration, but this ambivalence or paradox has a logical though polycentric explanation. To conclude:

> This ambivalence is a problem for policymakers, and for populists in particular, because it suggests that simple and straightforward conclusions about people's opinions cannot easily be drawn. . . . Because ambivalence about punishment and criminal justice seems inevitable, generalizations or global statements about 'the right punishment', 'the criminal justice system', and 'public opinion' should be treated with care.'
>
> (Verfaillie, 2012: 241)

Victims and legitimacy of penal policies

Many countries have witnessed the emergence of victim movements and a growing public support for and solidarity with victims of crime. This may lead to increased criminalisation at the level of legislation and practice. In the US, punitive laws have been passed in the name of particular victims, such as 'Megan's law' concerning the registration of sex offenders. Some politicians seem to consider that the rights of victims can only be defended through more punitive and exclusionary practices towards offenders ('zero-sum policy') (Garland, 2001). Other movements have, however, tried to foster both the interests and the rights of victims and of offenders and to avoid punitive reactions, such as the 'procedural justice' and the 'restorative justice' movements. So what does empirical research tell us about the legitimacy of penal policies for victims?

First of all, it should be stressed that the victimological literature has demonstrated the importance of the treatment of victims by criminal justice agencies in avoiding secondary victimisation (Wemmers, 1996; Shapland *et al.*, 1985). Victims expect decent information concerning judicial procedures, a respectful and correct treatment by penal actors, a not purely formalistic approach to the case, a greater personal implication and participation, receiving financial or material compensation and, finally, receiving psychological restoration by the attitude of the offender (Aertsen, 2012). Expectations seem hence more related to procedural aspects than to (punitive) results (Shapland *et al.*, 1985), although this aspect varies with the type of offence (violent offences versus property offences) and between individual victims (Lemonne *et al.*, 2007). Few victims want to influence sentencing, but many want to be informed about the sentence (ibid.). Victims are not more punitive than other members of the public, and the same variations in punitiveness exist as in the general public (Costelloe *et al.*, 2009; King and Maruna, 2009).

Avoiding secondary victimisation hence mainly entails respectful treatment, adequate information, more participation, support and assistance. Research on 'procedural justice' (cf. Tyler, 2006) and on 'restorative justice' indicates that fair and respectful treatment of the victim also leads to a better acceptance of the outcome of penal procedures (Aertsen, 2012). Much more controversial is the issue of 'participation' of the victim in penal procedures. In some European countries, victims can be added as 'civil parties' to the inquisitorial criminal process. This allows them to inform the court about the physical or emotional consequences of the offence, but this relates only to the civil compensation of damages and is in principle without influence on the punishment. In other, mainly Anglo-Saxon countries, where the accusatorial system does not provide many opportunities for participation by the victim, 'victim impact statements' have been introduced as a means to contribute to the penal decision-making. This has been strongly criticised, as different sensibilities of individual victims will lead to violation of the fundamental penal principles of equality and proportionality (Cesoni and Rechtman, 2005). Moreover, the increased emphasis on 'symbolic' or even 'psychological reparation' of victims through the criminal procedure may itself lead to secondary victimisation. Some research indicates that basic legal principles and guarantees such as the 'presumption of innocence' of the offender may lead to feelings of injustice for the victims, as some may feel that a 'presumption of good faith of the victim' should rather lead to a 'presumption of culpability' of the offender (Languin and Robert, 2012). This has been linked by Cesoni and Rechtman (2005: 163–5) to the psychiatric evolution concerning 'post traumatic stress disorder' ('PTSD') in the US in the 1960s. Pressured by lobbying from war veterans and feminists, the DSM III introduced 'PTSD' as a specific syndrome resulting from exceptional events (e.g., war, domestic violence). The new classification did not define such events, but emphasised that the victims had no responsibility whatsoever in their occurrence, thus moving away from the traditional 'clinic of suspicion' concerning post-traumatic pathologies towards a 'clinic of innocence'. This was then rapidly taken over by victim organisations in the US, and later in other countries such as France in the 1990s. Psychological trauma became the 'normal' hallmark of victimisation, and its psychological reparation a new collective obligation. However, claiming to help victims to cope with their traumas through penal procedures and punishment of the offender is also dangerous, as there is no medical or psychiatric evidence of the 'therapeutic' effects of the criminal procedure for victims, and penal actors are in general not competent to deal with psychic traumas (Cesoni and Rechtman, 2005: 167).

Victim movements themselves also represent a variety of ideologies, from an ideology of care, to an instrumental, retributive or abolitionist ideology. While victim movements in the US emphasised from the start the need to strengthen the rights of victims in different criminal procedures, European movements emphasised more the improvement of the provision of care to victims of crime. The involvement of probation staff and of academics in the European movements may also have contributed to a more balanced, less punitive approach (Aertsen, 2012). Moreover, empirical research has demonstrated that more punitive policies, such as the abolition of parole for serious offenders, do not enhance the legitimacy of the criminal justice system for victims, as their satisfaction with the sentence correlates primarily with 'procedural justice' aspects in the performance by the criminal justice professionals and with victim support (Mc Coy and McManimon, 2002). This emphasis on 'procedural justice' for victims can also be found at the European institutional level. Both the *European Union* (Council Framework Decision of 15 March 2001 on the standing of victims in criminal proceedings) and the *Council of Europe* (e.g., European Convention on Compensation of Victims of Violent Crime, 1983; Rec(2006)8 on assistance to crime victims) stress the rights of victims to be treated with respect for their dignity, to provide and receive information, to understand and be understood, to be protected at the various stages of the procedure and to receive compensation by the offender or by the state. The EU Framework Decision emphasises that this does not impose an obligation on Member States 'to ensure that victims will be treated in a manner equivalent to that of a party to proceedings' (Preamble, 9) and promotes mediation in appropriate criminal cases (art. 10). The Council of Europe insists on the importance of assistance to victims, including medical care, material support, psychological health services, social care and counselling, on compensation schemes by the state and on the potential benefits of mediation for victims (see also Rec(99)19 concerning mediation in penal matters).

Conclusion

The normative legitimacy of penal policies in democratic constitutional states requires policy-makers and courts to take into account the fundamental human rights of all persons, including unpopular minorities such as offenders or prisoners. European policies towards the abolition of the death penalty and the increased protection of prisoners' rights by the ECtHR illustrate such a normative approach to legitimacy. Although populist politicians often refer to 'the public' in order to justify more punitive policies, empirical research shows that public opinions concerning crime and punishment are much more complex and ambivalent than these politicians like to present. The example of the Dutch surveys illustrates that questions concerning the public legitimacy of penal actors such as the judiciary cannot be reduced to levels of punitiveness, but must be assessed within other basic values such as justice, fairness and independence. The fundamental importance of procedural justice in the opinions of the public and in the expectations of victims of crime seems much more in line with the normative arguments concerning fundamental human rights and the rule of law than is often assumed. Comparative studies also show that countries with the lowest levels of punitiveness but the highest investments in welfare and social equality enjoy the highest political legitimacy and trust. Politicians could hence develop less punitive penal policies, in accordance with the normative demands of democratic constitutional states, without necessarily loosing political legitimacy.

References

Abts, K. (2004) 'Het populistisch appel: voorbij de populaire communicatiestijl en ordinaire democratiekritiek', *Tijdschrift voor Sociologie*, 25(4): 451–76.

Aertsen, I. (2012) 'Punitivity from a victim's perspective', in S. Snacken and E. Dumortier (eds) *Resisting Punitiveness in Europe? Welfare, Human Rights and Democracy*, London, New York: Routledge, 202–24.

Akandji-Kombe, J.-F. (2007) *Positive Obligations under the European Convention of Human Rights. A guide to the implementation of the European Convention of Human Rights*, Human Rights Handbooks nr 7, Strasbourg: Council of Europe.

Apostel, L. (1993) '*Ethische vraagstukken rond het levenseinde*', Symposium met Leo Apostel en Wim Distelmans, Federatie Palliatieve Zorg Vlaanderen, 12 mei 1993.

Becket, K. and Western, B. (2001) 'Governing social marginality. Welfare, incarceration and the transformation of state policy', *Punishment and Society*, 1: 43–59.

Blommaert, J. (2005) *Discourse: A Critical Introduction*, Cambridge: Cambridge University Press.

Blommaert, J., Corijn, E., Holthof, M. and Lesage, D. (2004) *Populisme*, Berchem: EPO.

Bottoms, A. (1995) 'The philosophy and politics of punishment and sentencing', in C.M.V. Clarkson and R. Morgan (eds) *The Politics of Sentencing Reform*, Oxford: Clarendon Press Oxford, pp. 17–50.

Brants, C.H., Mevis, P.A.M. and Prakken, E. (2001) *Legitieme strafvordering. Rechten van de mens als inspiratie in de 21ste eeuw*, Antwerpen-Groningen: Intersentia Rechtsweten-schappen.

Brown, D. (2005) 'Continuity, rupture or more of the "volatile and contradictory"? Glimpses of New South Wales' penal practice behind and through the discursive', in J. Pratt, D. Brown, M. Brown, S. Hallsworth and W. Morrison, (eds) *The New Punitiveness: Trends, theories, perspectives*, Cullompton: Willan Publishing, pp. 27–46.

Cavadino, M. and Dignan, J. (2006) *Penal Systems: A Comparative Approach*, London: Sage Publications.

Cesoni, M.-L., and Rechtman, R. (2005) 'La "réparation psychologique" de la victime: une nouvelle fonction de la peine?', *Revue de Droit Pénal et de Criminologie*, 158–78.

Costelloe, M.T., Chiricos, T. and Gertz, M. (2009) 'Punitive attitudes towards criminals. Exploring the relevance of crime salience and economic security', *Punishment and Society*, 1: 25–49.

Council of Europe (2001) *La peine de mort hors la loi! Le Conseil de l'Europe et la peine de mort*, Direction Générale des Droits de l'Homme, Strasbourg: Conseil de l'Europe.

De Hert, P. and Gutwirth, S. (2004) 'Rawls' political conception of rights and liberties. An unliberal but pragmatic approach to the problems of harmonisation and globalisation', in M. Van Hoecke (ed.) *Epistemology and Methodology of Comparative Law*, Oxford and Portland, OR: Hart, pp. 317–57.

De Hert, P., Gutwirth, S., Snacken, S. and Dumortier, E. (2007) 'La montée de l'Etat pénal. Que peuvent les droits de l'homme?', in M. Van de Kerchove (ed.) *Les droits de l'homme, bouclier ou épée du droit penal?* Bruxelles: Facultés Universitaires Saint Louis, pp. 235–90.

De Tocqueville, A. (1956 [1835]) *Democracy in America* (ed. Richard D. Heffner), New York: Mentor Books.

Downes, D. and Hansen, K. (2006) 'Welfare and punishment in comparative perspective', in S. Amstrong and L. McAra (eds) *Perspectives on Punishment. The Contours of Control*, Oxford: Oxford University Press, pp. 133–54.

Elffers, H. and De Keijser, J.W. (2008) 'Different perspectives, different gaps. Does the general public demand a more responsive judge?', in H. Kury (ed.) *Fear of Crime – Punitivity. New Developments in Theory and Research*, Crime and Crime Policy Volume 3, Bochum: Universitätsverlag Brockmeyer, pp. 447–69.

European Union, Charter of Fundamental Rights of the European Union (2000) *Official Journal of the European Communities*, C 364/01–22.

Garapon, A. and Papadopoulos, I. (2003) *Juger en amérique et en France. Culture juridique et common law*, Paris: Odile Jacob.

Garapon, A. and Salas, D. (1996) *La République pénalisée*, Paris: Hachette.

Garland, D. (2001) *The Culture of Control. Crime and social order in contemporary society*, Oxford: Oxford University Press.

Girling, E., Loader, I. and Sparks, R. (2000) *Crime and Social Change in Middle England. Questions of Order in an English Town*, London: Routledge.

Green, D.A. (2007) 'Comparing penal cultures. Two responses to child-on-child homicide', in M. Tonry (ed.) *Crime, Punishment and Politics in Comparative Perspective, Crime and Justice, A Review of Research* Vol. 36, Chicago: Chicago University Press, pp. 591–643.

Gutwirth, S. (1998) 'De polyfonie van de democratische rechtsstaat (The polyphony of the democratic constitutional state)', in M. Elchardus (ed.) *Wantrouwen en onbehagen* (Distrust and uneasiness), Balans 14, Brussels: VUB Press, pp. 37–193.

Hood, R. and Hoyle, C. (2008) *The Death Penalty: A Worldwide Perspective* (4th edn), Oxford: Clarendon Press.

Hutton, N. (2005) 'Beyond populist punitiveness', *Punishment and Society*, 7(3): 243–58.

Kelk, C. (2008) *Nederlands detentierecht* (3rd edn), Deventer: Gouda Quint.

King, A. and Maruna, S. (2009) 'Is a conservative just a liberal who has been mugged? Exploring the origins of punitive views', *Punishment and Society*, 11(2): 147–69.

Lacey, N. (2008) *The Prisoner's Dilemma: political economy and punishment in contemporary democracies*, Cambridge: Cambridge University Press.

Lappi-Seppälä, T. (2007) 'Penal Policy in Scandinavia', in M. Tonry (ed.) *Crime, Punishment and Politics in Comparative Perspective, Crime and Justice, A Review of Research*, Vol. 36, Chicago: Chicago University Press.

—— (2008) 'Trust, welfare and political culture. Explaining difference in national penal policies', in M. Tonry (ed.) *Crime and Justice: A Review of Research*, Vol. 37, Chicago: Chicago University Press.

—— (2011) 'Explaining national differences in the use of imprisonment', in S. Snacken and E. Dumortier (eds) *Resisting Punitiveness in Europe? Welfare, Human Rights and Democracy*, London: Routledge, pp. 35–72.

Languin, N. and Robert, C.-N., with Abbiati, M. and Rauschenbach, M. (2012) 'Victims and the penal process: roles, expectations and disappointments', in S. Snacken and E. Dumortier (eds) *Resisting Punitiveness in Europe? Welfare, Human Rights and Democracy*, London: Routledge, pp. 190–201.

Lemonne, A., Van Camp, T. and Van Fraechem, I. (2007) *Onderzoek met betrekking tot de evaluatie van de voorzieningen ten behoeve van slachtoffers van inbreuken*, Brussel: Nationaal Instituut voor Criminalistiek en Criminologie.

Mary, Ph. (2003) *Insécurité et pénalisation du social*, Brussel: Labor.

McCoy, C. and McManimon, P.J. (2002) 'Harsher is not necessarily better: Victim satisfaction with sentences imposed under a "Truth in sentencing" law', in C. Tata and

N. Hutton (eds) *Sentencing and Society. International Perspectives*, Aldershot: Ashgate, pp. 197–218.

Meert, H., Blommaert, J., Stuyck, K., Peleman, K. and Dewilde, A. (2004) *Van Balen tot Onthalen: De geografische en discursieve dimensies van attitudes tegenover asielzoekers*, Gent: Academia Press.

Parmentier, S., Vervaeke, G., Goethals, J., Doutrelepont, R., Kellens, G., Lemaître, A., Cloet, B., Schoffelen, J., Vanderhallen, M., Biren, P., Sintobin, M., van Win, T. and Vandekeere, M. (2004) *Justitie doorgelicht. De resultaten van de eerste Belgische justitiebarometer*, Reeks: Actuele problemen met betrekking tot de sociale cohesie. Gent: Academia Press.

Pratt, J. (2008) 'Scandinavian exceptionalism in an era of penal excess', *British Journal of Criminology*, 48: 119–37.

Roberts, J.V. and Hough, M. (eds) (2002) *Changing Attitudes to Punishment. Public opinion, crime and justice*, Cullompton: Willan Publishing.

Roberts, J.V. and Hough, M. (2005) *Understanding Public Attitudes to Criminal Justice*. Maidenhead: Open University Press.

Roberts, J.V., Stalans, L.J., Indermauer, D. and Hough, M. (2003) *Penal Populism and Public Opinion*, Oxford: Oxford University Press.

Shapland, J., Willmore, J. and Duff, P. (1985) *Victims in the Criminal Justice System*, Aldershot: Gower.

Snacken, S. (1999) *Long-term prisoners and violent offenders*, in 12th Conference of Directors of Prison Administration, Strasbourg: Council of Europe Publishing, pp. 43–74.

—— (2006) 'A reductionist penal policy and European human rights standards', *European Journal of Criminal Policy and Research*, 12: 143–64.

—— (2007) 'Penal policy and practice in Belgium', in M. Tonry (ed.) *Crime, Punishment and Politics in Comparative Perspective, Crime and Justice, A Review of Research*, Chicago: Chicago University Press, pp. 127–216.

—— (2010) 'Resisting punitiveness in Europe?', *Theoretical Criminology*, 14(3): 273–92.

—— (2011) *Prisons en Europe. Pour une pénologie critique et humaniste*, Bruxelles: Larcier, Collection Crimen.

Snacken, S. and Dumortier, E. (eds) (2012) *Resisting Punitiveness in Europe? Welfare, Human Rights and Democracy*, London: Routledge.

Snacken, S. and Verfaillie, K. (2009) 'Media, "public opinion" and (criminological) research', in H. Eisendrath and J.P. Van Bendegem (eds) *It Takes Two to Do Science. The puzzling interactions between science and society*, Brussels: VUB Press, pp. 159–82.

Stalans, L. (2002) 'Measuring attitudes to sentencing', in J.V. Roberts and M. Hough (eds) *Changing Attitudes to Punishment. Public opinion, crime and justice*, Cullompton: Willan Publishing, pp. 15–32.

Sudre, F. (2005) *Droit international et européen des droits de l'homme* (7th edn), Paris: Presses Universitaires de France, Coll. droit fondamental.

Taggart, P. (2000) *Populism*, Buckingham: Open University Press.

Tonry, M. (2001) 'Symbol, substance and severity in western penal policies', *Punishment and Society*, 4: 517–36.

—— (2004) *Punishment and Politics: Evidence and Emulation in the making of the English Crime Control Policy*, Cullompton: Willan Publishing.

—— (ed.) (2007) *Crime, Punishment and Politics in Comparative Perspective, Crime and Justice, A Review of Research*, Chicago: Chicago University Press.

Tulkens, F. (2012) 'Human rights as the good and the bad conscience of criminal law', in S. Snacken and E. Dumortier (eds) *Resisting Punitiveness in Europe? Welfare, Human Rights and Democracy*, London: Routledge, pp. 156–74.

Tyler, T. R. (2006) *Why People Obey the Law*, Princeton: Princeton University Press.

Van Campenhoudt, L. (1999) 'L'insécurité est moins un problème qu'une solution', in Y. Cartuyvels and P. Mary (eds) *L'Etat face à l'insécurité. Dérives politiques des années 90*, Bruxelles, Labor, pp. 51–68.

van Zyl Smit, D. and Ashworth, A. (2004) 'Disproportionate sentences as human rights violations', *Modern Law Review*, 67: 541–60.

van Zyl Smit, D. and Snacken, S. (2009) *Principles of European Prison Law and Policy. Penology and Human Rights*, Oxford: Oxford University Press.

Verfaillie, K. (2009) 'Punitieve behoeften, samenleving en publieke opinie', in I. Aertsen, K. Beyens, T. Daems and E. Maes (eds) *Hoe punitief is België?* Gent: Maklu, pp. 85–106.

—— (2012) 'Punitive needs, society and public opinion: An explorative study of ambivalent attitudes to punishment and criminal justice', in S. Snacken and E. Dumortier (eds) *Resisting Punitiveness in Europe? Welfare, Human Rights and Democracy*, London: Routledge, pp. 225–46.

Wacquant, L. (2004) *Punir les pauvres. Le nouveau gouvernement de l'insécurité sociale*, Marseille: Agone.

Wemmers, J.A.M. (1996) *Victims in the Criminal Justice Systems*, The Hague: WODC, Ministry of Justice; Amsterdam: Kugler Publications.

Zimring, F.E. and Johnson, D.T. (2006) 'Public opinion and the governance of punishment in democratic political systems', in S. Karstedt and G. LaFree (eds) *Democracy, Crime and Justice, The Annals of the American Academy of Political and Social Sciences*, Thousand Oaks: Sage Publications, pp. 266–80.

Notes

1 Not to be confounded with the concept of 'normative' legitimacy versus 'procedural' legitimacy within the framework of 'procedural justice', see Tyler (2006 and this volume).

2 The concept of 'citizen' does not refer to citizenship of a national state in the narrow sense, but to the concept of '*rechtsburgerschap*' or legal citizenship as developed by Kelk (2008). Kelk defines the essence of *rechtsburgerschap* as the ability to participate in legal matters and the possibility of claiming that legal principles and values must be applied to them in a discursive process where belief in the rationality of the arguments prevails. Such process must allow claims and counter-claims to be made before an independent decision-making authority (Kelk, 2008: 15).

3 To give one illustration, in a survey I organised for the Council of Europe on the application of 'long term prison sentences', definitions in member states of such sentences ranged from 18 months in Norway to 10 years in most central and eastern European countries (Snacken, 1999).

4 The initial judgment in *Hatton* was overturned by a majority of the Grand Chamber, but this did not undermine the fundamental approach adopted by the initial chamber of the ECtHR towards the duty to minimise infringements of human rights (*Hatton and others v. United Kingdom* [GC], 8 July 2003).

5 'Punitiveness' refers in general to 'attitudes to punishment' and is a complex concept which has both a quantitative and a qualitative dimension which go beyond the often used prison population rates per 100,000 inhabitants (Snacken, 2011: 274).

4

QUESTIONING THE LEGITIMACY OF COMPLIANCE

A case study of the banking crisis[1]

Doreen McBarnet

Introduction

Discussion of the relationship between legitimacy and compliance is normally concerned with how those subject to the law perceive the legitimacy of legal institutions and processes and how this affects their approach to compliance (Tyler, 2006). This chapter reverses that focus, asking questions about the legitimacy of the approaches to compliance taken by those subject to the law.

'Compliance' is not a simple concept. Not only, as this book demonstrates, can there be an active choice exercised between complying and not complying, perhaps withholding compliance because of the perceived illegitimacy of the system or indeed more pragmatically because the likelihood of enforcement is seen to be low, but there is also a whole range of ways of 'complying'. Compliance may be 'committed', whether this involves commitment to the substantive law or to the legitimacy of the system. Legal requirements may be complied with on more pragmatic grounds – 'capitulative' rather than committed compliance (McBarnet, 2003). But the response can also be 'creative compliance'. It is this option which has been the focus of my research for some years, particularly in the context of big business, and which, for me, raises significant questions about the nature and legitimacy of compliance.

Creative compliance is the dominant culture of compliance in business, and indeed among those 'high net worth' individuals with the resources and power to manage law to suit their own interests. Rather than simply accepting and meeting the substantive obligations imposed by law, those opting for creative compliance focus on finding means of arguably complying with the technical drafting of the law, while simultaneously frustrating its purpose. Practices may well be adjusted, but they will be adjusted technically rather than substantively so that the same practice continues substantively, simply (or complicatedly, as we shall see) repackaged into another legal form, a form which arguably falls beyond the reach of legal control. Wholly innovative techniques may also be devised to similarly, arguably, fall beyond the ambit of law as currently drafted.

The word 'arguably' is significant. The argument may fail. Should the issue go to the courts, the judges may or may not accept the validity of the claim to technical compliance, and indeed, on rare occasions, may find ways to overrule mere technical compliance as unacceptable. There have been notable legal 'turning points' where this has occurred; for example, in the judges' 'new approach' in the 1984 case of *Ramsay v. Dawson* on what constituted legal tax avoidance. But the existence of an arguable case usually provides immunity from any suggestion of non-compliance. It is simply a legal case that failed rather than a fraud. Creative compliance thus provides 'fraud insurance', enabling business, as simple non-compliance does not, to simultaneously avoid both the criminal label and legal control. This is why I have in the past characterised creative compliance as 'whiter than white collar crime' (McBarnet, 1991, 2006).

This chapter seeks to take the notion of creative compliance further, focusing on it as a process of 'legal engineering', the practice of working on the material of law and regulation to design problem-solving constructs. The 'problems' being solved, however, are the legal policies and legal constraints that would be taken on board in committed or capitulative compliance. This not only has major implications for the efficacy of the rule of law, but also raises significant questions about the legitimacy of creative compliance. This chapter examines these issues in the context of the current financial crisis, assesses the significance of new regulatory and social developments, and explores the potential in current trends for a real, practical challenge to the legitimacy of creative compliance. Though the introduction and conclusion have been written for this book, the case study of the banking crisis which follows has been discussed elsewhere (McBarnet, 2010) and is republished here with the kind permission of the previous editors and publishers, Hart.

A case study of the banking crisis: financial engineering or legal engineering?

One strand of analysis in the banking crisis has been the issue of financial engineering gone wrong. Problems are attributed to innovative financial products that were too readily believed to disperse risk (Turner, 2009), backed by mathematical models (Teanor, 2008) that senior banking executives took at face value, without, it is said, questioning or even comprehending them (Hutter and Dodd, 2008). The financial structures set in place were so complex that risk, according to John McFall chairman of the House of Commons Treasury Committee (McDermid, 2008), and even ownership (Schwarcz, 2008) became untrackable. People were blinded by 'disaster myopia' (Plender, 2009) and indeed market ideology (Peston, 2009). There was a dominant belief in the rationality of the market and a collective failure to recognise the limits of market, maths and risk management. Regulators are portrayed as carried along on this tide of false confidence, regulating through only a light touch with the focus on internal and market controls, and encouraged, or instructed (Turner, 2009), by politicians to do so. People questioning the reality of the emperor's new clothes were dismissed as the ones who did not understand, lacking the sophistication to handle the magic of financial engineering. The subsequent crisis has revealed that the emperor was indeed unclothed, and the demand is for tougher regulation to stop this situation recurring, though with concerns, even in the throes of crisis, that regulation should not be so heavy handed as to stifle the lifeblood of financial innovation (IMF, 2007; Engelen *et al.*, 2009).

Characterising the financial products and transactions that led to the crisis primarily as financial engineering, however, tends to gloss over the other innovative skills and creative participants involved in their construction. A crucial component of the new banking products was legal creativity. The legal work behind such practices as securitisation was not confined to drafting the contracts to sell on risk. It was also about creatively removing the 'obstacles' of prudential regulation, accounting requirements and other legal and regulatory constraints intended to control or disclose risk. Indeed, circumventing capital adequacy regulation was a crucial driver behind much structured finance.

This analysis seeks to reconceptualise the significant practices behind the banking crisis as not just a matter of financial engineering but a matter of legal engineering, legal engineering that is common practice in all sophisticated business. It seeks to set the financial crisis in the context of the wider practice of creative transaction structuring in which the driving characteristic is to deliberately and systematically thwart regulation and bypass regulatory control. The analysis is based on documentary analysis and on interviews over a long period of years at major companies, banks, accountancy and law firms, in the context of a wide range of regulatory, tax and accounting issues, although the interviews quoted here relate specifically to banking. These were mainly conducted before the banking crisis, in 2004 and early 2007, and give some insight into the legal practice and culture that I would argue contributed to it. The focus is sociological rather than legal. It explores the practice of legal engineering and the attitude to law and compliance at its core. It is therefore concerned less with banking regulations than with how banks and their lawyers have reacted to them, and it is less about the financial instruments created than about the motivations behind them, depicting them as part of a pervasive strategic response to regulation, which itself needs to be critically reviewed.

Reconceptualising the issue as one of creative legal circumvention rather than simply financial innovation suggests a different set of issues that need to be addressed in the wake of the financial crisis. This chapter, first, analyses the role of legal engineering in the banking crisis, showing it to be a conscious strategy, in which regulatory circumvention, complexity and opacity were integral parts. It then sets out some specific implications for future practice in business, government, regulation and the professions, and argues the need not just for new law and regulation, but more fundamentally for a questioning of the legitimacy of creative compliance and a new respect for the rule of law, for a new legal integrity.

Legal engineering, intent and complexity

A prime excuse for the financial crisis has been that those involved simply did not understand the complex financial instruments in use or realise the risk, organisational and systemic, they were creating. It is hard not to see this incomprehension as, in the kindest interpretation, a willing suspension of disbelief. Like the courtiers in the tale of the emperor's new clothes, a lot of people were doing rather nicely out of this apparently misunderstood scenario. Indeed, it might be fairly argued that if senior banking executives – who were taking vast rewards for the steward-ship of their businesses – did not understand their own products, they ought to have, and their failure to probe was itself, to the layperson if not the lawyer, a failure of duty.

What is clear, however, is that the image of financial disaster as the result of ignorance or of unintended consequences simply does not wash when we view the innovative financial instruments through the lens of legal rather than just finan-cial creativity. The legal creativity involved was knowingly and deliberately aimed at avoiding laws and regulations put in place to control risk and to ensure its disclosure. Of course, regulators may have been lax and regulations insufficiently demanding, too permissive and perhaps naive. But the fact of the matter is that however the regulations had been formulated, they would have met with the same response: here is a constraint; how do we gain a competitive advantage by getting round it?

Finding arguably legal ways round legal and regulatory obstacles is a key function of the lawyer's role for clients such as banks, and sophisticated legal circumvention has been integral to the construction of innovative financial products in banking. As one banking lawyer put it in interview:

> The traders talk to people in the marketplace. 'What problems do you have at the moment, what would you really need if you could have something devised for you?' Then they look at pricing models, and mathematical models, and then the next stage is the law. This could be very good, very lucrative, what legal hurdles are there?

Or again:

> The credit group at [X] Bank is a specialist structured group in the capital markets which focuses on credit instruments to securitise and it's a wonderfully lucrative business, but there are lots of laws, regulations and concepts and natural justice principles which, you know, inconveniently get in the way and they have to be reformed or modified or creatively dealt with.

These quotations articulate particularly clearly a culture and approach to law which is not always so baldly verbalised but which is clearly and consistently demonstrated in the practice of legal work described to me over many years in corporate and professional interviews. Regulation is an obstacle to be overcome. In the particular context of banking, laws and regulations that obstruct financial engineering have to be removed by legal engineering: 'If law is inconvenient to the economic features of the proposal the lawyer must get round it.'

The banking crisis in context

Legal engineering lies at the heart of the banking crisis, and there is nothing new or unique about the practice. In that sense, the banking crisis needs to be seen in a wider context. It is just part of an approach to law that has been pervasive in business over a long period of time and in a range of contexts, and there have been warnings enough of the dangers inherent in it, notably via Enron (McBarnet, 2006).

The banking crisis has been particularly related to the practice of 'securitising' subprime assets. Simply put, this refers to the practice of providing mortgages to clients who could not afford them (so that the loans were subprime in terms of their creditworthiness), then packaging these mortgages together ('securitising' them) and transferring them to a legally separate entity. This allowed the banks to remove the loans from their books, or balance sheets, and to lend out more money than would otherwise be feasible under banking regulations. Securitisation is one of the many techniques of 'Off balance sheet financing' (OBSF), which constitute prime examples of a long-standing practice of legal engineering to deal with 'obstructive' laws. Though both securitisation and OBSF in general have been defended as, properly used, being of real value to business and society, they have also been systematically and pervasively exploited over a long period of years as a deliberate means of undermining attempts at regulatory control.

OBSF, particularly through the use of the 'special purpose entities' (SPEs) or 'vehicles' (SPVs) that feature so centrally in securitisation – separate companies or other legal forms that have been carefully constructed to be technically legally distinct from the originating company – has a long history. It has been widely used in corporate creative accounting as a technique for consciously circumventing company law obligations to disclose a 'true and fair view' of corporate finances to shareholders. It has been used to keep debts or liabilities out of the accounts, enhancing apparent performance and misleading the market. Since accounts are used as the basis of all sorts of further specific corporate governance controls, OBSF has also been used to circumvent them. Bank loan covenants might stipulate tolerance of only a certain level of debt to equity before a loan can be called in. Keeping debt off the books – even if it might ultimately come back to haunt the company in the future – removes this control. It has also meant the negation of shareholders' rights, often written into the company's memorandum and articles of association, to call an EGM if a particular debt/equity ratio is exceeded.

Performance-related pay and bonuses have also been magnified by profits and growth reported in the books, even if they had no fundamental economic substance (McBarnet and Whelan, 1999).

Banks have played a key role not only in engineering their own OBS practices but also in creating and very actively marketing schemes to corporate clients to relieve the client's books of liabilities and losses with all the advantages just noted. Many corporate interviewees in my research emphasised the active role of investment banks in corporate OBSF schemes, sometimes, in hindsight in more recent interviews, with some vituperation. One major bank's head of compliance complained about:

> the snake oil salesmen from the investment banks coming in and saying 'Everyone's doing this, why aren't you?', putting enormous pressure on young directors.

Banks were also active participants both in corporate-initiated schemes and in the schemes they were purveying themselves. They would, for example, play the crucial role of independent third party in the structuring of an SPV, this being a key element in meeting the criteria that would let the SPV be treated as a legal entity separate from the originating company. Or they might temporarily buy liabilities to get them off the client's balance sheet at a legally significant moment.

Banks could indeed be in the interesting situation where one department of the bank was actively marketing a device to take debts off a client's balance sheet, so undermining the covenants of the bank loans lent by another department of the same bank. It might be worth noting here the wider implications of the banks' role in general corporate off-balance sheet financing. It was not just bank risk which was disguised but also general corporate indebtedness and therefore corporate vulnerability in the face of the kind of credit crunch the banking crisis has produced. Banks' OBSF activities have played a part in the economic and not just the financial crisis.

Banks were also heavily implicated in Enron's OBSF practices, a fact that led to some interesting developments in the deferred prosecutions that followed, of which more later.

Enron famously, or infamously, used a host of SPEs, derivatives and other creative legal devices to hide liabilities and boost apparent profits, while at the same time constructing a vast range of tax avoidance devices to the point where it received tax rebates (McBarnet, 2006). Enron executives, of course, also resorted to, and were prosecuted for, fraud, but the reality is that the corporation was doing a pretty good job of misleading the market even without resort to fraud. Indeed, comments at Congressional investigations repeatedly drove this point home:

> The real scandal here may be not what is illegal, but what is totally permissible. If the GAAP [Generally Accepted Accounting Principles] allow the bookkeeping shenanigans that have been reported in the press then we

should all go into the derivative business. It seems that all too often the name of the corporate game is to conceal the true financial situation of the company while doing the minimum amount of disclosure to avoid legal exposure. (US Senate, 2002, Senator Thompson)

Many of the devices used by Enron were standard business practice. Indeed, at the 2002 annual meeting of the US Bond Market Association one member is reported as asking: 'How do we help the market distinguish between what we do and what Enron did?' The question was put to speaker Harvey Pitt, then chair of the SEC, and the report notes 'he had no ready answer' (Osterland, 2002). Enron's use of legal engineering to circumvent regulatory control was far from unique.

A single device of legal engineering can often circumvent multiple regulatory obstacles. SPEs have been used to circumvent all manner of other laws and regulations such as tax, disclosure rules in takeovers and trade embargoes. Synthetic securitisation, described in interview as 'the transfer of economic or credit risk associated with assets without transferring the assets', was credited by the interviewee as being:

helpful in the face of anti-assignment clauses, transfer restrictions under the laws or jurisdictions where the assets are located, securities law registration issues regarding transfers of assets or securities, legal investment restrictions, withholding tax and stamp duty.

A useful tool indeed.

And of course both synthetic securitisation and securitisation in general, along with derivatives and other innovative legal structuring, gave banks an escape route from the constraints of capital adequacy regulation, an escape route that was precisely the purpose of the innovation.

Creative legal responses to regulation

Regulation and regulators have been criticised strongly in the wake of the banking crisis, and with justification, but it is also important to remember that whatever regulation is put in place, business, in this case banks, will routinely respond by seeking out ways to circumvent it. Reviewing the history of off-balance sheet practices in banking, a 2003 report by one international bank noted:

The motivation [for OBSF] was heightened in the late 1980s by the introduction of risk-based capital guidelines for banks and thrifts. (Nomura Fixed Income Research, 2003: 2)

In this the banks were behaving no differently from any other big business. Introduce a new regulatory strategy and the business response will be a new circumvention strategy. Require companies to consolidate subsidiaries and the response is creative structures to constitute 'non-subsidiary subsidiaries' or SPVs that fall beyond the definition of subsidiaries. Capture in the tax net the practice of 'bed and breakfasting' shares (selling them on the last day of one tax year and buying them back on the first day of the next) to artificially crystallise tax losses and the response is share-'weekending' to tweak the technique using parallel but technically different criteria. Count the loans on the books as part of a regulatory risk assessment and the response is to come up with some creative legal engineering to get those loans off the books.

The first Basel concordat on banking regulation, in 1988, prompted a flurry of creativity to circumvent its constraints and, indeed, use it as an opportunity to secure competitive advantage through that circumvention. Legal engineering involves close scrutiny of the wording of laws and regulations in order to work out how to package a transaction in such a way that it can claim to meet the technical demands of the regulation even if the result is not what the creators of that regulation had in mind. Definitions and criteria involving clear rules or thresholds make particularly valuable material for legal engineers to work on. The criteria set out in Basel I were scrutinised in just this way and the distinction between tier 1 and tier 2 capital provided, said the *Financial Times* (6 December 1990), 'a rich vein of material with which financial engineers have, with, it should be noted, legal engineering integral to the process'.

Tier 1 capital was the safest capital with higher weighting, equity being the prime example since it did not have to be repaid in the event of crisis. The challenge therefore became how to invent an instrument which could claim to meet the tier 1 criteria while still attracting investors by offering them the kind of investor security that, for example, a bond would give. It had in short to do the magic trick of apparently involving no risk to either bank or investor.

One early response by Barclays was the construction of preference shares with dividends which could be interrupted if the bank got into trouble. They were also, in legal form, 'permanent', meaning that in theory they need never be repaid, all of this enabling them to be claimed as tier 1 capital, although in practice they were structured such that they could be redeemed after five years. The attraction of this instrument was that it raised money that, it was claimed, had the same tier 1 status as equity, while avoiding the rights issue that equity raising would involve and, since it was done through an SPV, also avoiding the need to seek the approval of shareholders (*Financial Times*, 9 May 1989). Reports on this instrument noted that the banking supervisors intended to keep a close eye on innovative instruments to prevent the Basel agreement being subverted. There were similar concerns with Royal Bank of Scotland (RBS) early innovative floating rate notes (also 1989). The Bank of England prevaricated on whether to accept the bank's claim that they qualified as upper tier 2 capital, allowing the first issue, only to disallow further issues when the Basel Committee made it clear it saw the instrument as a threat to the regime: it 'would open the door to a variety of innovations that might ultimately undermine the Basel Agreement' (*Independent*, 1 June 1989). From the beginning, in short, there were creative challenges for the regulators which only became more sophisticated over time in response to both competition and changing regulations.

In legal engineering any new regulation is seen simply as a new challenge to be overcome. OBSF regulation was significant for the banking industry in relation to both banks' own securitisation practices and, as we have seen, the lucrative services they were marketing to clients. So, when the US Federal Accounting Standards Board introduced new rulings on off-balance sheet financing after Enron (FASB, 2003), the banks' response was not to capitulate and to accept more activities would now go on the balance sheet, but, as one international bank noted in an analysis of current trends, to search for 'practical solutions to avoid consolidation' (Nomura Fixed Income Research, 2003).

In the same 2003 document, the bank analysed the new regulations to explore possible ways to avoid the consolidation they required. It suggested restructuring collateralised debt obligations (CDOs) and ABCP (Asset Backed Commercial Paper) programmes to fall within an exclusion in the rules, which did 'not apply to a "qualifying special purpose entity" or QSPE under FAS [Financial Accounting Standard] 140(14c)'. This approach was predictable, exploitation of exclusions and exemptions being a standard technique of legal engineering. Concern was expressed, however, that this would constrain the ability to actively market the asset portfolios backing the deals. Another route, the bank's researchers suggested, looking closely at the wording of the regulation, would be:

> to disperse a VIE's [Variable Interest Entity] economic risks and benefits among many parties, so that none holds a majority of variable interests requiring consolidation.

Though there would be problems with this:

> if third party holders of variable interests insist on having a measure of control proportionate to their economic stake.

The ideal way would be another route, finding an:

> aggressive (but not manifestly unreasonable) basis for measuring variable interests in a way which does not closely correspond to their economic risks and benefits . . . [then] . . . dispersing variable interests without dispersing the economic risks and benefits.

Such a device, the document noted, would be the 'holy grail' to search for. This is just one example of how every new regulation becomes a challenge to be creatively overcome, and to be scrutinised for escape routes, usually with some success. Certainly *Accountancy Age* in 2008 reported a general loss of confidence within the FASB on how to tackle off-balance sheet financing: though new rules were introduced in the US after Enron, 'the banks found a way round these' (Sukhraj, 2008).

Over time, regulatory initiatives to control or ensure the disclosure of risk have spawned a range of new and ever more complex securitisations which let banks expand their lending without having to increase their risk capital. This has of course been argued – for example, by former Chief Accountant of the Securities Exchange Council, Lynn Turner (2002) – to have real value:

> Structured finance allows people to raise money they might not otherwise be able to raise, and that access to capital contributes to productivity.

And where risk really has moved from the banks, the argument goes, then it is right to treat innovative forms as substantively and not just technically compliant. One question that arises from the current crisis, however, is how far were the risks truly removed? There is also the issue of how adequately they were disclosed. In addition, the apparently infinite capacity to lend off-balance sheet without the need for balancing capital encouraged much riskier lending than could otherwise have been undertaken. Indeed, the legal capacity to securitise itself stimulated a hunger for opportunities to create loans or other assets that could be securitised. Rather than securitisation being built on pre-existing assets with their own economic logic, the possibility of securitisation prompted the creation of assets – such as subprime loans – to securitise, regardless of their intrinsic economic logic. Small wonder there was concomitant expansion of systemic risk.

Economic risk issues are beyond the scope of this chapter, as is the adequacy of the regulations themselves. The focus of this chapter is the strategic approach taken to law and regulation by the regulated, and the point there is that regulatory attempts to control bank risk were – as is routine and pervasive practice in any big business context – consciously and deliberately met by attempts to innovate out of them, and that innovation involved not just mathematical or financial creativity but legal creativity. For banks, capital adequacy regulations, designed to control risk, were 'obstructions' to be 'dealt with' through creative legal engineering.

The role of tax in structured finance

This legal engineering was right at the core of structured finance. Legal engineering is what translated the financial whizz-kid's idea into a legally and therefore economically viable product. As it was put in interview:

> the potential of the product depends on the ratio of cost it would incur to get round legal, regulatory, tax or accounting difficulties.

The reference to tax is pertinent. Creative tax avoidance was a frequent driver of securitisation as well as a key element in profit and indeed in marketability. There was always a basic issue in any legal engineering of ensuring that devices intended to circumvent one set of regulations, such as capital adequacy rules, did not end up with adverse tax repercussions, and an equally basic practice of working to retain both tax and regulatory advantages even where logically the securing of one advantage should have been at the expense of the other.

Legal engineering is about having your cake and eating it too. Hybrid capital, for example, was designed to achieve both the capital adequacy advantages of equity and the tax advantages of debt. In normal usage, equity would be best for the capital adequacy count but equity does not generate the tax allowable costs of debt which boost the return on equity. 'Hybrid capital' was conjured up to claim qualification as tier 1 capital under the Basel framework while still being tax deductible. It is, as noted by a UK regulator:

> capital that acts like debt as far as the taxman is concerned, and capital that acts like equity as far as the depositor is concerned . . . Market participants have been quite imaginative in devising structures that meet diverse requirements in different jurisdictions to qualify as debt for tax purposes and equity for accounting purposes.
>
> (Huertas, 2008)

This indeed is parallel to the convertible bonds created in the corporate sector in the 1980s to simultaneously meet the apparently contradictory criteria of both debt and equity for different regulatory purposes.

Tax avoidance can itself be a primary driver of structured finance, and the source of the profit generated. In its 2009 'Tax Gap' series, the *Guardian* (13 March 2009) reported structured finance deals, such as those where:

> 'investments' of £6 billion at a time . . . moved in circles between RBS and other banks . . . [as] . . . an important factor in driving the 'securitisation' boom which led to worldwide financial calamity.

Creatively structuring in tax avoidance can also be key to the marketability of the underlying assets for securitisation – and it is important to remember here that assets have sometimes been created in order to securitise them rather than the securitisation following from the pre-existence of the assets. A securitisable insurance product for example, said one interviewee, might be dreamed up in the abstract, and successfully legally engineered. But then the insurance policies had to be sold – to give the product what an interviewee called 'an insurance wrap' – and constitute the underlying asset. In marketing the policies, the lure of tax avoidance for the purchasers proved key:

> The objective is the securitisation but we use the legal benefits to get the policies sold. It's sold as a cheap way for high net worth individuals to leave money to heirs, avoiding IHT [inheritance tax].

In a number of ways, then, the legal engineering of tax avoidance has also been a key driver of, and integral to the profit in, banks' securitisation and other structured finance transactions, and this has added further layers of complexity to transaction structures.

Legal engineering and the production of complexity

In highly structured transactions of any kind – and these instruments were, as one lawyer put it, 'hellishly structured' – there is typically complexity and opacity. So if the securitisation transactions behind the banking crisis were retrospectively deemed too complex and opaque for their risk to be comprehended, it is hardly surprising. But a key factor in why highly structured finance *became* highly structured was the desire to circumvent regulation.

Dealing with regulatory obstacles involves complex and sophisticated legal work in long chains of transaction structures, and this is neither accidental nor incidental but inherent in the task of regulatory circumvention. A solution to one regulatory problem will inevitably throw up new legal, regulatory, accounting and tax problems, which in turn need to be dealt with. Solving them will involve adding further complex steps or partners or legal entities or jurisdictions to the transaction structure and the final product may indeed be a 'labyrinthine' structure that is hard to comprehend. But if financial instruments are too complex to understand, it is important to recognise that one of the reasons for this is the legal engineering that lies behind them and the multiplicity of laws, regulations, taxes and jurisdictions that are being circumvented in order to avoid regulatory control.

The complexity, incomprehensibility and opacity of risk attributed to innovative financial instruments can then be characterised not simply as an unfortunate by-product of financial engineering but as an integral part of legal engineering. And whether or not there was awareness of the financial risk being created, there was most certainly a very clear awareness that the regulations intended to control and disclose financial risk were being systematically circumvented by legal engineering. That indeed was its purpose. In fact, my research over the years underlined to me that the risks that primarily concerned legal engineers, whether in the corporate or the banking sectors, were not financial risks at all but, interviews indicated, 'structural risks' – the risk that the regulatory and tax circumvention integral to the transactions might be challenged by the authorities.

Implications

Reconceptualising financial innovation as legal innovation gives a different take on some of the problems underlying the banking crisis and raises different issues that need to be addressed. I will consider the implications of this analysis for regulation, exploring the question of changing the regulations, and assessing the significance for the future of principles-based regulation. But I will also address the wider questions of responsibility and legitimacy.

Changing the regulations

Regulations and regulators have themselves come under fire as a result of the current financial crisis. Capital adequacy regulations have been described as inadequate and promises made that they will become more demanding (McCarthy, 2008). But as we have seen in the course of this chapter, any new regulation tends to be met with the same energetic drive to circumvent it, and there should be no expectation of a quick fix from increasing the capital adequacy ratios required or prohibiting specific instruments currently in use.

Legal engineering is all about getting round the rules, whatever shape they currently take. We saw instances of that earlier in this chapter in our discussion of the banks' response to the introduction of new regulations on off-balance sheet financing. New regulations can simply stimulate new devices to escape them. Financial innovation has been discussed as 'bricolage' (Engelen *et al.*, 2009; MacKenzie, 2003), with 'bricoleurs' using 'whatever is at hand' to construct new products from the current finite materials around them. One of those materials is law. Legal engineers use whatever law is available at any given moment, sometimes drawing from areas of law and regulation not hitherto seen as relevant to the context in hand, in order to construct new ways out of control. Law is both the obstacle to be overcome and the 'raw material to be worked on' (McBarnet, 2004) in order to achieve that. However regulations are changed, they will be complied with 'creatively' and there needs to be awareness that the same could happen in the current context with new regulations unless the whole approach to compliance is addressed.

That is not to say that regulations should not be enhanced, that creative compliance cannot be made a little more difficult, that legal engineers should not be challenged by presenting them with tougher obstacles to surmount. And the pleas of ignorance at the top could be addressed. On this, lessons might be learned from the post-Enron deferred prosecutions in the US (McBarnet, 2006).

Several banks which had been involved in Enron's schemes, along with KPMG, were not immediately prosecuted for their roles, but were monitored under deferred prosecution agreements. Prosecution was deferred so long the firms undertook a range of obligations, with the threat of prosecution dropped after a specified time. These agreements included some obligations of direct relevance to the kind of legal engineering discussed in this chapter. Firms were, for example, required to set up committees of senior executives ('Head of Group or experienced designee') from all the 'disciplines' in the firm to review and approve transactions, with the need for agreement of all Heads before a transaction structure was approved. This review obligation extended, to cite the Merrill Lynch agreement, to 'all complex structured finance transactions effected by a third party with Merrill Lynch' (US Department of Justice, 2003). This requirement for the direct involvement of top management is in line with the FSA's call for responsibility at the top of organisations, it is best practice in some organisations, and it might be a mechanism that should be given greater emphasis, especially in the wake of senior bankers' protests that they simply didn't realise what was going on or the risk it involved.

Under the deferred prosecution agreements, these committees were required not just to ensure that the transactions did not technically break the law but they also had to consider their wider effects. The agreements prohibited firms from engaging in any transaction intended to 'achieve a misleading earnings, revenue or balance sheet effect' (US Department of Justice, 2003) for the corporation involved. Note the reference to 'misleading' rather than just 'fraudulent' effects. There was also a demand that in assessing these structures, there should be a shift of focus from technical compliance to a concern with the 'objectives' of the structuring, with a purely accounting or tax objective deemed inappropriate.

Given the impact of Enron at the time, it is not surprising that the focus in these agreements was on the bank's role in facilitating OBSF deals for other corporations. Hence the concern with third-party transactions and with the effects on the third party's accounts. But there is no reason why the same standards could not be set for monitoring a bank's own transactions and the effect on its own balance sheet. The underlying concept was that it was not enough for a transaction to be, under a strict or literal reading of the law or regulation, technically not illegal. There needed to be some responsibility taken too for its wider purpose and effects. This reflected public concern at the time not just over Enron's fraud but also over the whole idea of legally engineered structures that could claim to be 'perfectly legal', or 'not illegal', but nonetheless defeated regulatory policy. The same public concern is clear now in relation to banking practice itself.

Principles-based regulation

As a result of the banking crisis, principles-based regulation – the flagship approach of the FSA – has come in for severe criticism. Julia Black (2008) has described the approach as having suffered 'a potentially fatal blow'. Indeed, FSA officials themselves have declared principles-based regulation a failure in that 'a principles-based approach does not work with individuals who have no principles' (Sants, 2009). But critics seem to be equating principles with soft-touch regulation and the two do not necessarily have to coincide.

There are different philosophies and strategies behind principles-based regulation. Sometimes the approach is to provide a broad goal in order to allow for variations in detail or implementation. This approach characterises regimes bent on harmonisation of different bodies of regulation, and is often a way of achieving broad harmonisation – or the appearance of harmonisation – without every party having to agree on every detail. It can be a product of political expediency, or of an approach which finds it more appropriate to delegate detail to a lower regulatory rung. The FSA's approach – and it was also bringing into one regime a range of different organisations with different regulations – was to set very broad behavioural standards but allow for variation in the methods used to achieve those standards, allowing a broad sweep of laissez-faire so long as the 'outcomes' met the goals. This exhibited a great deal of trust in the regulated and their ability to self-regulate, and it tied closely with the dominance of market ideology.

There can be another philosophy behind principles-based regulation however, where it is driven not so much by trust in the regulated and their capacity for restraint, but by distrust, based on experience, and by the need for constraint. Driving this approach is an explicit recognition that any specific rule will be met by legal engineering to circumvent it, and principles-based regulation is seen as the only realistic response, the only way to try to capture the spirit of the law in the face of constant creativity and technical challenge. This approach featured to some extent in the FSA's adoption of principles-based regulation but it was the overwhelming driving force behind the adoption of this style of regulation in the 1990s by the Accounting Standard Board (ASB). For the ASB, principles-based regulation was an essential bastion against opportunistic legal engineering.

It would be unwise in the extreme for the FSA to abandon the idea of principles-based regulation because of the current debacle. A reversion to rules will simply result in legal engineers developing ways out of them with bright line rules to point to in their defence. Creative compliance thrives on rule-based regulation, for tight specific rules provide particularly solid material for legal engineers to work with.

Importantly, though, principles will certainly not stop legal engineering if they are not strongly enforced. The ASB emphasised the need for principles to control creative compliance with law and regulation through legal and accounting engineering. However, the body responsible for enforcing accounting standards, the Financial Reporting Review Panel (FRRP), was not noted for its use of principles in its enforcement practices, tending instead to monitor for and enforce compliance with specific rules. ASB chairman David Tweedie frequently stated that the requirement in company law to give a true and fair view in accounts should override even compliance with specific rules if such compliance did not result in a true and fair view of the financial situation. However, research on the FRRP's enforcement practice showed that it did not use the 'true and fair' requirement in this way (McBarnet and Whelan, 1999). The Panel quite frequently refused to accept situations where a company had invoked the override as a reason for not following specific rules. But there were no instances of the Panel doing the opposite, that is, itself using the override to reject a company's technical compliance if it was not deemed to result in a true and fair view of the accounts, though it was for this situation that Tweedie had particularly advocated its use.

In dealing with Citigroup and Deutsche Bank in 2006, the FSA used principles as a means of enforcement in cases where there were deemed to be unacceptable effects even though there was arguably no breach of a relevant specific rule (McBarnet, 2007a). In one case, there was no specific rule to deal with the situation. In the other, the infringement took place outside FSA jurisdiction. Using principles in this way helps tackle the kind of legal engineering which takes advantage of an absence of rules, and innovates into a vacuum. But it would take more to challenge legal engineering based on a claim to technical compliance with extant rules, despite the fact that the net result is not what was intended. For that approach to be challenged, principles need to be brought in not just to fill a vacuum in the book of specific rules but also to override the rulebook if the principles have not been met. That is the only way to ensure technical compliance with the letter of the law is subjugated to a requirement to comply with its spirit. And to be meaningful this would have to be the basis not just of regulatory rhetoric but also of regulatory enforcement.

However, too much can be expected of principles-based regulation. It is difficult to enforce principles. There is not always agreement about whether a practice constitutes compliance with the spirit of the law. Some financial products seem to have left regulators stumped as to whether or not they are legitimate. Thomas Huertas, Director of the Banking Sector of the FSA, discussing hybrid capital, pondered on whether it was 'admirable alchemy or invidious innovation' (Huertas, 2008). There is a real reluctance to use principles in enforcement because of the criticisms of subjectivity, retrospectivity and too much power being usurped by regulators, and even principles and broad abstract concepts take the form of words which can still provide material for legal engineers to work on.

Principles should not be abandoned, but neither are they the panacea. Indeed, underlying the issue of principles or rules is a more fundamental problem: the culture that fosters legal engineering and its presumption of legitimacy.

Legal engineering, responsibility and legitimacy

The rule of law may be seen as a fundamental of democratic society, but that is not how it is approached in the practice of legal engineering. In the mindset of the legal engineer, law or regulation is not a legitimate and authoritative command to be taken at face value, respected and obeyed. It is simply a nuisance, an obstacle to be overcome, a material to be worked with and reshaped to one's advantage, a challenge in a regulatory cat and mouse game.

Legal engineers know they are not following the intentions or spirit of the law. Bankers and banking lawyers talk in interview about their legal practices as 'bullish' or 'sailing close to the wind'. Indeed, they are sometimes surprised when they succeed, when regulators fail to see through what a lawyer described as the 'fog' of complexity and opacity, a fog which indeed can be developed for just that purpose. In the mindset that underlies and fosters legal engineering, all the responsibility for control is being placed on the regulators. If they can't make regulations legal engineering proof or spot the failings in the schemes, it is fair game to exploit that situation. Ideas such as responsibility, the public good, morality, ethics or integrity do not enter into the equation. All, it seems, is fair in love and law.

But should all the responsibility for securing compliance rest with writers and enforcers of regulation? Or should the regulated too not be seen as having a responsibility to comply with the spirit of the law? Black (2008) describes the regulations on capital adequacy as too easy to get round. But that takes as given the culture of circumvention. The present crisis may indicate it is time to question that culture and its legitimacy and to place more responsibility for the efficacy of regulation on the regulated.

What this chapter has reminded us of too is the behind-the-scenes but active and crucial role of the legal profession in creative compliance. At the core of financial engineering is legal engineering which depends heavily on lawyers and legal work. Professional responsibility therefore also needs to be questioned and the meaning of professional ethics in relation to the rule of law addressed.

If the legitimacy of legal engineering and creative compliance is to be reassessed, politicians also need to put their own house in order since they have been as guilty of legal engineering, creative compliance and disrespect for the law as banks and corporations have. Politicians and governments have themselves thoroughly exploited this 'bullish', technical and literal approach to law, not just in such practices as the careful technical packaging of party donations as loans in the 'peerages for loans' scandal, but also in core financial policy. Gordon Brown, UK prime minister at the time of the banking crisis, appealed to:

> all companies to bring out their bad assets and put them back on their balance sheet so the financial system can move forward.
>
> (IFA 2008)

Yet for years the government itself used off-balance sheet financing techniques in the form of the Private Finance Initiative to enhance public accounts. There is more than a whiff of hypocrisy in politicians denouncing such activities as tax avoidance and off-balance sheet financing while themselves using the letter of the law to defeat its spirit. If a more responsible approach to the rule of law is to be encouraged, there must be more of what corporate responsibility consultants and regulators have referred to as 'tone at the top'.

Conclusion: questioning the legitimacy of creative compliance

This chapter has sought to question the legitimacy of creative compliance on the basis of empirical research and academic analysis. But the legitimacy of this approach to law and compliance is now being questioned not just academically but at the level of practice. In recent years there has been a growing regulatory rhetoric for a more ethical stance in relation to law and compliance and for greater emphasis on compliance with the spirit of the law (McBarnet, 2007b). Indeed, the earlier analysis of regulatory responses to creative compliance demonstrates how this has moved in some contexts beyond rhetoric to practice.

Nor is it just academics and regulators who are questioning the legitimacy of creative compliance. The banking crisis has added force to a public discontent with business that began to flourish with Enron, a discontent that demonstrates growing awareness of, and strong objections to, the practice of technical compliance with the letter but not the spirit of the law, and the lack of basic ethics in business and public life. Recent UK experience over politicians' approach to expenses, and above all the banking crisis, has strengthened this public mood to a level of public disgust that is beginning to be harnessed to demands for change. There is currently growing

NGO, media and popular criticism of such issues as tax avoidance, where all the skills of legal engineering are applied to transaction and corporate structuring in order to 'perfectly legally' escape paying tax. Questions about the legitimacy of this practice are being thrown into particularly sharp relief by the consequences of the banking crisis, and the economic crisis that has followed. Corporate practices which are seen to starve public revenues are being characterised as particularly iniquitous at a time of massive cuts in public services.

International accounting and consulting firm, KPMG, warned in 2004:

> Boards should recognise, when overseeing the design and monitoring of tax strategies and policies, that contemporary debates about governance, corporate social responsibility and ethics mean that even legal tax-minimisation activity can generate reputational liabilities that can destroy shareholder value.
>
> (KPMG, 2004)

But few might have anticipated that 2010 would see not only media and internet campaigns against tax avoidance, such as the *Guardian*'s sustained reporting of the 'Tax Gap' throughout 2009 to 2010, but also demonstrations outside the doors of major high street companies such as Topshop, protesting against the tax practices of household name companies and high net worth individuals. There was no claim by the protesters that the practices involved were illegal. They were acknowledged as tax avoidance, not tax evasion or fraud. But those practices were still giving rise to protest on the basis that, regardless of their technical compliance, they were not, particularly in an era of public austerity, socially or ethically legitimate (Pinkerman, 2010).

The legitimacy of corporate creative compliance is also being questioned more generally by the wider movement for corporate social responsibility, which has been expanding its agenda beyond pressures for environmental responsibility and human rights to concerns with a more ethical approach in business to finance and to legal compliance. This too has been expressed particularly in the context of tax avoidance but has the potential to be harnessed to a wider critique of cavalier approaches to law – by business, professions or politicians – and to a call for compliance with the spirit of the law (McBarnet, 2007a). The banking crisis has demonstrated that clever manipulation of law, and circumvention of regulation, may not be quite so clever after all, and that its economic and social costs can be devastating. There is a growing awareness of the unfairness by which those with the resources to do so can buy their way out of legal control at the expense of those who cannot.

The legitimacy of creative compliance is under challenge. The time may be appropriate for a new aspiration towards a greater respect for the rule of law, a greater respect for democracy in law, and a new legal integrity. Certainly it will require a shift as fundamental as that, and not just some tinkering with the rules, for there ever to be any hope of effectively regulating banking, or indeed business, in general.

References

Black, J. (2008) 'The death of credit, trust – and principles-based regulation?' *Risk and Regulation,* December: 8.

Engelen, E., Erturk, I., Froud, J., Leaver, A. and Williams, K. (2009) 'Reconceptualising Financial Innovation: frame, conjecture and bricolage', *Conference on the Future of Financial Regulation,* Glasgow University, 29–30 March.

Financial Accounting Standards Board (FASB) (2003) *FIN 46, FASB Interpretation No 46, Consolidation of Variable Interest Entities, an Interpretation of ARB No 51* (17 January 2003).

Huertas, T. (Director) (2008) 'Hybrid Capital', speech at City and Financial Bank Capital Seminar, 26 June (Banking Sector, FSA).

Hutter, B. and Dodd, N. (2008) 'Social Systems Failure? Trust and the credit crunch', *Risk and Regulation,* December: 4.

International Monetary Fund (IMF) (2007) *Global Financial Stability Report,* Washington, DC: IMF126.

Institute of Financial Accountants (2008) 'Gordon Brown has vowed to force banks and other businesses to put their off-balance sheet liabilities into their books', 25 September, www.ifa.org.uk/news.

KPMG (2004) 'Tax in the Boardroom', KPMG, p. 8.

MacKenzie, D. (2003) 'An equation and its worlds: bricolage, exemplars, disunity and performativity in financial economics', *Social Studies of Science,* 33(6): 831–68.

McBarnet, D. (1991) 'Whiter than white collar crime: tax, fraud insurance and the management of stigma', *British Journal of Sociology,* 42(3): 323–44.

—— (2003) 'When compliance is not the solution but the problem: from changes in law to changes in attitude', in V. Braithwaite (ed.) *Taxing Democracy,* Aldershot: Ashgate, pp. 229–44.

—— (2004) 'Law and capital: the role of legal form and legal actors', in McBarnet (ed.) *Law and Capital,* Special Issue of *International Journal of the Sociology of Law,* 231–38, Academic Press, 1984 (reprinted in McBarnet *Crime, Compliance and Control,* Aldershot: Ashgate Dartmouth, 2004).

—— (2006) 'After Enron: will whiter than white collar crime still wash?' *British Journal of Criminology* 46(6): 1091–1109.

—— (2007a) 'Compliance, ethics and responsibility: emergent governance strategies in the US and UK', in J. O'Brien (ed.) *Private Equity, Corporate Governance and the Dynamics of Capital Market Regulation,* London: Imperial College Press, pp. 213–29.

—— (2007b) 'Corporate Social Responsibility beyond law, through law, for law: the new corporate accountability', in D. McBarnet, A. Voiculescu and T. Campbell (eds) *The New Corporate Accountability: Corporate Social Responsibility and the Law,* Cambridge: Cambridge University Press, pp. 9–56.

—— (2010) 'Financial engineering or legal engineering? Legal work, legal integrity and the banking crisis', in Iain MacNeil and Justin O'Brien (eds) *The Future of Financial Regulation,* Oxford: Hart, pp. 68–72.

McBarnet, D. and Whelan, C. (1999) *Creative Accounting and the Cross-eyed Javelin Thrower,* Chichester: John Wiley.

McCarthy, C. (2008) 'Lessons from the financial crisis', speech at Manchester Business School, 13 May, 3, and Mansion House Speech, 18 Sept. 2008 (chairman FSA).

McDermid, A. (2008) 'Banks "refused to believe the good times were about to end"', *The Herald,* 3 March.

Nomura Fixed Income Research (2003) *Off-balance sheet update,* 11 March, p. 1.

Osterland, A. (2002) 'Commercial Paper Chase', *CFO Magazine,* 1 June at www.cfo. com/article.cfm.

Peston, R. (2009) *Today,* Radio 4, 18 March.

Pinkerman, A. (Pseudonym of spokesperson for UKUncut) (2010) 'Today make Topshop pay', *Guardian,* 4 December.

Plender, J. (2009) 'Analysis: Error laden machine', *Financial Times,* 3 March.

Sants, H. (2009) Speech at Thomson Reuters, 12 March, *Guardian,* 13 March (chief executive FSA).

Schwarcz, S. (2008) 'Protecting financial markets: lessons from the subprime mortgage meltdown', *Duke Law School Legal Studies Research Paper no 175,* March.

Sukhraj, P. (2008) 'FASB probes off-balance sheet rules', *Accountancy Age,* 29 February.

Teanor, J. (2008) 'Toxic shock: how the banking industry created a global crisis', *Guardian,* 8 April .

Turner, A. (2009) 'The financial crisis and the future of financial regulation', *The Economist's* Inaugural City Lecture, 21 January (chairman FSA).

Turner, L. (2002) quoted in *CFO magazine,* October, www.cfo.com.

Tyler, T. (2006) *Why People Obey the Law,* Princeton: Princeton University Press.

US Department of Justice (2003) *Enron Task Force Agreement with Merrill Lynch on Deferred Prosecution* at www.justice.gov/achive/dag/cftfcases.

US Senate (2002) 'The Fall of Enron: How Could It Have Happened', Committee on Homeland Security and Governmental Affairs Hearing, 107th Congress, S. Hrg. 107–376, 24 January.

Note

1   Thanks are due to the ESRC whose professorial fellowship award RES-051-0031 funded the research on which this analysis is based.

5

RESISTANT AND DISMISSIVE DEFIANCE TOWARDS TAX AUTHORITIES

Valerie Braithwaite

Introduction

This chapter approaches the topic of compliance and legitimacy from a motivational postures perspective. The starting point is empirical, that is, the signals that those being regulated send to regulators around questions of compliance and legitimacy. Armed with these data, referred to here as motivational postures (commitment, capitulation, resistance, disengagement and game playing), and drawing on existing social science theory, a framework is built to guide practitioners working toward compliance with regulatory regimes.

This chapter proposes two different kinds of defiance on the basis of an analysis of postures: resistant defiance and dismissive defiance. Both are negative responses to the threat posed by authority. The threat occurs by virtue of the power that authorities wield to coerce compliance. First, the moral self is threatened by possible unlawfulness: it seeks comfort in affirmation of law abidingness. Second, the democratic collective self is threatened when democratic rights are not respected: it will feel aggrieved until justice is restored. Third, the status seeking self is threatened by blocked aspirations: it seeks ways around or competes with authority in search of a win against its rules. The chapter shows how resistant defiance reflects a battle between psychological processes of moral obligation and grievance. Dismissive defiance reflects a battle between the psychological processes of moral obligation and competition with authority. When authority meets resistance, its chances for successfully winning over those being regulated are improved if the authority can be seen as having high integrity. A substantial part of high integrity is acting in a procedurally fair way (Tyler, 1989, 1990, 1997). When authority meets dismissiveness, however, relationships are not so easily turned around or built up. Dismissiveness may be associated with alternative authorities. If so, resolution may demand some form of power sharing, which is generally likely to mean a fundamental re-think in what the regulatory system stands for and what it hopes to control through deterrence.

Defining terms and ambitions

The term 'compliance' is used variously for a process or an outcome. When applied to process, compliance refers to the measures that entities put in place to make sure they undertake certain duties in order to comply with specific requirements. The term 'compliance process' can also be used to refer to the measures that a regulator puts in place in order to elicit compliance among those being regulated. Elements in such a process might be educating, monitoring, praising, applying penalties, or offering incentives.

In this chapter, compliance process describes the public's assessment and inter-pretation of a regulatory authority's efforts to steer the flow of events in supposedly socially desirable directions and how those being regulated choose to respond to regulatory influence. The compliance process is oriented to achieving certain compliance outcomes, but the journey toward these outcomes is often littered with contestation with regulator, regulatee and other parties all exerting influence on each other. The process is dynamic with different actors having the upper hand at different points of time and with authorities revamping strategy in response to the changing regulatory field.

Compliance outcomes may refer to either intention to act as requested (for example, I intend to comply) or the requested behaviour (for example, I complied). Cialdini and Goldstein (2004: 592) capture both meanings through defining compliance as responding favourably to an explicit or implicit request from others. Psychologists have put forward psycho-social strategies for improving the likelihood of compliance, be the context that of advertising, health routines, environmentally friendly behaviours, workplace performance, or law abidingness. What distinguishes compliance in relation to law abidingness is the presence of authority with capacity and obligation to enforce the law. In such circumstances, compliance is elicited against a backdrop of coercion. Compliance as outcome therefore may take the following minimalist form: 'Tell me what I must do and I will do it, whether I agree with it or not.' While recognizing this reality, every regulator would prefer that those they are regulating be committed to their objectives. Commitment brings with it possibilities for self-regulation and more cost-effective compliance processes on the part of the regulator.

Consideration of compliance with authorities that have coercive powers raises the question of legitimacy: has the authority the right to make the request; and, more importantly, has the authority the right to use coercion to ensure there is compliance with the request? Legitimacy according to Beetham (1991) encompasses the degree to which an authority is using its power in accordance with established rules, the degree to which shared social beliefs underpin these rules, and the degree to which those being coerced have consented to the power relations that give authority the right to make demands and enforce them. Beetham's conception of legitimacy emphasizes the normative, that is, how an authority should use its power under the law and what are the legal and moral constraints for doing so, while also making room for the subjective understandings of the public regarding the legitimacy of their authorities. It is this subjective understanding of legitimacy that frames the current study. As Suchman (1995: 574) explains, people have to believe that 'the actions of an entity are desirable . . . within some socially constructed system of norms, values, beliefs, and definitions'. If people do not accept the same socially constructed system, acceptance of authority and what it is expecting by way of compliance will be fragile.

The above uses of compliance and legitimacy all have their place. The approach outlined in this chapter uses the terms to frame the domain of enquiry – individuals' response to the tax authority in relation to payment of income tax. Other concepts will be used in this chapter to do the work in explaining how to create a tax system that has legitimacy with the public and has an effective compliance process. Legitimacy is overarching, describing public perceptions of government responsibilities including the legality and appropriateness of the tax code. The compliance process refers to the ways in which Australian taxpayers make sense of and respond to the Australian Tax Office as a statutory authority that requires them to pay income tax. In terms of this chapter, compliance may be thought of as framing the analysis of how authorities might go about eliciting public cooperation within a regulatory field. Legitimacy is broader, framing the analysis of whether or not the existence of the regulatory field is justified.

The perspective that underpins the empirical analysis presented in this chapter is the voice of the taxpayer. Of as much importance, however, if not more in certain contexts, are the tax professionals and financial advisers who are interpreting the tax code for ordinary taxpayers, sometimes aggressively, sometimes cautiously, all in a bid to ensure taxpayers are only paying the amount of tax that they have to pay while remaining inside the law. The arguments of tax professionals and the counter arguments of tax officials mean that the interpretation of the tax code is not infrequently placed before the courts. Within the tax domain, legitimacy has not only the complexity described by Beetham (1991) but also ambiguity (Picciotto, 2007), making the authority of the Australian Tax Office quite contestable among those with resources to challenge its decisions through the courts.

Theoretical propositions in motivational posturing theory

The starting point for motivational posturing theory is that authorities which make regulatory demands threaten our freedom. Through making demands they threaten our sense of ourselves as people who can act responsibly and do the right thing. The significant body of criminal justice literature on shame and humiliation illustrates the moral self that is threatened by authorities (Braithwaite, 2009; Harris, 2007; Scheff and Retzinger, 1991; Sherman, 1993). Demands also may threaten our sense of ourselves as part of a collective or community where the voices of individuals are listened to respectfully and heeded. The social justice and human rights literatures link injustice to identity threat and loss (Tyler, 1989, 1990, 1997; Young, 2000). And finally, regulatory demands may threaten through blocking pathways to successfully achieving personal goals. A substantial literature addresses the importance of goal achievement to human development (Rokeach, 1973; White, 1959).

These three selves that may come forward within any one of us to defend against a regulatory regime are referred to here in the tax context as the moral self, the democratic collective self and the status-seeking self. We all like to think of ourselves as good people, as having democratic rights, and as having the opportunity to pursue personal advancement. When tax authorities make their presence felt, taxpayers invariably pause to consider how they will be affected. Tax authorities, like all regulators, threaten because they have the potential to diminish conceptions that we have of ourselves – of our moral self which may be found wanting under closer scrutiny, of our democratic collective self that we may find is unacknowledged, even abused, and of a status-seeking self that may find future hopes and ambitions placed beyond reach.

Protecting the self through adjusting social distance

The immediate response to threats to our freedom is to find some way of regaining that freedom. Brehm and Brehm (1981) describe reactance as a response that directly counters attempts to rob individuals of particular freedoms. If people are pressured into expressing a certain attitude, for instance, they may persist in expressing the opposite attitude and become resistant to further efforts of persuasion. Behavioural examples abound. Among the most creative are breaking or circumventing computer codes that have been put in place to protect intellectual property rights. Each innovation of authorities to protect their material is an invitation to those resourceful enough to crack the code, often sharing their success with like-minded others.

Reactance is not the only tool we have in our repertoire of responses to those who want to curb our freedom. The early years of socialization equip us well for the task. We learn through trial and error that freedom can be best regained through control of social distance – or the distance of influence and attention – between self and authority. We keep our distance if we are fearful that the authority does not value our self as we do. If we are confident that our self is at one with authority or that we can convince the authority that our self is worthy of respectful treatment, we move closer, regarding such positioning as mutually favourable.

The social distance we place between self and authority provides us with comfort that we can manage any attention the authority directs towards us. As we step outside the reach of authority the fear that we may be made to do something we do not want to do lessens and the influence that authority has over us weakens. We also lose openness to persuasion and negotiation – or to changes the authority may make to win our cooperation. The closer we are, the more vulnerable we are to the authority's influence, but so too is the authority potentially vulnerable to ours.

Engaging the moral self

It is common for the moral self to be aligned with legitimate authorities. We refer to this phenomenon in individuals as law abidingness. If authorities ask something of us, we assume they have good reason and that it is the right thing to do. By meeting the request, we further assume that we will be free from further intrusion and domination. We regain freedom through appeasing authority. In the process, our moral self receives the affirmation it needs. We do what authorities want us to do, the authorities do not bother us because we have done the right thing, and we feel affirmed in the knowledge that we are good law-abiding people.

The moral self has capacity to be the regulator's best friend. But is this always the case? There are occasions when individuals find it impossible to restore the moral self through alignment with authority. Authorities may punish or treat people disrespectfully in an indiscriminate fashion – those doing the right thing as well as those not. Should these conditions prevail, the moral self will be denied the acknowledgement and assurances it requires. In time, it may lose its salience and the authority may be unable to engage it in processes to either re-affirm legitimacy or build compliance. Greater social distance between self and the regulator may follow, with the moral self withdrawing from engagement, making way for a threatened democratic collective self or status-seeking self to become dominant.

Engaging the democratic collective self

The democratic collective self enters into a compact with government. That compact involves being an active and responsible citizen – including paying taxes. In response, the government is expected to maintain order and provide security and look after people's needs – for education, health care, jobs and infrastructure. No group of people is expected to have special privileges nor does any group expect to be discriminated against. Governments are expected to act in accordance with principles of justice, in terms of both outcomes and processes. When governments or their agent – for example, the tax authority – deviate from acting justly, the democratic collective self sees the behaviour as a breach of trust, as an offence that breaks the compact. The democratic collective self enters unsafe territory and fears the onset of further injustice. Under such circumstances, putting social distance between self and the authority becomes a way of dealing with a sense of betrayal by the authority and avoiding unwanted intrusions on freedom. Restoration of the democratic collective self involves removing injustice from the system.

Engaging the status-seeking self

The status-seeking self is an expression of an individual's journey of accomplishment and fulfilment. Individuals have aspirations and life goals, shaped and directed by culture and background most certainly, but internalized and tailored to individual circumstance to the point of being personally owned and giving individual's purpose and meaning in their lives. When these goals are blocked by events of any kind, individuals experience threat or loss as they re-adjust to their new circumstances.

In the context of the payment of income tax, a tax authority threatens the accumulation of capital, and therefore those with aspirations for improving their socio-economic status in society. Where paying tax is seen to hold back an individual aspiring to expand a business, or having discretionary income to enjoy some luxuries, or even having enough money to house, feed and clothe a family, individuals might be expected to adopt a negative attitude to both taxation and the authority that administers it. Viewing the tax system unfavourably is likely to result in increased social distance between self and the authority, adopting an 'out of sight, out of mind' position until a way is found to beat the system. Status seeking involves competition and there is no reason why a competitive challenge should not be launched against government if it is blocking advancement.

Motivational posturing

As individuals assess the tax system – the authority as well as the taxation levels, payment methods and sanctioning procedures for self and others – they develop postures that sum up what they think of this regulatory system. Postures are signals or messages to self, others and authorities about their comfort with the regulatory system. They are composite narratives made up of attitudes, beliefs, emotions, expectations and norms. They inform us of how individuals and groups of individuals are likely to position themselves to deal with messages from the authority that try to educate, persuade or threaten people into adopting compliant behaviours. The term 'motivational' is pertinent because there is a purpose to the posturing – to defend the self from regulatory assault. But unlike the more traditional meaning of the term 'motive', the response of those being regulated is not hidden from view or buried amidst other beliefs and values. The threat is social – domination by an outside entity – and the response is social, although undoubtedly shaped by an individual's long-held personal values, beliefs and experiences. The response, be it one of social distancing or social alignment, is a statement for others to see. It will more than likely be shared with others, fine-tuned through dialogue with others, and used to justify the social distance that the individual has placed between self and the authority. The purpose of protecting the self is to feel good about the self, to be comforted by the support of others, and to find a way around the feared constraints of the system.

Five motivational postures have been identified in the taxation field. They have parallels in other regulatory fields such as child protection, occupational health and safety, peace building, nursing home regulation and agricultural reform. The postures have been empirically derived through factor analysing inventories measuring attitudes to authority and to regulatory systems and through listening to the accounts that people provide for their interactions with authority.

Two postures reflect a degree of alignment with authority or what Losoncz (2010) has called *accommodation to the demands of the system*. The first is called *commitment* because it conveys a belief that the regulatory purpose is sound and that the regulatory system should be valued and supported by everyone. The second is called *capitulation*. Similar to McBarnet's (2003) usage, capitulation reflects acquiescence to the powers that be, along with general acceptance that it must be right because they are the authority.

Whether one believes in the authority because it has sound purpose or because it has the force of the law behind it, the motivational posturing response is likely to be alignment. Postures of commitment and capitulation are likely to be buttressed by a moral self that is dealing with the potential threat of regulation through the following line of thought: 'They must know this is the right thing to do, I will support them and do the right thing, then I will have nothing to fear from the authority because I am a good citizen.'

In contrast to the postures of accommodation are the postures of defiance. Defiance is defined as a signal that individuals express towards an authority (and shared with others) that communicates unwillingness to follow the authority's prescribed path without question or protest. Defiance may take two forms. In the first form, defiance is an expression of dislike for or hostility towards an authority, while accepting that the authority has legitimate power that may be used to coerce cooperation. This is called *resistant defiance* because the need for the system is accepted. The source of discontent lies with power being used inappropriately and poor decisions made. The posture of resistance is at the core of defiance of the same name. Resistance is the motivational posture of grievance with insistence that authorities fix the problems of their making and honour their compact with the people. This is also the essence of resistant defiance – fix the problems so that the tax system functions as it should.

While resistance is directed at how the system operates, the other form of defiance, *dismissiveness*, is directed at whether or not the system should exist. Dismissiveness is a form of defiance that credits neither the authority nor the system with soundness of purpose. Dismissive defiance reflects lack of deference for the authority. For the dismissively defiant, a good outcome would be no regulatory system. Two postures are associated with dismissive defiance – *disengagement* and *game playing*. Disengagement is a posture of anomie where people have lost their connection with the norms and values of the regulatory system and continue living their lives paying no heed to the demands of the regulator. In keeping with Durkheim's (1952) formulation of anomie, it is not simply a case of not knowing what the regulator expects: it is often a consequence of a mismatch between the rigid norms of a regulator on the one hand, and individual circumstances and larger social norms on the other.

While disengagement has a degree of fatalism about it (for example, the authority will do what it will do and I am not going to lose any sleep over it), game playing has a combative agenda of beating the authority at its own game. Game playing has an element of extreme reactance. The posture of game playing shows no respect for the spirit of the regulation, but observes technical requirements as part of a game of beating the designers of the system, finding loopholes and creative ways of working around the regulation. The game becomes personally satisfying and liberating for self and others, because it involves challenge and competition, often through cleverly deconstructing the rules.

The postures of commitment, capitulation, resistance, disengagement and game playing are familiar to and readily used by most of us. They will be used when authority intrudes on our freedom and threatens our moral, democratic collective or status-seeking self. In the course of experiencing some intrusion from authority, we may use one or all of the postures. Postures are not mutually exclusive and may emerge at different times depending on the context we find ourselves in and depending on how the authority deals with us. For example, take a small business owner who has left her business in the capable hands of her nephew while she takes an overseas trip. She returns to find that her quarterly business tax returns have not been filed while she has been away. The tax office has written to her threatening fines. She has never been in trouble before. She rings to explain the situation, but fails to gain leniency or sympathy – or even a hearing. She writes a letter of complaint. The unpaid tax accrues interest. Her desire for a fair hearing and to make amends changes when her plea for a little more time to sort things out falls on deaf ears. She needs money fast to pay her debt to the tax office. As she begins to grow her business again, she remembers the problems she had with the tax office and decides to keep some of the profits out of view. She finds an aggressive tax planning adviser who is prepared to help her avoid as much tax as possible. She pays the tax she owes and her penalty, but she has also developed a defiant posture to tax office authority. She will capitulate when there is no other way. But she will also game play when the opportunity presents itself and disengage when gains from evading tax are too great to forfeit. Posturing is a function of who we are, our social milieu and the treatment we receive at the hands of the regulator.

The integrity of the regulator

Motivational posturing theory allows individuals to choose their comfort zone in relation to a regulator such as the tax office. The social distance between regulator and the regulated may be high or low. It follows that the actions of a regulator, particularly positive initiatives to improve relations with those being regulated, are going to make a difference and influence posturing, although most impact is likely to be felt by those whose social distance is not too great. They will be the ones who are attentive, while those who are more socially distant are more likely to be 'deaf' to the regulator's message. Nevertheless, efforts to build relationships with the socially distant in a regulatory community need not be counterproductive. So long as someone notices the positive engagement of the authority with the community, the message can be carried along networks that include those who have positioned themselves beyond the authority's reach (Braithwaite and Drahos,

2000). In time, those beyond reach may become more open as they are exposed to third parties carrying a more conciliatory message from the authority.

Building relationships with regulatory communities is an essential part of the process of building the integrity of the regulatory agency. Integrity refers to soundness of purpose, a willingness to be open and accountable to the public for actions, capacity to acknowledge shortcomings and lead with new solutions, and finally commitment to respectful treatment of citizens through adherence to principles of procedural justice (Selznick, 1992; Braithwaite, V. 2003). Integrity can be measured by an independent overseeing agent that routinely scrutinizes the tax authority's actions (for example, an ombudsman) or by the people whom the tax office serves (i.e., the general public, taxpayers and citizens alike).

As is the case with legitimacy, both the objectively assessed and subjectively evaluated faces of integrity are important. There is little integrity in being popular with the public but wanting in substance when an independent overseer undertakes a more meticulous, evidence-based review; and it would be an odd sort of integrity that is evident to an independent overseer but not to the people one serves. Yet in periods where integrity has been in a slump, integrity in the public's eye and integrity as observed by the overseeing agent are likely to be out of step because of lag times in detecting improvements or decrements on the various dimensions. For this reason, both the objective (evidence assessed by an overseer) and subjective (perceptions of the public) are important facets of integrity to monitor. In this particular chapter, the focus is on the subjective.

When the public perceive an authority acting with integrity, social distance should decrease between regulatees and the regulator, that is, the postures of accommodation (commitment, capitulation) should become stronger and the postures of defiance weaker (resistance in particular, disengagement and game playing depending on circumstances). The circumstances in which integrity may fail will be those where all hope is lost that any good can come of showing the authority deference. The postures of disengagement and game playing are most likely to be implicated in this way of thinking about the authority. If individuals, or more likely a group of individuals, have already come to the conclusion that an authority is irrelevant in their lives, it may not matter whether or not that authority acts with integrity. The objective for these so-called regulatees is to keep the ties broken so that the authority remains irrelevant. Integrity only matters to those who have ceded regulatory control to an authority and have accepted a subordinate role within the system – or can see some advantage in doing so.

Psychological processes by which threats to the moral, democratic collective and status-seeking self become postures

Two processes have been useful in explaining how threat to the moral self, democratic collective self, or status-seeking self are processed and how appraisal of such threat is related to motivational postures. One of these processes focuses on emotions, cognitions and reasoning with the objective of removing threat and protecting self. The second has the same objective, but the process relies less on thinking about the threat and more on copying those who seem to have come up with the best response to the threat.

Cognitive appraisal

Perceptions of threat may be dealt with through analysing thoughts and feelings, that is, through reason – for example, we might say to ourselves 'I feel afraid or unhappy in response to the authority, why is that, what can I do to make myself feel better, what are my best options for resolving this situation?' Through this appraisal process that has been examined at length in the stress and coping literature (Pearlin and Schooler, 1978; Lazarus and Folkman, 1984), response options are reviewed and decisions made. In the regulatory context, this is often a social process where stories are exchanged, people look to others to make sense of the threat they feel, and come up with solutions or possible responses. Injustice is often the rallying point for exchanging regulatory stories. Authorities become the out-group in storytelling and regulatees unite around the themes of unfair treatment, unreasonable demands, and the authority's poor judgement. The process may not be evidence-based or strictly logical, but it has the quality of psycho-logic. A number of theories address such processes in decision-making, for example, belief-attitude-value consistency theories (Rokeach, 1968), reasoned action and planned behaviour theories (Ajzen, 1985; Ajzen and Fishbein, 1980), stress and coping theories (Pearlin and Schooler, 1978; Lazarus and Folkman, 1984) and rationalization theories (Sykes and Matza, 1957). These theories rely on a process of reasoning that brings consistency between beliefs, attitudes, feelings and actions, including what Harris (2007) calls our ethical identity – those attributes about ourselves that we like, strive for, and feel proud of.

Resistant defiance, at least in the tax context, is best explained by such rational processing (Braithwaite, 2009). In the case of resistant defiance, defending against regulatory threat and protecting ethical identity gives rise to a battle that looks like this. On the one hand is a moral self that wants to be law abiding and will align itself with an authority that has credibility and legitimacy. The proper postures for this self are commitment or capitulation. On the other hand is an offended democratic collective self that favours the posture of resistance. These two selves compete for dominance – is the moral self the more reasonable and sensible self to adopt, all things considered; or has the democratic collective self been so offended that no decent person could turn away from fighting such injustice? For the postures of commitment, capitulation and resistance, a form of deliberation can take place in the tax context about what is the most reasonable response. Persuasion is possible, through reasoning with self or reasoning with others. This includes dialogue with authority. It is in this context that the integrity of the authority becomes paramount as a way of establishing credibility and trustworthiness with the public. There is no assumption here that the sense of grievance is justified. It may be a rationalization to avoid facing up to wrongdoing. Authorities with integrity can work through misplaced as well as justified grievance.

Social modelling – or contagion

Sometimes the threat context is so complex and bereft of explanation that there is too little information to form a judgement. The threat from authority, while registering, is not conducive to understanding through the process of reasoning. Just as psychology has been instrumental in promoting explanations of human behaviour based on cognitions and reasoning, it has a strong tradition in learning theory and social modelling (Bandura, 1977, 1986). Sometimes we do not need to understand – we just look at what others are doing – particularly those who are successful and well regarded, and emulate their actions. Copying others need not be incompatible with some level of reasoning of course. We choose role models on the basis of their similarity to who we are or who we want to be. The important point here is that sometimes individuals are expected to adapt in environments where they do not have resources to permit sound reasoning; for example, where individuals do not understand what the regulatory authority is doing or wants them to do. In such circumstances, feelings of threat can be dealt with through watching others, observing consequences, and following in the footsteps of those getting the best outcomes.

In the area of taxation, it appears that threat to the status-seeking self triggers a modelling process whereby people turn to an alternative authority on tax matters, putting their faith in aggressive tax planners and advisers. The process that takes hold in this context resembles what economists call contagion (Braithwaite, 2005), whereby the individual does what others are doing to improve their economic position and beat the system. Contagion and the desire to pay as little tax as possible fuels the postures of disengagement and game playing. Dialogue is likely to be irrelevant in this context, as is the integrity of the regulator. All eyes are turned elsewhere, towards an alternative authority that has found a pathway for outsmarting the tax office and denying them control.

Generalizability?

It is a question for further enquiry whether, in other regulatory contexts, resistant defiance is based on reasoning and dismissive defiance is based on modelling. The assertion may be generalizable on the following grounds. Where authorities are effective and use coercion to enforce compliance, most people who are concerned for their own well-being will reason that when the costs of non-compliance are too high, compliance is the better option (Ayres and Braithwaite, 1992). Regulatory institutions use various kinds of messaging to remind those whom they are regulating to think of the risk of getting caught and the costs, and do the right thing. With framing of this kind, regulatees, if they want to fight back, are most likely to develop reasoning around injustice and unreasonableness on the part of authorities and push for change within the democratic system. Most will consider it foolhardy to challenge the formal authorities head on. That is, unless the authority loses credibility and legitimacy on a grand scale.

In circumstances where authorities have either lost coercive power or lost all credibility and legitimacy, the government lacks an institutional frame for putting forward a convincing case for compliance. Individuals who are estranged from government institutions must find it difficult to explain to themselves why they should comply, particularly if they consider the chances of being caught minimal, and if they are conscious of sacrificing goals and aspirations for no good reason. Individuals are likely to experience a degree of cognitive dissonance in this situation. The assumption is that processes of socialization into law abidingness continue to be influential even in our individualistic and socially heterogeneous society, and even when our institutions are failing. This means that it is not so easy to adopt the persona of someone who genuinely does not care about authority as is the case with disengagement, or is prepared to challenge the power of authority as is the case with game playing. In order for dismissiveness to be embraced and confidently displayed, individuals need exposure to role models with leadership qualities that quell the nerves of those not accustomed to defiance, and with capacity to inspire a new definition of a moral self. In taxation, this has been successfully accomplished by some within the financial planning industry – tax minimization and avoidance advisers find savings within the law, while avoiding the intended control of authorities.

Evidence to support the theory from the field of taxation

Three surveys of Australians' views about and experiences of taxation and the Australian Tax Office were conducted in 2000, 2002 and 2005. The surveys were conducted at a time when tax reform was being undertaken in Australia and the public were being introduced to a new tax, a goods-and-services tax, for the first time. A total of 511 respondents completed the survey at all three time points providing a panel for looking at the development of posturing over an extended period of time. (See Braithwaite and Reinhart (2005a, 2005b) and Braithwaite *et al.* (2001) for a description of the sampling frame and final sample.)

The methodological approach of this study was exploratory and broad-brushed. Various theoretical approaches were tested in developing the theoretical framework presented in this chapter. Each set of hypotheses, once tested, led to theoretical modifications, further testing, and further model building using regression analyses, path analyses and structural equation modelling. It is the end result of this process that is presented here. (For further information on the theoretical building blocks and empirical modelling, see Braithwaite, 2009.)

For reasons of parsimony, structural equation models for the two kinds of defiance are presented separately. In time, more data analysis and theory building will bring simplification of these models and possibly the capacity to combine the two types of defiance into one model. At this stage, the complexity and detail of the two path models serve an important function – ensuring the theory is well grounded in the data.

The measures that made their way into the final models of resistant defiance and dismissive defiance are described briefly below and in detail elsewhere (Braithwaite, 2009; http://vab.anu.edu.au). Various scales and indices were combined into composite measures of core constructs. It is the composite core constructs and their constituent parts that are outlined below.

Measures of the moral self, expressed in terms of alignment with authority

Perceptions of deterrence: the index for measuring perceived deterrence was a multiplicative term comprising 'likelihood of being caught X, likelihood of sanctioning X, perceived problems resulting from being caught and sanctioned'. Respondents' assessments of these deterrence components were made in relation to two scenarios: (a) Imagine you have been paid $5,000 in cash for work that you have done outside your regular job. You don't declare it on your income tax return; and (b) Imagine you have claimed $5,000 as work deductions when the expenses have nothing to do with work. For each scenario, one question assessed likelihood of being caught, while likelihood of sanctioning and resulting problems were assessed in relation to four possible sanctioning outcomes.

Thinking morally: this construct represented commitment to law abidingness on tax issues. Four measures were combined to represent the construct: (a) an honest taxpayer identity index (two questions); (b) a personal honest taxpaying ethic scale (four questions); (c) disapproval of tax cheating scale (three questions); and (d) a willingness to report and confront tax cheating scale (two questions).

Honest no-risk adviser as ideal choice: respondents were asked to imagine that they were choosing a tax adviser and to indicate the priority they would place on finding someone who was honest, no-risk and no-fuss (three questions).

Measures of the democratic collective self, expressed in terms of grievance

Disillusionment with the democracy: six questions assessed level of agreement with the view that democracy had lost much of its original meaning, the government was not allowing ordinary people opportunity for input, that the democracy, including the legal system, had been captured by those with resources and money, and that cynicism of all government processes was warranted.

Feeling oppressed: this measure was a composite of three measures of an individual's sense of victimization at the hands of the tax system: (a) economic disadvantage through taxation (three questions); (b) self-rating on the dimension of paying more than one's fair share of tax (one question); and (c) receiving unfavourable decisions from the tax office (two questions).

Measures of the status-seeking self, expressed in terms of pursuit of economic and social aspirations

Status-seeking values: values represent goal states and ways of behaving that we consider desirable and that we strive for. Of most relevance in the tax context are values associated with being financially well off, entrepreneurial and successful. A five-item value scale was used for the analyses below.

Aggressive tax planning adviser as ideal choice: respondents were asked to imagine that they were choosing a tax adviser and to indicate the priority they would place on finding someone who was creative, well-networked and could deliver on aggressive tax planning (three questions).

Measure of integrity

Integrity describes the degree to which the community regards an authority as acting with soundness of purpose, executing its operations competently, reasonably and fairly with awareness of and consideration for those affected by them. In the context of taxation, three measures were particularly relevant and were combined to form a composite integrity index: (a) an index of taxation's benefit to the community (two questions); (b) a scale measuring commitment to the Taxpayers' Charter (twelve questions); and (c) a scale measuring showing respect (six questions, four drawn from Tyler's (1997) respect and trustworthiness scales and two representing consultation measures).

Measures of motivational postures and defiance

The motivational postures of commitment, capitulation, resistance, disengagement and game playing were measured through a set of scales that were first developed in the context of nursing home regulation and have been adapted for use in occupational health and safety, child protection, governance more generally and taxation. The tax version of the scales and descriptive statistics is given in Table 5.1 in the Appendix. The profile of postures for the sample followed the traditional pattern – very high endorsement for the system through commitment, high acknowledgement of a capitulation posture, over half acknowledging resistance, and a much smaller proportion (less than 20 per cent) laying claim to the postures of disengagement and game playing. When the postures were factor analysed, two distinct dimensions emerged in the taxation context. The first, with one pole defined by commitment and capitulation and the other by resistance, represented a mindset that was highly critical but accepting of the existence of the power of the system – resistant defiance. The second defined by disengagement and game playing represented a mindset that was cynical and rejecting of the power of the system – dismissive defiance.

Structural equation modelling

The process of building models involved initially thinking about the variables in terms of being instigators or mediators. The term 'instigator' refers to variables measured in 2000 that represented a mental state that was envisaged as the beginning of a path to defiance. *Disillusionment with the democracy, perceived deterrence,* and *status seeking* were instigators in so far as they were variables that explained why some individuals might feel more threatened than most just by the thought of government taxation.

After a period of appraisal of how taxation was likely to impact on them personally, individuals were expected to come up with a coping style. *Thinking morally* and *feeling oppressed* were examples of such coping styles and were expected to prove useful in defending the moral and democratic collective selves. They were likely to be shaped by the instigators mentioned above – *status seeking, perceived deterrence* and *disillusionment with democracy. Thinking morally* and *feeling oppressed* were also measured in 2000.

The tax authority's *perceived integrity* was measured in 2002, eighteen months into the tax reform process. It was reasonable to suppose that by this time, Australians would have formed some view of how the tax authority was performing as it implemented the tax reform package. Individual predispositions (*status-seeking* values, *disillusionment, feeling oppressed* and *thinking morally*) and perceptions of how the tax office operated (*perceived deterrence*) were assumed to function as a lens through which the tax authority's efforts to improve its performance would be interpreted. Even so, perceptions of integrity were unlikely to be determined solely by perceptual bias. Interventions that affected integrity should have registered with the public and made a difference to how much defiance individuals felt.

By 2005, individuals were able to look at the tax reform process with some distance and perspective. They were in a position to decide whether they were on side with the tax authority or not. The 2005 measures included attraction to *honest no-risk advisers* or *aggressive tax planning advisers* and the measures of *resistant* and *dismissive defiance*.

A structural equation model for resistance

From Figure 5.1, resistant defiance was best explained through a pathway connecting disillusionment with the democracy to feeling oppressed. Feeling oppressed directly and indirectly influenced resistant defiance, indirectly through failing to see integrity in the tax authority. This pathway reflects grievance, a response to injustice when the democratic collective self is threatened. Such a threat raises doubts about government's good faith in honouring the contract of cooperation between state and citizen/taxpayer. Importantly, this pathway shows the performances of government and the tax authority connected in the minds of the public.

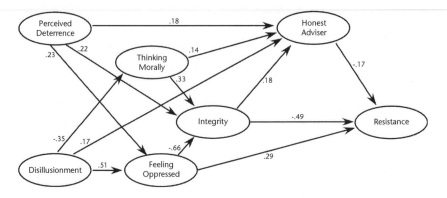

FIGURE 5.1 A composite structural equation model predicting resistance

Reining in resistant defiance in Figure 5.1 is law abidingness. The moral obligation pathway is not as strong as the grievance pathway, but nevertheless is significant and captures the way in which individuals are most likely to protect their moral self when it is under threat. Thinking morally strengthens a preference for an honest tax adviser. Perceived deterrence also strengthens a preference for an honest tax adviser. An honest tax adviser, in turn, lowers resistant defiance.

Contrary to expectations, perceived deterrence did not strengthen the coping style of thinking morally. Perceived deterrence, however, was important to both the grievance and the moral obligation pathways. Perceived deterrence was connected to feeling oppressed, suggesting that it was a threat to the democratic collective self. Given that fear of deterrence and feeling oppressed were measured at the same time, it is probably not surprising that the measures correlated: both could be interpreted as manifestations of victimization. More interesting is what happens over time. Perceived deterrence positively affected perceptions of tax integrity two years on and preference for an honest no-risk adviser five years on. Deterrence strengthens the morally obligated pathway in the long term and the grievance pathway in the short term. Deterrence may not be flavour of the month when one is struggling to find the money to pay a tax bill, but believing that a deterrence system is operating and that it is risky to cheat on tax appears to pay dividends for authorities in the long term.

Integrity, like deterrence, is of great interest because it is an institutional characteristic over which tax authorities have some control. Figure 5.1 also shows how pivotal the perceptual measure of integrity is in the expression of resistant defiance. Those thinking morally are more likely to have a positive view of tax office integrity two years later. The effects of integrity extend into 2005. High integrity protects against resistant defiance and increases prospects of wanting an honest adviser. Integrity therefore boosts the moral obligation pathway. By the same token, an authority's best efforts to practice integrity will not always be appreciated by the public. In Figure 5.1, those who feel oppressed by taxation have a more negative view of the tax authority's integrity.

The variance accounted for in resistant defiance was 58 per cent. The model had satisfactory goodness of fit indices (see Tables 5.2 and 5.3 in Appendix). In developing a model for resistant defiance, the variables associated with the status-seeking self were not significant and therefore do not appear in the model in Figure 5.1. Of the other relationships appearing in Figure 5.1, those involving disillusionment are intriguing in what they reveal about individual adaptation to perceived institutional failure.

Disillusionment with the democracy mainly fuelled grievance, but it also was relevant to moral obligation. Faith in (as opposed to disillusionment with) the democracy was associated with thinking morally. The finding is important. Nurturance of the moral self was not sparked by fear of punishment but by pride in the democracy and pride in the democratic collective self. With this in mind, the next finding is an interesting adaptive strategy. At least some of those disappointed in the way the democracy functioned maintained good faith with the democracy through idealizing an honest no-risk adviser. They were willing to hand their citizenship responsibilities over to an agent who would ensure that tax obligations were properly met, thereby imposing constraints on any temptation they might have to be non-compliant.

A structural equation model for dismissiveness

In contrast to resistant defiance, the model for dismissive defiance did not include integrity. Various attempts to accommodate integrity in the dismissive defiant model failed. Integrity was neither directly nor indirectly related to dismissiveness. Instead, status seeking and preferring an aggressive tax adviser, variables that represented a challenge to the tax office and attraction to an alternative authority, emerged as significant predictors of dismissiveness.

In Figure 5.2, the moral obligation pathway shows thinking morally and perceived deterrence increasing preference for an honest adviser, which, in turn, lowers dismissiveness. Feeling disillusioned with the democracy weakened the moral obligation pathway. It was negatively related to thinking morally.

Figure 5.2 features the grievance pathway in its early stages with the variables, disillusionment with the democracy and feeling oppressed by taxation. They combine with other variables to define an alternative pathway, a way of overcoming a victimized state. Status-seeking values work through perceived oppression to increase preference for an aggressive adviser and dismissiveness. This competitive pathway serves the interests of the status-seeking self. It also attracts interest from those who feel aggrieved about treatment of the democratic collective self.

As was the case with the resistant defiance model, some variables linked the moral obligation and grievance-cum-competitive pathways. Thinking morally made it unlikely that a person would look to aggressive tax planning. Perceived deterrence once again had a complex set of relationships, strengthening both the moral obligation pathway and the grievance-cum-competitive pathway. Notably, perceived deterrence in 2000 was directly linked to lower dismissiveness five years later in 2005, albeit weakly.

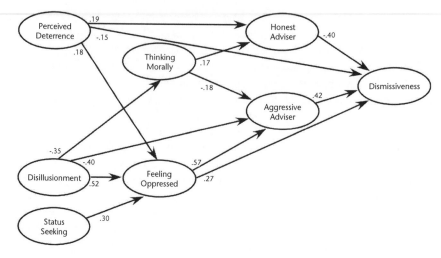

FIGURE 5.2 A composite structural equation model predicting dismissiveness

Finally, disillusionment with the democracy worsened dismissive defiance along some pathways and guarded against it along others. Disillusionment dampened the moral obligation pathway while strengthening grievance. In this sense, it exacerbated dismissiveness. But for some, disillusionment placed constraints on the pathway to dismissiveness by leaving them with a distaste for aggressive tax planning. Disillusionment in 2000 was negatively related to holding as an ideal an aggressive tax adviser in 2005. If not open to the possibilities of aggressive tax planning, it would be difficult for most individuals to successfully pursue a pathway to dismissiveness.

The structural equation model depicted in Figure 5.2 explained 50 per cent of the variance in dismissive defiance. The data fitted the model well producing satisfactory goodness of fit indices (see Tables 5.2 and 5.3 in the Appendix).

Implications of findings

The most important contribution of this chapter is to demonstrate why regulation is a costly and difficult business when carried out without appreciation for how adept individuals are in protecting their freedom. Studying defiance shows individuals as capable of choosing their social distance from the regulator. This determines how much cooperation they will offer and are capable of offering. It is true that cooperation is not synonymous with compliance. Often regulators focus on key performance indicators of 'outcomes', and mistakenly conclude that a tick in a series of compliance boxes is good enough. Increasingly, this approach is found to be wanting (see Gunningham and Sinclair's (2002) leaders-to-laggards typology and Braithwaite, Makkai and Braithwaite (2007) on the dangers of ritualism). Individuals can meet basic legal requirements to comply without agreeing with the rules (Kagan and Scholz's (1984) political citizen) or having respect for them (McBarnet's (2003) creative compliance) or appreciating their purpose (Braithwaite *et al.*'s (2007) ritualism). In many domains, minimal compliance of this kind does not make a regulatory system effective. The reality is that in order to fulfil the purposes of the regulation, cooperation and effort from regulator, regulatee and other third parties is required. Sometimes such cooperation is even necessary to understand what the law means (see Picciotto (2007) on the difficulties surrounding tax law). Recent high-profile examples where law abounds, but cooperation does not, include financial regulation, environmental regulation, intellectual property regulation, child protection, and sanctioning of nation-states for violation of international law.

Once cooperation is accepted as an important goal of regulation, we are in a better position to understand how regulatory regimes can fail, in spite of being backed up by law and enforcement capability. Importantly, there is no one best way for a regulatory body to manage defiance. Resistant defiance will respond best to being given a fair hearing, dialogue and reform. Deterrence can make matters worse for those whose resistance should be resolved through addressing grievances and respectful treatment; but at the same time, it may be necessary to communicate to people that compliance is important and for nudging those sitting on the fence over to the right side. Dismissive defiance is far harder to break down with persuasive strategies or even through the use of power. The authority may have become an irrelevancy to be ignored, or exploited should any sign of weakness in the system be exposed. In such circumstances, seeing an authority with credible deterrence capability becomes imperative.

In yet other circumstances, the use of, as opposed to the threat of, deterrence may be essential (Braithwaite, J., 2009). When authorities are trying to curb dismissiveness that is being led by an alternative authority (in this case the financial planning industry), authorities sometimes need to intercede to call a halt to contagious outbreaks of defiance through high-profile prosecutions. At the same time, deterrence may be counterproductive if the so-called legitimate authority does not hold the higher moral ground in the minds of the public. In such situations, if democratic debate, deliberation and due process through the legal system do not deliver moral legitimacy to the authority, a settlement of some kind will have to be reached, essentially involving power sharing. The alternative authority will have earned its place at the table to decide on future governance arrangements when it is supported by the democracy and the courts.

This study demonstrates how the triggers for defiance, which are to some degree controlled by the authority − in this case, disillusionment in the democracy, tax integrity, and deterrence, are interconnected through people's interpretation of events and storytelling. Authority's control, however, is seriously limited by the fact that the context for sense making is personal: individuals are trying to manage the threat they feel to their freedom when faced with an authority's demands. Doubts about the authority's authenticity (Selznick, 1992) be they sown by the authority, other community leaders, self or significant others, can acquire traction and weaken moral obligation pathways, while consolidating grievance and competitive pathways. These psychological processes are comforting, particularly when individuals need justification or rationalization for their non-cooperative stance. Convincing oneself that the moral self should not be engaged and that the collective democratic self and status-seeking self have been treated badly by the authority is a satisfying outcome for regaining a sense of moral superiority and freedom from control.

Regulatory authorities, mindful of their coercive powers, understandably have a vested interest in projecting an image of being in control. Recognizing limitations, however, also has survival value institutionally. One of the most confronting findings for a tax authority is that as disillusionment with government goes up, many other elements contributing to cooperation with the tax system go off the rails. The findings are consistent with work that has come out of the area of crime control. LaFree (1998) has linked crime rates in the US to loss of trust in political institutions and to the use of law to impose change from the top to the detriment of community social capital and equal opportunity. Efforts to regulate that fail to connect with people's moral compass and that create grievance give rise to a culture of suspicion and wariness where individual propensity for dismissive defiance has a comfortable home. This psychological state of readiness to dismissively defy is related to what Hagan *et al.* (1998) describe as anomic amorality and Sampson and Bartusch (1998) as legal cynicism (Braithwaite, V., 2009).

Integrity and the acceptable use of deterrence might be considered measures that will fix these problems. For some yes, for others no. Institutional integrity is something that authorities can and should pledge and deliver. In the context of this research, the aspect of institutional integrity that did most of the work was Tyler's (1989, 1990, 1997) procedural justice. This is likely to be the case in most settings in mature democracies where institutional soundness of purpose is not under a cloud. But as this research shows, people are capable of putting themselves at such distance from authority that they can deflect procedural justice or worse still take advantage of it. This is not to say procedural justice is a negotiable quality in a regulatory system. It is not. The findings of Tyler and his colleagues are compelling in this regard. Without everyone being assured of and receiving procedural justice, a regulatory authority will be in even more strife, providing ready ammunition for the grievance and competitive pathways and for silencing any remnants of a moral obligation pathway. This research affirms the pivotal role that integrity (an expanded conception of procedural justice) plays in managing defiance.

Nevertheless, for the regulator at the coal-face doing his or her job, the cases where procedural justice does not produce the desired benefits are not easy. As we see from Figure 5.2, this may occur when individuals are seeing authority blocking their hopes and aspirations for improving the quality of their lives. Or from Figure 5.1, procedural justice may not register when people are so aggrieved over what they see as the authority's unsound purpose that they are unable to see anything positive in the authority's actions. These regulators need other strategies.

This may include restorative justice conferencing that brings in third parties, and where the soundness of purpose can be scrutinized as well as procedures. Equally important are a range of credible deterrence measures. In short, regulators need to be responsive. How and when these various options should be introduced depends on context, and as this chapter argues, context includes the sense making of those being regulated.

Regulatory fora that allow for exchange of views and sharing of goals seem paramount to overcoming problems of non-cooperation. Both responsive regulation and restorative justice provide opportunity for this kind of meaningful dialogue between those who enforce law and those expected to obey it. Unless these conversations take place, it is difficult to see how the key elements in defiance pathways will be ameliorated. Perceptions of low integrity, disillusionment with the democracy and grievance over deterrence depend, for their resolution, on sharing understandings, agreeing on goals and processes, and airing misunderstandings.

In discussions with regulatees, appropriate regulatory pyramids can be designed not only to enforce compliance but also to build cooperation and social capital through recognizing strengths (Braithwaite *et al.*, 2007). Providing there are institutional opportunities for regulatees to understand regulators and regulators to understand regulatees, prospects for building cooperation remain high. Moreover, in arriving at mutual understanding, defiance will come to be seen not as a nuisance, but rather as an adaptive resource, as a way of protecting the self that we all should be able to relate to. Through the insights gained through connecting with these selves, it should be possible to reap benefits all round, including designing a better regulatory system that attracts consent. Consenting to a regulatory system that is explained and accessible provides the best possible platform for building compliance and legitimacy.

References

Ajzen, I. (1985) 'From intentions to actions: A theory of planned behavior', in J. Kuhl and J. Beckmann (eds) *Action-Control: From cognition to behavior*, Heidelberg: Springer-Verlag, pp. 11–39.

Ajzen, I. and Fishbein, M. (1980) *Understanding Attitudes and Predicting Social Behaviour*, Englewood Cliffs: Prentice Hall.

Ayres, I. and Braithwaite, J. (1992) *Responsive Regulation: Transcending the deregulation debate*, New York: Oxford University Press.

Bandura, A. (1977) *Social Learning Theory*, Englewood Cliffs: Prentice-Hall.

—— (1986) *Social Foundations of Thought and Action: A social cognitive theory*, Englewood Cliffs: Prentice-Hall.

Beetham, D. (1991) *The Legitimation of Power*, Basingstoke: Macmillan Education.

Braithwaite, J. (2005) *Markets in Vice, Markets in Virtue*, Sydney: The Federation Press.

—— (2009) 'Restorative justice for banks through negative licensing', *The British Journal of Criminology*, 49(2): 439–50.

Braithwaite, J. and Drahos, P. (2000) *Global Business Regulation*, Cambridge: Cambridge University Press.

Braithwaite, J., Makkai, T. and Braithwaite, V.A. (2007) *Regulating Aged Care: Ritualism and the new pyramid*, Cheltenham, UK and Northampton, MA: Edward Elgar.

Braithwaite, V. (2003) 'Tax System Integrity and Compliance: The democratic management of the tax system', in V. Braithwaite (ed.) *Taxing Democracy: Understanding tax avoidance and evasion*, Aldershot: Ashgate Publishing Company, pp. 271–90.

—— (2009) *Defiance in Taxation and Governance: Resisting and Dismissing Authority in a Democracy*, Cheltenham: Edward Elgar Publishing.

Braithwaite, V. and Reinhart, M. (2005a) 'Preliminary Findings and Codebook for the Australian Tax System – Fair or Not Survey', Centre for Tax System Integrity Working Paper 79, Australian National University, http://ctsi.anu.edu.au/publications/WP/WPlist.html.

—— (2005b) 'Preliminary Findings and Codebook for the How Fair, How Effective Survey: The Collection and Use of Taxation in Australia', Centre for Tax System Integrity Working Paper 84, Australian National University, http://ctsi.anu.edu.au/publications/WP/WPlist.html.

Braithwaite, V., Reinhart, M., Mearns, M. and Graham, R. (2001) 'Preliminary Findings from the Community Hopes, Fears, and Actions Survey', Centre for Tax System Integrity Working Paper No 3, Australian National University, http://ctsi/publications/WP/3.pdf.

Brehm, S.S. and Brehm, J.W. (1981) *Psychological Reactance: A Theory of Freedom and Control*, New York: Academic Press.

Cialdini, R.B. and Goldstein, N.J. (2004) 'Social influence: compliance and conformity', *Annual Review of Psychology*, 55: 591–621.

Durkheim, E. (1952) *Suicide: A study in sociology*, London: Routledge and Kegan Paul.

Fishbein, M. and Ajzen, I. (1980) *Belief, Attitude, Intention, and Behavior*, Reading, MA: Addison-Wesley.

Gunningham, N. and Sinclair, D. (2002) *Leaders and Laggards: Next Generation Environmental Regulation*, Sheffield: Greenleaf Publishing.

Hagan, J., Hefler, G., Classen, C., Boehnke, G., K. and Merkens, H. (1998), 'Subterranean sources of sub-cultural delinquency beyond the American dream', *Criminology*, 36(2): 309–42.

Harris, N. (2007) 'Shame, ethical identity and conformity: lessons from research on the psychology of social influence', *Regulatory Institutions Network Occasional Paper 12*, http://ctsi.anu.edu.au/publications/OccPaper12.pdf.

Kagan, R.A. and Scholz, J.T. (1984) 'The "criminology of the corporation" and regulatory enforcement strategies', in K. Hawkins and J.M. Thomas (eds) *Enforcing Regulation*, The Hague: Kluwer-Nijhoff Publishing, pp. 67–95

LaFree, G. (1998) *Losing Legitimacy: Street Crime and the Decline of Social Institutions in America*, Boulder, CO: Westview Press.

Lazarus, R.S. and Folkman, S. (1984) *Stress, Appraisal and Coping*, New York: Springer.

Losoncz, I. (2010) 'Respect and community inclusion – post-settlement Sudanese experiences', paper presented at *Engaging Africa/Engaging Africans: Knowledge, Representation, Politics Conference*, Victoria University, Melbourne, 2–4 December.

McBarnet, D. (2003) 'When compliance is not the solution but the problem: from changes in the law to changes in attitude', in V. Braithwaite (ed.) *Taxing Democracy: Understanding Tax Avoidance and Evasion*, Aldershot: Ashgate, pp. 229–44.

Pearlin, L.I. and Schooler, C. (1978) 'The structure of coping', *Journal of Health and Social Behavior*, 19(1): 2–21.

Picciotto, S. (2007) 'Constructing compliance: game playing, tax law and the regulatory state', *Law and Policy*, 29(1): 11–30.

Rokeach, M. (1968) *Beliefs, Attitudes and Values: A Theory of Organization and Change*, San Francisco: Jossey-Bass.

—— (1973) *The Nature of Human Values*, New York: Free Press.

Sampson, R.J. and Bartusch, D.J. (1998) 'Legal cynicism and (subcultural?) tolerance of deviance: the neighbourhood context of racial differences', *Law and Society Review*, 32(4): 777–804.

Scheff, T.J. and Retzinger, S.M. (1991) *Emotions and Violence: Shame and rage in destructive conflicts*, Lexington, MA: Lexington Books.

Selznick, P. (1992) *The Moral Commonwealth: Social theory and the promise of community*, Berkeley: University of California Press.

Sherman, L.W. (1993) 'Defiance, deterrence, and irrelevance: a theory of the criminal sanction', *Journal of Research in Crime and Delinquency*, 30(4): 445–73.

Suchman, M.C. (1995) 'Managing Legitimacy: strategic and institutional approaches', *Academy of Management Review*, 20(3): 571–610.

Sykes, G.M. and Matza, D. (1957) 'Techniques of neutralization: a theory of delinquency', *American Sociological Review*, 22(6): 664–70.

Tyler, T.R. (1989) 'The psychology of procedural justice: a test of the group-value model', *Journal of Personality and Social Psychology*, 57(5): 830–8.

—— (1990) *Why People Obey the Law*, New Haven: Yale University Press.

—— (1997) 'The psychology of legitimacy: a relational perspective on voluntary deference to authorities', *Personality and Social Psychology Review*, 1(4): 323–45.

White, R.W. (1959) 'Motivation reconsidered: the concept of competence', *Psychological Review*, 66(5): 297–333.

Young, I.M. (2000) *Inclusion and Democracy*, Oxford: Oxford University Press.

Appendix

TABLE 5.1 Statements representing the motivational postures of commitment, capitulation, resistance, disengagement and game playing

---

Commitment (M = 3.85, S D = .54, alpha reliability coefficient = .82, homogeneity ratio = .43)

Paying tax is the right thing to do.
Paying tax is a responsibility that should be willingly accepted by all Australians.
I feel a moral obligation to pay my tax.
Paying my tax ultimately advantages everyone.
I think of tax paying as helping the government do worthwhile things.
Overall, I pay my tax with good will.
I resent paying tax. (reversed)
I accept responsibility for paying my fair share of tax.

Capitulation (M = 3.40, SD = .54, alpha reliability coefficient = .63, homogeneity ratio = .27)

No matter how cooperative or uncooperative the Tax Office is, the best policy is to always be cooperative with them.
If you cooperate with the Tax Office, they are likely to be cooperative with you.
Even if the Tax office finds that I am doing something wrong, they will respect me in the long run as long as I admit my mistakes.
The Tax Office is encouraging to those who have difficulty meeting their obligations through no fault of their own.
The tax system may not be perfect, but it works well enough for most of us.

Resistance (M = 3.18, SD = .54, alpha reliability coefficient = .68, homogeneity ratio = .31)

As a society, we need more people willing to take a stand against the Tax Office.
It's important not to let the Tax Office push you around.
The Tax Office is more interested in catching you for doing the wrong thing, than helping you do the right thing.
It's impossible to satisfy the Tax Office completely.
Once the Tax Office has you branded as a non-compliant taxpayer, they will never change their mind.
If you don't cooperate with the Tax Office, they will get tough with you.

Disengagement (M = 2.31, SD = .52, alpha reliability coefficient = .64, homogeneity ratio = .27)

I don't really know what the Tax Office expects of me and I'm not about to ask.
I don't care if I am not doing the right thing by the Tax Office.
If I find out that I am not doing what the Tax Office wants, I'm not going to lose any sleep over it.
I personally don't think that there is much the Tax Office can do to me to make me pay tax if I don't want to.
If the Tax Office gets tough with me, I will become uncooperative with them.

Game playing (M = 2.42, SD = .62, alpha reliability coefficient = .69, homogeneity ratio = .32)

I enjoy talking to friends about loopholes in the tax system.
I like the game of finding the grey area of tax law.
I enjoy the challenge of minimizing the tax I have to pay.
I enjoy spending time working out how changes in the tax system will affect me.
The Tax Office respects taxpayers who can give them a run for their money.

Note: Respondents were asked to rate each statement on a five-point scale from strongly disagree (1) to strongly agree (5).

TABLE 5.2 Indicators of fit for models predicting *Resistance* and *Dismissiveness*

Model for Resistance
Chi-square (χ^2) = 6.164, df = 5, p < .291
Goodness-of-Fit Index (GFI) = .997
Adjusted Goodness-of-Fit Index (AGFI) = .981
Root Mean-Square Error of Approximation (RMSEA) = .021

Model for Dismissiveness
Chi-square (χ^2) = 12.220, df = 10, p < .271
Goodness-of-Fit Index (GFI) = .994
Adjusted Goodness-of-Fit Index (AGFI) = .978
Root Mean-Square Error of Approximation (RMSEA) = .021

TABLE 5.3 Squared multiple correlations for the latent variables in the SEM models predicting *Resistance* and *Dismissiveness*

	Estimate	
	Predicting Resistance	*Predicting Dismissiveness*
Thinking Morally	.123	.123
Feeling Oppressed	.306	.412
Integrity	.613	NA
Honest No-risk Adviser	.096	.065
Aggressive Adviser	NA	.274
Resistance	.576	NA
Dismissiveness	NA	.503

6

LIQUID LEGITIMACY AND COMMUNITY SANCTIONS

Fergus McNeill and Gwen Robinson

Introduction

Though imprisonment tends to dominate our conceptions of punishment, it is not and has never been the principal mode of criminal sanctioning in most jurisdictions (Sparks and McNeill, 2009). Even taking the most extreme example, it remains the case that at the end of 2007 there were more than twice as many people on probation as in custody in the USA; 5.1 million people were under probation or parole supervision at that time (Glaze and Bonczar, 2009). European figures are harder to establish given the wide range of definitions and forms of community sanctions and differences in the official recording of their use. However, on the basis of Van Kalmthout and Durnescu's (2008) extensive recent survey, Durnescu (2007) estimates that when in 2006 the prison population in Europe was about 2 million people, the population serving community sanctions and measures was about 3.5 million. Moreover, in many jurisdictions this is a rapidly growing population. In England and Wales, the *total caseload of offenders* supervised by the Probation Service grew from 175,600 in 2000 to 243,400 in 2008; a 39 per cent increase (Wheatley, 2010). In Scotland, the *numbers of community sanctions imposed* in Scotland rose from about 11,000 in 1999–2000 to over 17,800 by 2008–09 – a 62 per cent increase (Scottish Government, 2010).

In contrast with the academic time and effort (rightly) devoted to analysing the causes and consequences of rising prison populations (with all of their associated costs), increases in both the scale and the range of forms of community sanctions have been relatively under-analysed. This is not the place to remedy that neglect. However, these basic statistics, particularly when set alongside concerns that non-compliance with such sanctions is a key factor in prison growth (Padfield and Maruna, 2006; Scottish Prisons Commission, 2008; Ministry of Justice, 2009), help to make the case that questions around compliance, legitimacy and community sanctions now demand urgent attention.

In this chapter, we examine how compliance with community sanctions has been theorised and discussed hitherto and explore the limited extent to which questions about the legitimacy of such penalties have been addressed. Drawing on our own 'dynamic' model of compliance with community sanctions developed elsewhere (Robinson and McNeill, 2008), we focus in this chapter on the ways in which legitimacy might ebb and flow during the life of a community sanction, and the associated implications for compliance. We focus in particular on the problems presented both by the perennially contested purposes of such sanctions and from the inherent tensions that exist between the pursuit of what Bottoms (2003) has referred to as 'external' and 'internal' legitimacy. Our analysis, which focuses primarily on the latter (i.e., legitimacy vis-à-vis the subject group rather than external audiences), suggests that from the view of offenders subject to community sanctions, legitimacy is highly fluid or 'liquid'. The notion of 'liquid legitimacy' in our title is thus intended as a fairly straightforward metaphor. However, it also recalls Bauman's (2000a) discussion of 'liquid modernity' because, like Bauman, we are concerned with how the object of our analysis (in our case, legitimacy) changes its forms and shapes as a community sanction is negotiated, constructed, contested and reconstructed by the various actors and audiences involved – all of them navigating uncertainties, risks and problems of trust. Our central argument is that, to the extent that community sanctions are oriented to purposes beyond the purely retributive, and to the extent that they seek to encourage active engagement or what we call substantive compliance on the part of offenders, attention to legitimacy is crucial.

Compliance with community sanctions: some peculiarities

Although by no means the most coercive of sanctions which may be meted out by the criminal courts, community sanctions and measures (CSM) nonetheless involve the exercise of (state-authorised) power over those individual offenders who are made subject to them. CSM include a range of measures used as alternatives to criminal prosecution (e.g., mediation), sanctions imposed at the point of sentencing which are administered within the community (e.g., probation or community service) and measures surrounding the early release of prisoners on some form of supervision (e.g., parole).[1] Our principal concern here is with the second and third of these three forms – that is, court-imposed community sanctions and post-release licences.

In recent years, those community sanctions imposed at the point of sentencing in some jurisdictions (England and Wales being a prime example) have explicitly developed their punitive credentials – that is, they are legally constituted in terms that are in part retributive, involving an explicit restriction of the offender's liberty. This aspect of community sanctions has been characterised in terms of their 'punitive weight' (Halliday, 2001). Thus community sanctions typically involve requiring offenders to do things they might not freely choose to do; for example, completing hours of unpaid work, meeting regularly with a supervisor, or attending therapeutic group sessions. Community sanctions may also involve prohibitions such that offenders are required *not* to do certain things which they might normally wish to do; for example, visiting particular locations, or socialising in the evenings. Crucially however, whether the punitive weight of community sanctions is realised depends to a large degree on the compliance of offenders. This is because whatever requirements or restrictions community sanctions involve, these are imposed on offenders in conditions of relative liberty: there are no bars and no other substantive physical restraints. As Mair and Canton (2007) have noted, the prisoner who resists the fact or the conditions of his confinement is nonetheless still being punished (see also Crewe, 2009); the same cannot be said of the offender who fails to comply with the conditions of a community sanction.

In thinking about whether the punitive elements of a sentence have been discharged, the notion of compliance can be and is generally understood in *quantitative* terms; for example, how many hours of unpaid work have been carried out, how many appointments with a supervisor or at groupwork sessions have been attended, etc. However, the purposes of community sanctions are not usually confined to the punitive or retributive: despite the gloomy predictions of some criminological and social theorists (e.g., Feeley and Simon, 1992, 1994; Bauman, 2000b; Hallsworth, 2002; Pratt, 2000) at least some community sanctions in most jurisdictions continue to be oriented towards promoting positive change in (and sometimes even *for*) offenders (rehabilitation, desistance) (e.g., Robinson and McNeill, 2004; Robinson, 2008). In order to achieve these sorts of objectives, quantitatively measurable compliance is clearly crucial, but the *quality* of compliance is also important. That the offender attends appointments or group sessions is necessary but it is not sufficient where there are objectives over and above the deprivation of liberty. Here we can draw a parallel with the distinction made by Tom Tyler in his chapter (this volume) between *compliance* and *cooperation*. Tyler's work clearly suggests that the latter is much more likely when individuals experience and perceive authorities as *legitimate*.

In what remains of this chapter therefore, we explore the notion of 'legitimacy' in the context of community sanctions from the purview of offenders subject to those sanctions. We consider questions both about why legitimacy is important, and how and under what conditions it may be developed, maintained or eroded. As noted above, throughout the chapter we focus in particular on those community sanctions which have a supervisory component, whether this supervision is part of a community-based sentence in its own right, or part of a period on licence that follows a prison sentence. We argue that, to the extent that community sanctions purport to have purposes over and above the punitive or retributive, legitimacy is crucial, but it is also potentially fragile. Our exploration of compliance and legitimacy in the community penalties context is grounded in and further develops a model of compliance we have outlined elsewhere (Robinson and McNeill, 2008). This model brings together and explores the interfaces between existing theoretical schema developed by criminological and socio-legal scholars with particular reference to the work of Bottoms (2001) and Braithwaite (2003).

We begin by briefly reviewing the key components of our model, with particular reference to legitimacy, before going on to consider in turn how legitimacy can be built, how it can be lost or damaged, and how legitimacy within community sanctions might relate to the development of longer-term compliance with the law.

Understanding compliance with community sanctions: a dynamic model

A key feature of community sanctions is their duration: unlike a fine, which can be paid in one instalment and then forgotten about, community sanctions will impact on the offender for a period of time which may be measured out in hours (of community service), months (of probation supervision) or in some cases years (on a licence). In thinking about compliance with a community sanction, then, it makes little intuitive sense to consider compliance as a static quality of offenders' behaviour, or as something that is simply present or absent – hence the logic of a dynamic model.

This basic notion of compliance as a dynamic concept is in fact to be found in Bottoms' (2001) theoretical model of compliance with community sanctions. Bottoms describes four possible 'mechanisms' capable of explaining compliance: instrumental; constraint-based; routinised or habitual; and normative mechanisms. Bottoms argues that the salience or power of these mechanisms may, for any individual offender, change over time. He also draws a useful distinction between 'short-term' and 'longer-term' compliance, which refers to compliance during the life of the order or sanction versus compliance with the law beyond the life of the order (i.e., desistance from further offending). He argues (rightly, in our view), that those responsible for administering community penalties ought to be interested in working towards both short- and longer-term compliance – not just the former.

But the duration of community sanctions also raises questions about the *quality* of compliance. Might this also fluctuate over a period of time? We have found little in the existing literature on community sanctions touching on this issue; nor have we managed to identify any empirical research directly addressing the development or quality of offenders' compliance (Ugwudike's (2010) study is an interesting exception). We did, however, find some clues in the existing research literature which seemed to point to the possibility of different levels or types of compliance. For example, in Monica Barry's (2000) interview-based study of offenders who had completed a community sanction in Scotland, a distinction was drawn between 'reactive' and 'proactive' experiences of supervision, and 'tokenistic' versus 'genuine' contact between supervisors and offenders. Looking further afield to the wider socio-legal literature, we have also drawn on Christine Parker's distinction between 'legalistic/rule compliance' and 'goal-oriented/ substantive' compliance in the corporate context. For Parker, substantive compliance denotes a company's engagement with its legal, social, environmental and ethical responsibilities (e.g., creating a more healthy environment, a safer or more equitable workplace), whilst rule compliance implies 'simplistic obedience to rules' (2002: 27).

Reflecting this notion of 'depth' in relation to compliance, and Parker's work in particular, we have proposed, in the community sanctions context, a distinction between *formal* and *substantive* compliance. Formal compliance denotes behaviour which technically meets the minimum specified requirements of a community sanction and is a necessary component of Bottoms' short-term requirement compliance. The most obvious example of formal compliance is attending appointments (or work placements) at designated times. Substantive compliance, on the other hand, implies the active engagement and cooperation of the offender with the requirements of the sanction. It is evident when (for example) the offender on probation shows a genuine desire to desist from offending. Substantive compliance implies the *active engagement* of offenders with the (productive) purposes of the sanction: the offender who is substantively compliant thus *buys in* (or, in Beetham's (1991: 19) terms, is 'bound in') to the sanction in a way that the offender who is merely formally compliant does not.

In constructing our dynamic model of compliance with community sanctions, we were also inspired by the work of Valerie Braithwaite (2003) and Doreen McBarnet (2003). Their research in relation to (Australian) tax payers and corporations usefully problematises compliance in a way that is absent in the extant literature on community sanctions. In this work, attention is drawn to the range of attitudinal stances or dispositions that may lie behind 'compliant' behaviour. McBarnet has argued that (formally) compliant behaviour is not an automatic 'good': it can in fact mask an attitude or stance toward authority that is negative or hostile. In such circumstances, the individual or company formally complies but only for 'instrumental' reasons (as in Bottoms' framework), doing the bare minimum in order to avoid further penalties. They may in fact attempt to evade substantive compliance to a significant extent, without actually going so far as to break the law. Thus McBarnet notes the prevalence of what she calls 'creative compliance' among resourceful taxpayers, who deploy sophisticated legal strategies to 'accomplish compliance with the letter of the law while totally undermining the policy behind the words' (2003: 229).

Braithwaite's work was particularly useful in informing our emerging model because, unlike much of the socio-legal literature, it deals with the behaviour of individuals in relation to legal authority – specifically the Australian tax office. Braithwaite's research revealed that compliant (i.e., tax-paying) behaviour tells us little about the attitudes or 'motivational postures' of individual tax-payers, which can vary considerably. Her research revealed five relatively distinct postures, which group into two categories: postures of deference and postures of defiance. These motivational postures reflect varying degrees of 'social distance' between regulator and regulatee, which in turn reflect an appraisal of the regulator on the part of the regulatee.[2] Braithwaite's central argument is that although regulators enjoy legal legitimacy, they do not necessarily enjoy psychological legitimacy from the perspective of the regulatee: postures of deference ('commitment' and 'capitulation') reflect an acceptance of the psychological legitimacy of the authority, whilst postures of defiance are indicative of varying degrees of resistance to or denial of legitimacy at the individual level. Indeed, only one of the five motivational postures outlined by Braithwaite (commitment) reflects the genuine endowment of psychological legitimacy and a feeling of moral obligation to comply: capitulation more closely resembles a 'resigned acceptance' on the part of the regulatee.

Whilst applying the findings of research on Australian tax payers directly to populations of offenders is perhaps not entirely unproblematic, there is some empirical evidence to suggest that broadly analogous motivational postures are evident amongst prisoners. Crewe's (2009) typology of compliance with prison regimes identifies four types of compliance which he describes as 'committed', 'fatalistic/instrumental', 'detached' and 'strategic'. Of these, only the first resembles Braithwaite's posture of 'deference'; the other three all contain elements of resistance, disengagement or manipulation.

Braithwaite's 'posture of commitment' also resonates with Bottoms' notion of 'normative compliance' – that is, compliance which reflects a judgement on the part of the individual that what is being asked or required of him or her is 'right' or reasonable. In Bottoms' model, 'legitimacy' is one of three possible grounds for normative compliance. Drawing on the theoretical work of David Beetham (1991) as well as empirical work on procedural justice by Tom Tyler (1990; see also Tyler and Huo, 2002; Tyler, 2003; Tyler, this volume), Bottoms proposes that legitimacy stems from the proper exercise of formal authority on the part of the probation officer who, he argues, is thus able to influence the offender's behaviour in and through the recognition that her authority is legitimate and, moreover, that its exercise is fair and reasonable. In common with Braithwaite, then, Bottoms theorises (psychological) legitimacy as a product of evaluation or 'cognitive construal' (Johnson *et al.*, 2006) on the part of the offender.

Our model, presented in diagrammatic form in Figure 6.1, brings together these various theoretical strands and represents an attempt to capture the reality of a diverse population of offenders subject to community sanctions of various kinds, recognising that probation staff are dealing every day with people who could be at a variety of points on this multi-dimensional spectrum. Our model is not, however, entirely descriptive: it also has a normative aspect. In our model, the 'ideal type', as far as what Bottoms (2001) terms 'short term requirement compliance' is concerned, is represented by the offender for whom compliance has both *formal* and *substantive* components; for whom compliance is underpinned principally by *normative mechanisms*; and whose motivational posture is one of *commitment*. To the extent that the life of a community sanction is intended to be productive, and to the extent that it seeks to engage the offender as an active agent in the process, it is this model towards which community sanctions should arguably be striving. It therefore follows that the supervisor ought to be engaged in

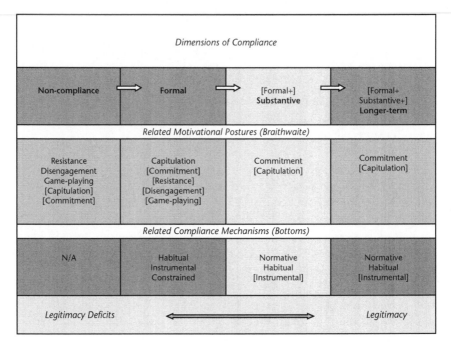

FIGURE 6.1 A dynamic model of compliance with community sanctions

encouraging individuals to move from those states characteristic of the left-hand side of the diagram, towards the (highlighted) 'ideal type': hence the direction of the arrows in the main part of the diagram.

We hypothesise that legitimacy, or the building of legitimacy, is a crucial part of that process, hence our reference to it in the bottom part of the diagram. However, the two-way arrow in that box is very important, and it serves to remind us that legitimacy is something that can be lost or damaged as well as something that can be channelled, developed or maintained. Precisely where and how it may flow into or ebb away in community sanctions is the subject of the next two parts of this chapter. However, we posit that the principal context in which the quest for legitimacy will be pursued, is a relational one. Specifically, we think that the relationship(s) the offender has with the individual(s) responsible for the administration or management of the community sanction is likely to be crucial. The relationship between the offender and the worker(s) with supervisory responsibility for him or her can thus be thought of as the key site or resource within which to develop legitimacy.

How legitimacy flows in

The notion that, in regulatory contexts, legitimacy has a potentially unstable or fluid quality means that it cannot be taken for granted by those in regulatory roles.

Individuals and groups evaluate authorities in terms of what they stand for and how they perform. As evaluations are made, revised, shared and accumulated over time, individuals and groups develop positions in relation to the authority.

(Braithwaite, 2003: 18)

In the community sanctions context, the relevant 'authority' is the probation service or other equivalent agency which assumes legal responsibility for the management or administration of the sentence of the court (Robinson and Dignan, 2004). However, this authority has traditionally been vested in an individual worker (probation officer, social worker, case worker, case manager) to whom the offender is expected to be accountable. In thinking, then, about the individual offender's propensity to evaluate the performance and values of the authority to which they are subject, this key or core relationship is heavily implicated. It is possible to draw a parallel here with research in the prisons context, which has demonstrated that prisoners' overall evaluations of fairness in the prison setting owes more to their perceptions of the fairness of treatment by individual uniformed prison staff, and to staff–prisoner relationships more generally, than to any objective features of the prison regime. This finding has led researchers to conclude that 'staff actually embody, in prisoners' eyes, the regime of the prison, and its fairness' (Bottoms and Rose, 1998, cited in Liebling, 2004: 264). Given that community sanctions lack the physical architecture of the prison, and perhaps cannot be said to be characterised by 'regimes' in the way that prisons are,[3] it seems even more likely that the relational features of community sanctions will be particularly salient when it comes to offenders' evaluations of legitimacy.

However, as important as the relational context of community sanctions may be – and in some jurisdictions it is increasingly likely that offenders will experience community sanctions via relationships with not just one but several workers (see further below) – it is important to recognise that offenders are unlikely to commence supervision as 'blank slates'. Their evaluations are likely to pre-date the commencement of the sanction and to pre-date any contact at all with probation staff of any sort, and there are good reasons to suspect that for a substantial proportion of offenders commencing community sanctions, those initial evaluations may not be wholly positive.

One reason why we think this may be the case – certainly in the context of community sanctions in England and Wales – is that in the majority of cases offenders are no longer required to give their explicit consent to being made subject to a community sanction. Thus some may not regard the sentence imposed by the court as legitimate in their case. For others, consent may be characterised by a degree of coercion or at least constraint – as when an offender sees a community sanction as the lesser evil compared with a possible prison sentence. There is thus little sense in which the community sanction resembles an ideal contract, freely entered into. Others may bring negative experiences of a previous community sanction, or of pre-sentence contact with the relevant authority (e.g., the process of being the subject of a pre-sentence report), or may be influenced by prejudicial reports about the community sanctions agency from their peers or even from the media. Importantly, none of these reasons necessarily means that the offender will not be compliant (as Braithwaite's research, discussed above, indicates); but compliance is unlikely to be normative, and is likely to be formal/superficial at best (see Figure 6.1).

Another reason why we might not expect a large proportion of offenders commencing community sanctions to exhibit positive motivational postures or substantive compliance relates to the problem of defining precisely what it is that offenders are being expected to comply with. We have argued elsewhere that the purposes of community sanctions tend to be multiple, somewhat opaque and fluid. Unsurprisingly, they are also sometimes contested (Robinson and McNeill, 2004). 'Official' purposes may be protective, punitive, rehabilitative, reparative, deterrent and/or surveillant. Part of the process of building or establishing legitimacy will therefore involve effective communication about the salience of such purposes in particular cases, about their relative priority, and about their operationalisation. Indeed, good practice would arguably involve the negotiation, or perhaps the *co-construction*, of purposes in the context of early interactions between the supervisors and the supervised (Barber, 1991).

The fluid nature of the purposes of community sanctions is of course compounded by the fact that, compared with some other sanctions, they are relatively invisible (or at best opaque) in cultural terms. Depictions of community sanctions in the news or entertainment media, for example, are relatively rare and usually misrepresentative. If, as Braithwaite argues, offenders are likely to make judgements about the legitimacy of community sanctions with regard to 'what they stand for', then a lack of clarity about purposes could potentially stand in the way of a positive evaluation. A related issue of course is that compliance itself is an elastic concept. Both the purposes of community sanctions and the definitions of compliance are subject to the interpretations and re-interpretations of both policy-makers and professionals.

For all of these reasons, offenders may wish to maximise or maintain the 'social distance' between themselves and the authority charged with implementing the sanction (McNeill, 2009, 2010). In order to reduce that gap, there is an onus on the worker or case manager to conduct him or herself, particularly in initial meetings with the offender, in a manner that will not damage and may begin to channel legitimacy into the community sanction in the eyes of the offender (see Trotter, 2006). It is their job to effectively communicate both the statutory purposes of the order and the specific requirements of the sanction.[4] One warm recollection of such an encounter was provided to one of us by a former probationer, interviewed as part of a small study gathering oral histories of Scottish probation in the 1960s:[5]

> FM: [H]ow did he explain how, what the whole thing was going to be about, if you can remember?
>
> Luke: I do remember. He actually explained that it was about helping me change my life and not to get into any sort of further trouble. And *his language*

was very, very acceptable and understandable because he didn't kind of jargonise words, he basically said – 'This is to keep you, helping you to stay out of any more trouble' and I said 'Oh'. He said 'It's as simple as that'. And *there was an immediate bond developed from that point, I knew that this wasn't somebody that was coming into my home and telling me how to live my life. It was somebody that was saying 'I'm here to support you and help you'*. (emphasis added)

(McNeill, 2009: 3–4)

Here, the probation officer was appealing to instrumental mechanisms (Bottoms, 2001): not so much what the probationer had to lose if he did not comply, but rather what he might gain if he did. In a much more recent study of compliance with probation in a Welsh probation area, Ugwudike (2010) found that most offenders related their compliance to such incentive-based instrumental mechanisms.

It has of course been argued – most vociferously by Tyler – that instrumental mechanisms are not the ideal basis for *durable* compliance, since they are only effective for as long as incentives are in place and demonstrable. Instrumental mechanisms are thus unlikely to underpin *substantive* compliance, as Figure 6.1 illustrates. Nonetheless, appeals to instrumental mechanisms could have potential longer-term benefits in the community sanctions context. First, it is likely that appealing to self-interest may be an effective initial step or building block towards establishing the sort of psychological legitimacy to which Braithwaite refers, and thus to establishing formal compliance on the part of the offender.

We also think that there could be useful subsequent 'interaction effects' (Bottoms, 2001) between instrumental and normative mechanisms, which could ultimately render substantive compliance more likely. Hypothetically, where the offender is persuaded that the community sanction offers some concrete benefit and the supervisor demonstrates a commitment to realising that benefit (e.g., by arranging accommodation, or making an appropriate referral), it is possible that the offender may come to develop an *attachment* to the supervisor which then forms the basis of, or acts as a bridge towards, normative compliance. A possible 'bridging' mechanism here could be the development of trust and respect in the key supervisory relationship. In this example, the offender's positive evaluation of the worker functions to reduce the social distance between regulator and regulatee, thereby increasing the offender's openness to (positive) influence by the worker. Again the Scottish probation history study provides a clear example of this:

Mary: And it was really good, you know, I was able to tell her about my home life, you know, and how miserable that I felt and she asked me what I wanted to do with my life and, you know, we just hit it off, we just hit it off. And on the occasions, you know, she'd say occasionally to come to Osborne Street and I would go to Osborne Street and she'd take me to tea in town, it was called Miss Cranstoun's. Now, you must remember here I was, a 17 year old, terrible background, you know, I never had any money and she would take me into this beautiful tearoom, you know, where all these well dressed people were sitting and with the cake stand the waiter coming and you know, I'd be sitting – I was absolutely overawed – overawed with it! And I thought '*Gosh, she's brought me here!', you know, she's brought me here*. So then –

FM: Just a bit – what did that convey to you, that she'd brought you there? What did it mean to you?

Mary: *I think it said that she liked me and, you know, and she listened to what I was saying and also sitting there and looking round as well and I thought 'I could be here too, I could do this as well', you know – 'This is what I want to do, this is what I want to do.'* (emphasis added)

(McNeill, 2009: 4)

More generally, this hypothesis finds some support in a small but growing body of research which has sought to identify what offenders value and find helpful about statutory supervision. Put another way, it is possible to 're-read' a number of studies in the context of the present discussion and a theoretical framework with legitimacy at its core. There is, for example, a small body of research on offenders' views of statutory supervision which has indicated that they value a consistent supervisory relationship to which they feel some commitment (see Robinson, 2005; Burnett and McNeill, 2005 for reviews). This sense of commitment is likely to be underpinned by an attachment to the supervisor, which in turn is an indication of legitimacy.

How legitimacy ebbs away

Summarising a body of research on policing and legitimacy, David Smith (2007) has observed that the police can, with relative ease, lower people's opinions of the police by treating them badly, but it is much more difficult to alter people's negative opinions by treating them well. In other words, it seems to be easier to spoil a positive motivational posture than to build one from a negative baseline. Whilst it is not clear whether this is true of offenders subject to community penalties, there is every reason to suspect that it probably is.

Just as legitimacy may be earned or accrued, therefore, so it may also be jeopardised or damaged, perhaps prompting the development of defiant postures towards authorities. But how might legitimacy ebb away? One answer to this question recalls the body of research by Tyler and others on the importance of procedural justice in offenders' encounters with legal authorities. In the community sanctions context, the aspect of policy and practice which is arguably most vulnerable to accusations of procedural injustice is enforcement; that is, action taken in response to non-compliance, which can result in a return to court for resentencing or (in the case of post-release licences) executive recall to prison. In England and Wales in particular, the 'toughening' of enforcement policy and practice is one of the most significant developments in the recent history of community sanctions, and is intimately tied up with the punitive credentials accorded to such sanctions following the Criminal Justice Act 1991. The toughening of enforcement has also been associated with the diminution of workers' discretion to make decisions concerning when offenders' behaviour constitutes compliance or non-compliance and about the appropriateness of deterrent sanctions in individual cases. Thus, workers have themselves been increasingly constrained by managerial oversight of their own 'compliance' with centrally determined definitions of 'acceptable' behaviour and appropriate responses to lapses on the part of offenders on their caseload. In this context, the likelihood that enforcement action may be perceived by those on the receiving end as inflexible and/or impersonal is almost certainly heightened.

As we have argued elsewhere, where enforcement policies (such as those in England and Wales) privilege formal compliance over substantive engagement, they pose significant threats to the legitimacy of community sanctions and to positive supervisory relationships (Robinson and McNeill, 2008). Where offenders have begun to buy into the 'spirit' of an order or sanction but find themselves nonetheless penalised for failing to abide by the letter of the law, it is easy to see how a positive motivational posture – and a positive working relationship – could begin to go sour. This is all the more likely when centrally imposed policies serve to raise the bar of compliance – as, for example, when in 2000 revised National Standards in England and Wales made breach (i.e., a return to court for resentencing) an expectation after a maximum of two, rather than three, 'failures to comply'.

An increasingly robust approach to the enforcement of post-custodial licences has also attracted the attention of researchers (e.g., Padfield and Maruna, 2006), and a recent study of offenders' perceptions of the prison recall system is illuminating in the context of the present discussion. Digard (2010) interviewed twenty sex offenders who had been recalled to prison, all of whom questioned the fairness of the recall process (as well as, incidentally, the legitimacy of the extended sentences to which they were subject).[6] Digard reports that the majority of offenders discussed their experiences of recall with 'vehemence', whilst a minority had 'sunk into a depressed apathy'. Several of Digard's sample had been recalled for technical violations rather than reoffending and considered the consequences in terms of recall to be out of proportion to the seriousness or 'riskiness' of their actions. Recalls were experienced as entirely punitive. Half of the sample further felt it was unfair that they were being recalled on the authority of their offender manager, rather than of a court. Sixteen offenders said they were upset because there was no formal investigation of the circumstances of their recall until after re-imprisonment: they were thus denied a 'voice' until much later down the line when an oral hearing could (eventually) be arranged. There were also criticisms of the vague/subjective nature of certain licence conditions, which were thought to make compliance difficult and breach therefore hard to avoid.

Worryingly, eight of Digard's sample of twenty said that they would be disinclined to comply with state sanctions in the future as a result of the procedural injustices they had experienced. As one offender put it: 'I'm going to be less cooperative with [the Probation Service], because if they're going to go out and help stitch people up, why should I cooperate with them?' Four others said that they would actively resist any attempt on the part of probation staff to forge a constructive working relationship with them. There are indications, then, that perceptions of procedural injustice could damage future compliance, or at least convert formerly substantive compliers into formal compliers, as Digard notes.

The force and durability of the kind of resentment Digard describes, and its consequences in terms of disengagement, have also been regular themes in the oral histories study to which we have already referred. Even forty years on, some of these ex-probationers recounted with great indignation their sense of betrayal and injustice about enforcement action. Matthew, for example, described poignantly his sense of betrayal when a young probation officer (to whom he related well as a sort of elder brother figure trying to steer him right) agreed with a magistrate that he needed the short, sharp shock of a custodial remand. His sense of abandonment was powerful enough to disengage him not just from this relationship but also from almost all future interactions with social workers.

In another interview, Peter expressed his rage at a probation officer who, twelve months into a two year order, had him 'jailed' for three months for not attending AA meetings, despite the fact that he was sober, was working and had not committed any new offences. He recollected his experience of being arrested and sentenced for the breach as follows:

> I said 'I've no done fuck all!' He [one of two police officers] said 'I don't know but we've to come for you' he said 'you go in front of the sheriff at 2 o'clock today'. . . . So I went in front of him, oh, and I said 'Look –' and I said – 'He [the probation officer] doesn't agree with some people and I'm one of them', I said 'I've no done any harm, I've not – I'll need to have a chance of [keeping my] job'. He said 'You can get a job in three months', and three months he gave me. That really fucking burst me – do you know what I mean? . . . Because *it was something for nothing, that was as far as I was concerned, you know.* I was really upset about it, I really was flaming after it. (emphasis added)
>
> (McNeill, 2009: 6)

A key theme in these and other accounts concerns the difficulty that probationers had in understanding why someone who was supposed to be trying to help them (i.e., to whom they imputed a rehabilitative purpose) could treat them this way (i.e., in a manner perceived to be officious and unduly punitive). To their minds, the enforcement action did not make sense to them in terms of the psychological contracts that the probation officers had developed with them. For Matthew, this soured not just his subsequent interactions with probation officers and social workers, but also his subsequent view of the entire social work profession:

> Now I am still very bitter towards them . . . That prevents me from encouraging anybody to get involved with them . . . Because I always

thought people like that could help me. And I feel as if they let me down.

(McNeill, 2009: 150)

Turning to more contemporary expressions of these difficulties, it is clear that policies which seek to bolster the *external* legitimacy of legal authorities can backfire at the level of *internal* legitimacy with the individual offender (and indeed, potentially, with workers) (see Bottoms, 2003). Whereas much of our argument here has been necessarily about the internal dynamics of compliance and legitimacy *within* the supervision process and between the actors directly involved, these actors of course operate in a broader social and political context; regulators have external 'audiences' and are necessarily concerned with their credibility, reputation and status. Often these concerns bear down upon their individual interactions with regulatees (see Halliday *et al.*, 2009; McNeill *et al.*, 2009). Conceivably, 'tough' enforcement policies, aimed at building credibility with the courts and the wider public, particularly when impersonally executed, could render community sanctions and the relationships through which they are enacted vulnerable to 'legitimacy deficits' (Beetham, 1991) in offenders' eyes. Indeed, scholars and researchers in the field of community sanctions have been critical of this policy turn in favour of tougher enforcement, arguing that it is not grounded in an understanding or appreciation of the dynamics of compliance (e.g., Ellis, 2000; Hedderman and Hough, 2004; Raynor, 2004; Robinson and McNeill, 2008). A considerable body of socio-legal research warns against the indiscriminate use of sanctions which can expose regulatory bodies to accusations of unreasonableness and unfairness and thus jeopardise the future compliance of regulatees (e.g., Bardach and Kagan, 1982; Ayres and Braithwaite, 1992; Sherman, 1993; Murphy, 2005).

Another contemporary example of the sort of difficulty for internal (offender) legitimacy created by the pressures of external (judicial or public) legitimacy is the recent introduction in England and Wales of high-visibility jackets for offenders carrying out unpaid work in the community. A recent Cabinet Review recommended that unpaid work should be more visible and demanding in the interest of improving public confidence in community sanctions (Casey, 2008). As a result, the wearing of high-visibility jackets by adult offenders performing unpaid work became a compulsory requirement in England and Wales in December 2008. For offenders formerly persuaded of the rehabilitative and reparative benefits of unpaid work, and for workers keen to promote these more positive purposes to those individuals under their supervision, it is easy to see how policy developments that alter the nature of the work – and perhaps lead to it being seen by offenders as degrading or even just pointless – may prompt confusion, resistance and perhaps conflict (see McCulloch, 2010).

Another potential threat to legitimacy in the community sanctions context recalls our preceding discussion of the potential importance of the offender/worker relationship. As we have already discussed, this relationship arguably constitutes the prime site within which legitimacy is negotiated. However, where there is discontinuity in supervision, problems may arise. If we assume that legitimacy is endowed by the offender on the basis of his or her experience of interactions with a specific individual supervisor, and that the endowment of legitimacy probably reflects the establishment of mutual respect and trust between the principal parties, then we cannot assume that a transfer of supervisory responsibility will be accompanied by an unproblematic transfer of psychological legitimacy. Even where normative compliance has previously been achieved, it will not necessarily continue in the context of the new supervisory arrangement. Similar problems may also arise in the context of supervisory arrangements that are experienced as fragmented or confusing because the different actors involved in different aspects of the administration of a sanction (e.g., offender managers, offender supervisors, drugs workers, employment advisers, housing support workers, probation hostel staff) lack a consistent approach. The journey towards normative compliance may be rendered still more complex in each of these sorts of situations. If the loss of one supervisor involves any sense of abandonment or betrayal, or inconsistency across the involved actors promotes a sense of confusion or capriciousness, then further obstacles to compliance have been created.

In various ways, these problems – around the negotiable meanings of community sanctions, of the disputed priorities within them, of relational disruptions and resentments, and of mixed messages about what matters and what is really being asked of the offender – invoke the notion of 'legitimacy deficits' in Beetham's (1991) model: referring to a withdrawal of implicit consent to authority. It is not difficult to see how these sorts of problems could account for such withdrawal.

Legitimacy and longer-term compliance

So far we have presented a number of hypotheses about compliance and legitimacy in the community sanctions context, our central argument being that where such sanctions seek to encourage substantive compliance and an engagement with their more positive and ambitious purposes, attention to legitimacy is important. We have, in other words, emphasised the importance of legitimacy – from the offender's perspective – to the 'quality' of compliance; that is, to cooperation and engagement with the short- and longer-term purposes of the sanction.

This link between legitimacy and the quality of compliance is one which is emphasised in Beetham's work. Beetham (1991: 28–34) discusses the effect a lack of legitimacy has on the degree of cooperation or quality of performance of the subordinate, and therefore on the ability of the powerful to achieve goals over and above simply maintaining their position. He gives the example of a classroom teacher whose pupils do not share a belief in the value of education, on which the justification for the teacher's power is based, or who do not have respect for the individual teacher. The teacher in this scenario will have to expend most of her energy on maintaining order rather than on teaching her class: to that extent the purposes for which power is held (i.e., education) will not be achieved, and this may feed into a further erosion of legitimacy. One might equally think about the priority that a prison officer might have to accord to just maintaining good order in custody.

In the community sanctions context, the corollary is that the supervisor struggling with a legitimacy deficit may also be tempted to revert to a focus on securing formal compliance. For some community sanctions, this may be less of a problem than for others but it is likely to be highly problematic where there are goals over and above the deprivation of liberty or the punishment of offenders: goals such as changing attitudes or behaviour. In connection with these more rehabilitative and reintegrative aspirations, there is obvious salience in Beetham's argument that power is more effective when it is psychologically and morally legitimate. Where the quality of performance is important (as in unpaid work, or group programmes), legitimacy is more important than when quality matters less.

But what about longer-term compliance (Bottoms, 2001)? One might expect that law-abiding behaviour is more likely to be maintained in the longer term following the completion of a community sanction that was experienced as legitimate. Indeed, some of the desistance literature (which is concerned with how and why people stop offending) – and more specifically much of the literature on assisted desistance (which is concerned with which kinds of interventions support the process) – suggests that calling forth change in an offender requires much more than legal legitimacy. Indeed, the literature suggests that the quality of the relationships between the supervisor and the supervised is critical in supporting desistance. Some studies have gone so far as to suggest that where these relationships are strong and are characterised by mutual respect and trust, probation officers significantly underestimate the degree of influence that they may be able to exert (Rex, 1999). Elsewhere, one of us has suggested that evidence about desistance from crime might suggest a range of 'practice virtues' that might be required to prompt or support desistance (McNeill, 2006). Speculative though this is, similar themes are also emerging in the literature on therapeutic jurisprudence and specifically drug courts; McIvor (2009) has recently suggested that some of the findings in recent drug court evaluations can be interpreted through the lens of Tyler's (1990) work on procedural justice, specifically in its focus on the salience of ethicality, efforts to be fair and representation. Wexler (2001) has gone further still in suggesting that the quality of offender–judge interactions facilitated by drug courts may play a role in the generation and/or certification of desistance narratives.

However, it seems important here to add the caveat that an offender can desist from crime without formally or substantively complying with sanctions at all. Neither formal nor substantive compliance is a necessary prerequisite of desistance or longer-term compliance. Indeed, in some cases, offenders' determination to desist on their own terms might reflect the sometimes powerful motivation of proving the formal authorities wrong. Leaving aside this possibility of 'desistance as spite', there is ample evidence that for many offenders it is more a case of 'desistance in spite' of the best efforts of the criminal justice system. Again it is interesting to note in this context that some desistance scholars have suggested that the unintended but nonetheless unjust consequences of system involvement can effectively encourage recidivism (Halsey, 2006; McAra and McVie, 2007, 2010). Ultimately, this line of argument takes us beyond the realms of procedural justice and into the territory of social (in)justice, as well as requiring us to attend more carefully to the relationships between the two. Where there are failures on *both* sides of the social contract, the problems of the legitimacy of state punishment run much deeper than we have been able to excavate in our discussion here merely of the proper administration of sanctions (cf. Duff, 2003).

Conclusions: 'moral performance' in community sanctions

In a recent book which has attempted to conceptualise and evaluate prisons using a framework informed by prisoners' and prison staff members' views about the aspects of prison life which they value, Alison Liebling introduces the notion of 'moral performance' (Liebling, 2004). The concept of moral performance brings together a number of dimensions of prison life, among them justice, fairness, safety, order, humanity, trust, and opportunities for personal development. Liebling presents this notion of moral performance as an alternative and more meaningful measure of 'what matters' in the prison context, and of the quality of prison life, than those measures which have arisen from the managerialist 'performance agenda' of the 1980s and 1990s.

Although the specific measures of 'moral performance' developed by Liebling do not translate unproblematically to the community sanctions context, we nonetheless think that the concept of moral performance is a potentially very useful one, and it is one which chimes with the limited research which has, to date, been conducted on offenders' views of statutory supervision. Like good sociologies of prison life (most recently Crewe, 2009), studies of offenders' experiences of community sanctions reveal that structures and systems are only part of the story of how justice or punishment works out in practice. The narratives of supervision collected for the oral history study discussed above, for example, ultimately reveal the extent to which the meanings and natures of such sanctions are negotiated between the people involved (McNeill, 2009).

As we noted at the outset, if community sanctions have a definable form or architecture, it is much less obvious than that of the prison. It is not just that legitimacy can ebb and flow for all of the reasons discussed above; the shape of the sanction itself is malleable. It is true that there are places and times where those on such sanctions must be and, perhaps more importantly, where they are expected to do *something* (whether unpaid work or participation in programmes or individual supervision) or even to be a particular kind of *someone* (a willing worker paying back, a remorseful offender making good, a recovering drug user staying clean). There may be no locks and keys, but there are borders and checkpoints to negotiate here, each of which opens up the possibility of interactions perceived as legitimate and illegitimate (Rose, 2000). The sentencing process is the first of these, in which the would-be subject of such a sanction must yield to (or better still facilitate) their construction as a suitable subject for a community sanction (perhaps even a suitable subject for leniency) – and hence for passage into the community sanction and, by implication, away from the prison door (McNeill *et al.*, 2009).

Once in the process of the community sanction, there are important and subtle forms and rituals to be observed in the numerous disciplinary passages through which the subject must pass in the process of supervision. The supervisor is the 'key-holder'; each point of passage involves them in disciplinary judgements about the offender's successful negotiation of assessment, intervention and review processes.

Probation law or 'rules', such as prison law or 'rules', may represent other forms of 'code' (Lessig, 1999) or architecture (Jones, 2006) that lend a certain form to the experience of community sanctions. In any jurisdiction, the law may determine the formal parameters of obligations (and perhaps entitlements) that community sanctions create. But beyond this legal scaffold, community sanctions have remarkable malleability and thus vulnerability in their character; whereas the prison physically frames the lived experience of imprisonment, the community sanction has no such obvious 'frame', except in the interactions between its executor (the probation officer) and its subject (the probationer). Thus it is in these interactions that such sanctions are continually invented and reinvented. The physical locus of such interpersonal engagement is important, but it is not in and of itself definitive of the experience of the sanctions that these actors co-construct (however equally or unequally).

But equally importantly, the probation officer or social worker is influenced in their crucial contribution to the construction of the sanction by the political, social, cultural and professional worlds that they inhabit. As we have noted throughout, where these conditions generate pressures to pursue external legitimacy or credibility (e.g., McNeill *et al.*, 2009), they may impact adversely on the internal quest for those same qualities (cf. Ugwudike, 2010). A key message of our analysis is that, particularly where sanctions aim to elicit change, the skills of the practitioner in bridging the social distance between the 'punished' and the 'punishers' are likely to be critical to the process. However, the conditions under which the 'punishers' labour can create countervailing forces, driving the parties apart. Especially in this context, the quality and the authenticity of the practitioner's moral performance seem likely to lie at the heart of the matter, since these moral qualities will profoundly affect the meaning, nature and experience of the sanction. Within this context, the legitimacy of the practitioner – on which his or her influence depends – is hard-won, easily lost, and almost impossible to recover. Put another way, it is as difficult to enable legitimacy to flow into a community sanction as it is easy to let it ebb away.

References

Ayres, I. and Braithwaite, J. (1992) *Responsive Regulation: Transcending the Deregulation Debate.* Oxford: Oxford University Press.

Barber, J. (1991) *Beyond Casework.* London: Macmillan.

Bardach, E. and Kagan, R.A. (1982) *Going by the Book: the Problem of Regulatory Unreasonableness.* Philadelphia: Temple University Press.

Barry, M. (2000) 'The mentor/monitor debate in criminal justice: "what works" for offenders', *British Journal of Social Work*, 30: 575–95.

Bauman, Z. (2000a) *Liquid Modernity*. Cambridge: Polity Press.

—— (2000b) 'Social issues of law and order', *British Journal of Criminology*, 40: 205–21.

Beetham, D. (1991) *The Legitimation of Power*. London: Macmillan.

Bogardus, E.S. (1928) *Immigration and Race Attitudes*. Boston: D.C. Heath and Company.

Bottoms, A. (2001) 'Compliance with community penalties', in A. Bottoms, L. Gelsthorpe and S. Rex (eds) *Community Penalties: Change and Challenges*. Cullompton: Willan.

—— (2003) 'Theoretical reflections on the evaluation of a penal policy initiative', in L. Zedner and A. Ashworth (eds) *The Criminological Foundations of Penal Policy*. Oxford: Oxford University Press.

Braithwaite, V. (2003) 'Dancing with tax authorities: motivational postures and non-compliant actions', in V. Braithwaite (ed.) *Taxing Democracy: Understanding Tax Avoidance and Evasion*. Aldershot: Ashgate.

Burnett, R. and McNeill, F. (2005) 'The place of the officer-offender relationship in assisting offenders to desist from crime' *Probation Journal*, 52(3): 221–42.

Casey, L. (2008) *Engaging Communities in Fighting Crime*. London: Cabinet Office.

Crewe, B. (2009) *The Prisoner Society: Power, Adaptation and Social Life in an English Prison*. Oxford: Clarendon.

Digard, L. (2010) 'When legitimacy is denied: Sex offenders' perceptions and experiences of prison recall', *Probation Journal*, 57(1): 1–19.

Duff, A. (2003) 'Probation, punishment and restorative justice: Should altruism be engaged in punishment?', *The Howard Journal*, 42(1): 181–97.

Durnescu, I. (2007) 'Community sanctions and measures in Europe: Interim results from a recent survey'. Paper presented at the first annual meeting of the European Society of Criminology Working Group on Community Sanctions, Barcelona, 18th April.

Ellis, T. (2000) 'Enforcement policy and practice: Evidence-based or rhetoric-based?', *Criminal Justice Matters*, 39: 6–7.

Feeley, M. and Simon, J. (1992) 'The new penology: notes on the emerging strategy of corrections and its implications', *Criminology*, 30: 449–74.

—— (1994) 'Actuarial justice: the emerging new criminal law', in D. Nelken (ed.) *The Futures of Criminology*. London: Sage.

Glaze, L. and Bonczar, T. (2009) *Probation and Parole in the United States, 2007 Statistical Tables*, August 2009, NCJ 224707, US Department of Justice, Office of Justice Programs. Available at: http://www.ojp.usdoj.gov/bjs/pub/pdf/ppus07st.pdf (accessed 10 December 2009).

Halliday, J. (2001) *Making Punishments Work: Report of a Review of the Sentencing Framework for England and Wales*. London: Home Office Communication Directorate.

Halliday, S., Burns, N., Hutton, N., McNeill, F. and Tata, C. (2009) 'Street-level bureaucracy, interprofessional relations and coping mechanisms: A study of criminal justice social workers in the sentencing process' *Law and Policy*, 31(4): 405–28.

Hallsworth, S. (2002) 'The case for a postmodern penality', *Theoretical Criminology*, 6(2): 145–63.

Halsey, M. (2006) 'Negotiating conditional release: Juvenile narratives of repeat incarceration', *Punishment and Society*, 8: 147–81.

Hedderman, C. and Hough, M. (2004) 'Getting tough or being effective: What matters?', in G. Mair (ed.) *What Matters in Probation*. Cullompton: Willan.

Johnson, C., Dowd, T. and Ridgeway, C. (2006) 'Legitimacy as a social process', *Annual Review of Sociology*, 32: 53–78.

Jones, R. (2006) '"Architecture", criminal justice, and control', in S. Armstrong and L. McAra (eds) *Perspectives on Punishment: The Contours of Control*. Oxford: Oxford University Press, pp. 175–96.

Lessig, N. (1999) *Code and Other Laws of Cyberspace*. New York: Basic Books.

Liebling, A. (2004) *Prisons and their Moral Performance*. Oxford: Clarendon Press.

Mair, G. and Canton, R. (2007) 'Sentencing, community penalties and the role of the Probation Service', in L. Gelsthorpe and R. Morgan (eds) *Handbook of Probation*. Devon: Willan.

McAra, L. and McVie, S. (2007) 'Youth justice? The impact of agency contact on desistance from offending', *European Journal of Criminology*, 4(3): 315–45.

—— (2010) 'Youth crime and justice: Key messages from the Edinburgh Study of Youth Transitions and Crime', *Criminology and Criminal Justice*, 10(2): 179–210.

McBarnet, D. (2003) 'When compliance is not the solution but the problem: from changes in law to changes in attitude', in V. Braithwaite (ed.) *Taxing Democracy: Understanding Tax Avoidance and Evasion*. Aldershot: Ashgate.

McCulloch, T. (2010) 'Exploring community service, understanding compliance', in F. McNeill, P. Raynor and C. Trotter (eds) *Offender Supervision: New Directions in Theory, Research and Practice*. Cullompton: Willan, pp. 384–406.

McIvor, G. (2009) 'Therapeutic jurisprudence and procedural justice in Scottish drug courts', *Criminology and Criminal Justice*, 9(1): 29–49.

McNeill, F. (2006) 'A desistance paradigm for offender management', *Criminology and Criminal Justice*, 6(1): 39–62.

—— (2009) '*Helping, holding, hurting: Recalling and reforming punishment*', the 6th annual Apex Lecture, at the Signet Library, Parliament Square, Edinburgh, 8 September.

—— (2010) 'Supervision in historical context: learning the lessons of (oral) history' in F. McNeill, P. Raynor and C. Trotter (eds) *Offender Supervision: New Directions in Theory, Research and Practice*. Cullompton: Willan.

McNeill, F., Burns, N., Halliday, S., Hutton, N. and Tata, C. (2009) 'Risk, responsibility and reconfiguration: Penal adaptation and misadaptation', *Punishment and Society*, 11(4): 419–42.

Ministry of Justice (2008) *Prison Policy Update*. London: Ministry of Justice.

—— (2009) *Story of the Prison Population 1995–2009 England and Wales*. Ministry of Justice Statistics Bulletin. London: Ministry of Justice.

—— (2010) 'Community compacts – for use in the community', *Probation Instruction 04/2010*. London: Ministry of Justice.

Murphy, K. (2005) 'Regulating more effectively: The relationship between procedural justice, legitimacy and tax non-compliance', *Journal of Law and Society*, 32(4): 562–89.

Padfield, N. and Maruna, S. (2006) 'The revolving door at the prison gate', *Criminology and Criminal Justice*, 6(3): 329–52.

Parker, C. (2002) *The Open Corporation*. Cambridge: Cambridge University Press.

Pratt, J. (2000) 'Emotive and ostentatious punishment: its decline and resurgence in modern society', *Punishment and Society*, 4: 417–40,

Raynor, P. (2004) 'Rehabilitative and reintegrative approaches', in A. Bottoms, S. Rex and G. Robinson (eds) *Alternatives to Prison: Options for an Insecure Society*. Cullompton: Willan, pp. 195–223.

Rex, S. (1999) 'Desistance from offending: experiences of probation', *Howard Journal of Criminal Justice*, 38(4): 366–83.

Robinson, G. (2005) 'What works in offender management?', *Howard Journal of Criminal Justice*, 44(3): 307–18.

—— (2008) 'Late-modern rehabilitation: The evolution of a penal strategy', *Punishment and Society*, 10(4): 429–45.

Robinson, G. and Dignan, J. (2004) 'Sentence management', in A. Bottoms, S. Rex and G. Robinson (eds) *Alternatives to Prison: Options for an insecure society*. Cullompton: Willan.

Robinson, G. and McNeill, F. (2004) 'Purposes matter: Examining the "ends" of probation practice', in G. Mair (ed.) *What Matters in Probation*. Cullompton: Willan, pp. 277–304.

—— (2008) 'Exploring the dynamics of compliance with community penalties', *Theoretical Criminology*, 12(4): 431–49.

Rose, N. (2000) 'Government and control', *British Journal of Criminology,* 40(2): 321–39.

Scottish Government (2010) *Statistical Bulletin: Criminal Proceedings In Scottish Courts, 2008/09*. Available at: http://www.scotland.gov.uk/Publications/2010/03/03114034/0 (accessed 27 April 2010).

Scottish Prisons Commission (2008) *Scotland's Choice*. Edinburgh: Scottish Prisons Commission.

Sherman, L.W. (1993) 'Defiance, deterrence and irrelevance: A theory of the criminal sanction', *Journal of Research in Crime and Delinquency*, 30(4): 445–73.

Smith, D.J. (2007) 'The foundations of legitimacy', in T. Tyler (ed.) *Legitimacy and Criminal Justice: International Perspectives*. New York: Russell Sage Foundation, pp. 30–58.

Sparks, R. and McNeill, F. (2009) 'Incarceration, Social Control and Human Rights', a research paper prepared as part of the International Council on Human Rights Policy's Project on Social Control and Human Rights. Published online by the ICHRP at: www.ichrp.org/files/papers/175/punishment_and_incarceration_sparks_and_mcneill.pdf.

Trotter, C. (2006) *Working with Involuntary Client,* 2nd edn. London: Sage.

Tyler, T.R. (1990) *Why People Obey the Law*. Princeton: Princeton University Press.

Tyler, T.R. (2003) 'Procedural justice, legitimacy and the effective rule of law', *Crime and Justice*, 30: 283–357.

Tyler, T.R. and Huo, Y.J. (2002) *Trust in the Law: Encouraging public cooperation with the police and courts*. New York: Russell Sage.

Ugwudike, P. (2010) 'Compliance with community penalties, the importance of interactional dynamics', in F. McNeill, P. Raynor and C. Trotter (eds) *Offender Supervision: New Directions in Theory, Research and Practice*. Cullompton: Willan.

Van Kalmthout, A M. and Durnescu, I. (eds) (2008) *Probation in Europe*. Nijmegen, The Netherlands: Wolf Legal Publishers/CEP.

Wexler, D.B (2001) 'Robes and rehabilitation: How judges can help offenders "make good"', *Court Review*, Spring, 18–23.

Wheatley, P. (2010) 'Speech to the Annual Conference of the National Offender Management Service of England and Wales', Palace Hotel, Manchester, 19 March.

Notes

1 Community sanctions and measures (CSM) imposed in lieu of prosecution or as sentences in their own right are sometimes referred to as 'front-door' CSM, those imposed as early release measures are referred to as 'back-door' CSM. The Council of Europe defines CSM thus: 'sanctions and measures which maintain the offender in the community and involve some restriction of his/her liberty through the imposition of conditions and/or obligations, and which are implemented by bodies designated in law for that purpose'. The term 'designates any sanction imposed by a court or a judge, and any measure taken before or instead of a decision on a sanction as well as ways of enforcing a sentence of imprisonment outside a prison establishment' (Rec. (92)16 on the European Rules on Community Sanctions and Measures).

2   Braithwaite (2003: 18) draws on the social-psychological work of Bogardus (1928), and specifically his notion of 'social distance'. Bogardus initially used this term to refer to the degree to which individuals or groups had positive feelings for, and ascribed status to, other ethnic groups. Taking this into the regulatory context, Braithwaite refers to social distance as a measure of liking and the ascription of status to the regulatory authority: the degree of social distance is thus determined by the subjective judgement of the regulatee, who decides how much he wants to be associated or aligned with the regulator and how much (or how little) he wants to be out of contact with the regulator.

3   Bottoms has, however, put forward the interesting suggestion that unpaid work could be said to operate according to a 'regime' (personal communication, 2009).

4   It is interesting to note the recent introduction of 'Community Compacts' which constitute a voluntary agreement between the offender and the supervising officer in the context of community sanctions in England and Wales (Ministry of Justice, 2010; see also Ministry of Justice, 2008).

5   'Oral Histories of Scottish Probation' was funded by the British Academy (award number SG:48403).

6   As Digard notes, offenders serving extended sentences are among those who stand to be hardest hit by prison recall because recall means serving the entirety of their sentence, including the 'extension period' of up to eight years.

7

COMPLIANCE WITH ELECTRONICALLY MONITORED CURFEW ORDERS

Some empirical findings

Anthea Hucklesby

Introduction

Since its introduction in the mid-1990s, electronic monitoring (EM) has become an important component in the criminal justice process in England and Wales. It is used as a condition of bail, as a sentence and for early release. In 2010, 52,000 offenders were subject to EM requirements on community orders (Ministry of Justice, 2011). Stand-alone EM use is common in England and Wales and differentiates it from many other jurisdictions which are much more likely to integrate the use of EM with probation supervision. Just under three-quarters of sentences using EM in England and Wales are single-condition community orders (Rogers, 2011). In 2010, a further 13,000 offenders were released from prison on Home Detention Curfews and 26,000 defendants were released on bail with an EM curfew condition (Ministry of Justice, 2011). EMs growth in England and Wales has been rapid rising from 2,500 in 2000 and it has expanded elsewhere in terms of both the number of countries using it and the number of offenders subject to it. The growing significance of EM at several stages of the criminal justice process means that explanations of compliance must be able to take account of it. Not considering EM and concentrating on other measures and community sentences is likely to mean that compliance theories are incomplete. Furthermore, studying compliance in relation to EM may elucidate how compliance is achieved, or could be enhanced, for other types of community sentence.

This chapter focuses on the use of EM as a sentence either as a stand-alone sentence or as a requirement of a community order. Despite this, many of the issues which are discussed are relevant to its other uses as a condition of bail or as a requirement for early release from prison. EM is the means by which curfew conditions or requirements are enforced. In relation to sentencing, EM curfew orders were introduced in the late 1990s and became one of the twelve conditions which may be attached to community orders under the Criminal Justice Act 2003. Curfew orders can be imposed for up to twelve hours a day for a maximum of six months either as a stand-alone sentence or in conjunction with other conditions. Curfews orders incorporation into the community order demonstrates most visibly that it is one of the suite of community sentences. It is not another form of imprisonment as some politicians have likened it to (Hucklesby, 2008; Nellis, 2004). The principle difference between prison and EM is that EM does not incapacitate offenders in the same way as prison does. Offenders can break their curfews as well as offend, even when formally complying, by either offending at home or changing their modus operandi to accommodate curfew times. Only in one respect is EM akin to a term of imprisonment. Recently, curfews imposed as a condition of bail count towards time served if defendants are subsequently convicted and given a custodial sentence. Consequently, the time spent subject to EM is taken off any prison sentence subsequently imposed with one day's curfew equating to half a day's imprisonment. This measure is a clear attempt to signal that EM is an alternative to custodial remands and not bail and to limit the extent of 'net-widening'. It may also have an impact on levels of compliance because defendants might view serving time on EM as preferable to serving time in prison once convicted.

Electronic monitoring in the UK is operated by the private sector. This currently demarcates it from other conditions of community orders which are overseen by the statutory sector although this may change with proposals for a wider range of providers to be involved in the provision of criminal justice services (Ministry of Justice, 2010a). The two private companies involved (G4S and Serco) have been running EM in England and Wales since it started in the 1990s (albeit under several different names). They provide the equipment and all the supporting services and are involved in investigating, and in some cases prosecuting, breaches. EM in England and Wales currently uses radio frequency technology and requires offenders to stay at a specified address. The technology does not track offenders away from their homes but alerts the companies if offenders leave their address. It is also unable to monitor what offenders are doing at the address during the curfew period.

This chapter explores what Bottoms (2001) terms 'short-term compliance', that is, whether offenders abide by the restrictions and/or obligations placed upon them by the sentence. It is not concerned with long-term compliance relating to whether offenders reoffend and abide by the law more generally. The latter form of compliance has been the primary focus of criminal justice policy and research most notably through the 'What Works' movement (Chapman and Hough, 1998; Harper and Chitty, 2005; McGuire, 1995). By contrast, short-term compliance has until recently largely been ignored in relation to criminal justice and remains under-researched and under theorised (for exceptions see Bottoms, 2001; Robinson and McNeill, 2008).

Spending time and resources in order to maximise offenders' compliance has a number of benefits. One of the most important of these is financial cost. Non-compliance has costs for the agency supervising offenders in terms of the resources required to instigate breach proceedings, for the police and for the courts who have to process the offenders and, potentially, for the prison service if the offender is imprisoned as a result of a breach. In terms of EM specifically, non-compliance reduces the income that private monitoring companies receive because they are only paid for the days that a person is actually monitored successfully so they have a vested interest in trying to increase levels of compliance. Non-compliance also reduces the legitimacy for the criminal justice system. It arguably demonstrates that offenders have little regard for the authority and legitimacy of the system. High levels of non-compliance, or highly publicised one-off cases of non-compliance, are likely to dent confidence in, and the legitimacy of, the system more generally. Non-compliance also has costs for offenders and potentially their families. It is likely to result in additional punishment not only in relation to the current sentence but it may also impact on any future encounters with the criminal justice system leading to offenders being less likely to be bailed and receive a non-custodial sentence. A final reason for focusing upon short-term compliance is that it is linked to desistance. Research evidence on the link between compliance and desistance is limited (see Hearnden and Millie, 2003 for an exception). However, the 'What Works' literature suggests that offenders who fail to complete their programmes have higher reconviction rates than those who complete programmes and those who do not participate in programmes (see, for example, Harper and Chitty, 2005). Such findings support a common-sense notion that offenders who comply with the requirements of the order are more likely to be the ones who will desist in the future. However, the link may not be causal and, certainly, compliance is not a sufficient or a necessary condition for desistance to take place.

There are no published data on EM compliance and very little on compliance with community orders generally. The Joint Inspectorate Report (CJJI, 2008) suggested that the non-compliance rate for stand-alone curfews was around a quarter and that a third of multiple requirements cases involving EM reached the point requiring breach action. This picture is similar to completion rates for community orders generally. Around two-thirds (64 per cent) of community orders are successfully completed or terminated as a result of good progress (Ministry of Justice, 2010b). Completion rates for orders of less than one year, which arguably are comparable with EM curfew orders, are slightly higher at 66 per cent. These figures appear to suggest that stand-alone curfew orders are less likely to be breached than EM as part of a multiple requirements sentence or community sentences without EM. However, differences between cases, offenders and which agency has responsibility for breach may account for the variations.

The remainder of this chapter explores compliance in the context of EM. Its first task is to draw out the similarities and differences between EM and other community sentences. Next it briefly reviews the theoretical frameworks relating to compliance proposed by Bottoms (2001) and Nellis (2006a). It then provides an overview of the research findings focusing specifically on the influences on compliance with areas which are particularly pertinent to EM or which differ in some respects from other community sentences. Before this, the research design and methodology of an empirical study are briefly described.

Research design and methodology

This chapter draws on the research findings of a study of compliance with electronically monitored curfew orders (see Hucklesby, 2008, 2009, 2011). The research was conducted in the North of England with offenders who were subject to stand-alone curfew orders as a single sentence or running concurrently with other community sentences. This chapter uses data gleaned from case files on 217 offenders which included demographic data, offenders' living arrangements, violation and breach data and records of communications between the monitoring company and the offenders. It also draws on interviews with seventy-eight offenders which took place at the end of their sentence when the equipment was decommissioned. Despite the fact that they had reached the end of their sentence, this did not mean that interviewees had complied fully with their orders. Because of the leeway built into breach procedures for EM (see NAO, 2006), all but two offenders of the 217 offenders and all offenders in the interview sample had not complied fully with the requirements of their curfews but may not have reached the point at which they were breached. For example, most non-compliance resulted from time violations when offenders were missing for short intervals during their curfew periods (Hucklesby, 2009). Short time violations do not result in immediate formal breach action but are accumulated until they reach a certain level when breach action is instigated (Hucklesby, 2009; CJJI, 2008). In the same way, tampering with, or minor damage to, monitoring equipment would not result in immediate breach action.

The research provides a snapshot of offenders' explanations for compliance and non-compliance. Interviews with offenders took place at the end of offenders' sentences and it may be that this influenced their views and perceptions about compliance. It is likely that offenders accounts of their behaviour whilst under curfew change over time and vary during their sentence and afterwards. Offenders also have an interest in minimising their non-compliant behaviour because of the possible repercussions but these would have been lessened because their sentences were ending when they were interviewed and breach action could no longer be taken.

Interviews were also undertaken with monitoring officers who are responsible for the day-to-day operation of EM. Twenty monitoring officers from two field branches were interviewed about their work. The interviews lasted between an hour and a half and three hours and usually took place before shifts began. Interviewees were asked about their employment backgrounds, their reasons for applying to be monitoring officers, the training they had received, their views on supervision and management, EM and offenders as well as how they went about their work, how they dealt with specific events and any problems or concerns they had relating to their work. Formal interviews were supplemented with observations of monitoring officers at work (see Hucklesby, 2011 for more details).

EM and community sentences

The legitimacy of community penalties as sentences of the court has been questioned perennially but particularly in the age of 'penal populism' with its calls for increasing levels of severity in all aspects of sentencing (Cavadino and Dignan, 2007; Pratt *et al.*, 2005). The criticisms of community sentences have focused primarily on four main concerns. First, that community sentences are 'too soft' and do not provide sufficient punishment. Second, that they provide only limited control over offenders so that offenders are able to reoffend if they so wish. Third, that compliance relies on trust rather than incapacitation. Finally, questions have been raised about whether offenders are breached when they should be and also about variations in breach practices. The representation of community sentences as too lenient relates to suggestions that they provide insufficient punishment. These assessments are usually made by comparing prison and community sentences – a practice which was explicitly acknowledged by using the terminology of 'alternatives to prison' to describe community sentences officially until the 1980s. In these circumstances, prison is always the yardstick by which the punitive credentials of any community sentence are measured thus elevating prison to the primary tier of punishment whilst relegating community sentences to the second tier (Mair, 2009). The basis of claims that community sentences are lenient is that they do not remove offenders from society and separate them from 'law-abiding' members of society. Instead, on the surface, offenders' lives appear to be largely unaffected by the sentence. The requirements on offenders vary depending on the type of sentence imposed but may be limited to reporting to the Probation Service once a week or less often for someone with a supervision requirement. Certainly, offenders have significant amounts of time when they are not under direct supervision and/or surveillance of the criminal justice process. This is viewed as providing an opportunity for them to do as they wish and perhaps offend. Community sentences rely heavily on trust-based compliance (Nellis, 2006a), which can be viewed with suspicion in light of the fact that offenders have already breached society's trust by offending in the first place. Offender managers' discretion inherent in decisions to breach offenders has also caused concern. As a result of criticisms of lax and variable enforcement practices, offender managers have often been portrayed as giving offenders the benefit of the doubt too often. This has resulted in the tightening up of enforcement practices which has reduced the amount of discretion available to them and aim to make decisions more consistent and transparent.

In many respects, EM is just another community sentence because it shares many of the characteristics of community sentences. EM is a home-based community sentence. Offenders are usually able to stay in their normal residence with significant others and undertake usual domestic and non-domestic activities within the confines of curfew hours. EM is also a trust-based sentence. Offenders have to choose to comply. They are able to remove their tag and leave the house although there are likely to be consequences for doing so. Partly for these two reasons, EM suffers from being viewed as a soft option – as not proper punishment. As Nellis (2003a, 2003b) notes, electronic monitoring has a public image problem with media reports nearly always being negative. Such concerns have been bolstered by a number of high-profile cases in which serious offences have been committed by individuals who were being electronically monitored at the time (Nellis, 2006b). Breaches of EM curfews are dealt with in a similar way to other community sentences, although the agency which is responsible for bringing breach proceedings differs depending on whether the EM curfew is a single (EM contractors responsibility) or multiple (Probation Service) requirement of a community order. Breaches of community sentences result in proceedings being brought to court sometime after the breach has occurred. It is not immediate and the time lapse may mean that the order has been completed before proceedings are concluded and/or that the link between non-compliance and the consequences in tenuous. Furthermore, penalties for breach are usually minimal, often involving a fine (Hucklesby, 2009).

At the same time, EM differs from other community sentences. This emanates most visibly from the fact that it is operated by the private sector rather than the Probation Service who currently oversee most other community sentences. Whether the supervisor of the sentence impacts upon the extent to which non-compliance is uncovered, officially recognised and acted upon is a question we will return to later in the chapter. Certainly the involvement of the private sector raises legitimacy issues which themselves may impact upon compliance. For instance, offenders may view the private sector as more or less legitimate enforcer of punishment than public sector agencies. Accordingly, it could be surmised, for example, that offenders who have had bad experiences of the state agencies and who do not hold them in high regard may view the EM contractors more favourable or visa versa. Alternatively, it may be that most offenders do not distinguish between EM contractors and public sector criminal justice agencies and view them as 'all the same'. Evidence suggests that offenders are able to distinguish between the sectors in relation to prisons (see, for example, Liebling, 2004) but similar questions have not yet been asked of offenders who are electronically monitored.

In terms of compliance, EM has some added value over and above that offered by other community sentences. Whereas most community sentences require offenders' attendance at a specified place sporadically often no more than once or twice a week, offenders subject to EM are monitored for up to twelve hours a day (longer if they are on bail). During this period, offenders are monitored to see if they are where they are supposed to be. If they are not, the EM contractor is alerted almost immediately. So, EM provides a greater level of surveillance of offenders as well as heightening the likelihood of being caught if offenders fail to comply. It also provides concrete evidence of non-compliance speedily. Technology provides the necessary evidence of breach so the role of human discretion is minimised coming into play only in terms of whether any explanations provided by offenders are valid. In theory, this should also increase consistency of treatment between individuals. In short, EM provides a greater level of control and monitoring over offenders, its enforceability is greater than other community sentences and as a result it should have increased credibility amongst criminal justice professionals and the general public. However, there is a mismatch between what EM actually does and expectations of it. EM has been oversold in many respects, being portrayed as providing constant surveillance of offenders and tracking their movements. Whilst satellite tracking, using GPS technology, is available and is in use in the US and other jurisdictions such as Portugal, it has not officially reappeared in England and Wales (although a small pilot scheme is taking place in Hertfordshire at the time of writing) after the mixed findings of the pilots which took place in the mid-2000s (Shute, 2007). Constant active tracking is far removed from the radio frequency technology which is in use in the UK and elsewhere.

Recently Robinson and McNeill (2008) have made a useful distinction between two types of short-term compliance: formal and substantive. Formal compliance is complying with the letter of the law, that is, meeting the minimum requirements of an order. Substantive compliance requires more commitment from offenders and involves them actively engaging whilst subject to an order. The extent to which offenders formally comply is measureable because what is required is clearly defined; for example, whether they turn up for supervision meetings or keep to their curfew hours. However, what constitutes substantive compliance is more nebulous. Defining what active engagement looks like and then measuring it is more difficult and can result in breach action being taken only when offenders do not formally comply with the requirements of their orders. A lack of active participation and engagement may remain unchallenged officially despite the fact that it may be a barrier to effective work with offenders simply because what it is cannot easily be defined and measured and therefore reported to courts (see Hucklesby, 2010 for an example related to drug treatment).

Unlike other community sentences, EM does not require offenders to actively engage whilst under sentence. Consequently, as long as offenders abide by their curfew hours, they can continue to drink, take drugs or offend within the confines of staying in during specific times. Although all community sentences can be criticised to some extent for not requiring substantive compliance, EM stands alone amongst community sentences in not even attempting to actively engage offenders. Consequently, it is criticised for being unconstructive and unlikely to result in desistance (Nellis, 2003a). Such concerns may be unfounded in some cases because research suggests that EM can play a role in desistance but that is has more impact on offenders who are actively seeking to change (Hucklesby, 2008). How EM's role in desistance could be enhanced by working alongside offender managers is not clear because we do not know enough about the interrelationship between EM and offender managers to say with certainty what their relative merits might be and how they might work together to enhance compliance and desistance. Whatever the merits of increased cooperation, the troubled history of EM and the Probation Service alongside evidence that offender managers still have someway to go before they fully embrace EM (see, for example, Rogers, 2011) suggests that there are significant obstacles to overcome before such an approach is realised.

Indeed, the evidence is that EM companies and the rest of the criminal justice system work in parallel worlds where information exchange between the two sectors is limited (see, for example, Bottomley *et al.*, 2004; CJJI, 2008).

This section has drawn some similarities and differences between EM and other community sentences/requirements. The next section reviews theories of compliance and how they might relate to EM.

Compliance theories and electronic monitoring

Bottoms' (2001) original conceptualisation of compliance with community sentences is well known and is discussed by other authors in the volume. For this reason, this section only discusses his work briefly, concentrating instead on Nellis' (2006a) insights into compliance with EM and how some of the motivations for offenders' compliance whilst on EM might differ from other community sentences. The aims of Bottoms and Nellis differed, with the former producing an abstract, theoretical framework whilst the latter views compliance from the perspective of supervisors of community sentences and how they work with offenders to bring about their compliance.

Bottoms' (2001) identifies four sources of compliance: instrumental, normative, constraint, and habit and routine. Instrumental compliance is based on deterrence whereby offenders comply either because they are concerned about the possible consequences of non-compliance or because of the positive outcomes which might result from complying. Normative compliance arises from offenders' moral obligation, commitment or attachment. Bottoms identifies three sub-groups of compliance in this category. The first of these is moral acceptance of a norm which arises through socialisation. The second group stresses the importance of attachments and social relations and the role of significant others. The third group relates to legitimacy which is linked to distributive and procedural justice, that is, whether offenders perceive the outcome of their sentence to be fair and justice and whether they perceive their treatment by the criminal justice process both pre-trial and whilst under sentence to be respectful, just and fair (see, for example, Tyler, this volume). Constraint-based compliance is the third of Bottoms' categories of compliance which relates to the various mechanisms which might be imposed on offenders to reduce their opportunities to offend. The final source of compliance according to Bottoms is habit and routine whereby compliance occurs 'unthinkingly' and derives from, and is linked with, other sources of compliance.

Nellis (2006a) identifies five types of compliance: incentive-based, threat-based, trust-based, surveillance-based and incapacitation-based. There are clear areas of convergence between Bottoms' and Nellis' frameworks, particularly around the role of instrumental reasons for compliance with incentive and threat-based compliance mapping onto Bottoms' instrumental compliance. Nellis' concept of trust-based compliance, which he suggests is linked to offenders' sense of obligation to courts or supervisors, links into some aspects of Bottoms' concept of normative compliance. There are also areas where the two theoretical frameworks diverge which are particularly important when discussing electronic monitoring. The first area of divergence is in relation to constraint-based compliance. What Bottoms means by constraint is not clear but the term itself suggests that the degree of restriction can differ between individuals and over time and place as well as for different sentences. By contrast, Nellis' use of the term 'incapacitation' suggests total restriction and relates only to the use of imprisonment. This is surprising given that Nellis (2004) himself points out that EM (and other community sentences) is not totally incapacitative. Conceptualising EM as constraining rather than incapacitative fits more comfortably with how EM might enhance compliance and militates against it being sold by politicians as 'a prison without bars'.

The major divergence between the two compliance theories is that Nellis (2006a) includes a category of surveillance-based compliance to take account of the particular nature of EM. He suggests that the principle mechanism for ensuring compliance with EM is surveillance and the fact that offenders are watched, albeit remotely, whilst they are being monitored. He defines surveillance-based compliance as 'instilling an awareness of immediate, here-and-now regulation as a result of being perpetually or intermittently watched, close up or at a distance, with one's trials and traces retrievable from databases' (Nellis, 2006a: 104). There is no disagreement that EM is a surveillance-based sentence in that the technology requires offenders to comply with the requirements of the technology in a precise way, in terms of both location and time, which other community sentences do not, making it unique amongst available punishments. However, how the technology contributes to increasing or reducing compliance is open to some debate. The central issue is the difficulty, practically and conceptually, of untangling the impact that increased surveillance has on getting caught and the subsequent effect this might have on instrumental reasons for compliance (Hucklesby, 2009).

Nellis (2006a) ignores a number of important areas of Bottoms' original work. The first of these is compliance arising from habit and routine. EM was never envisaged as a rehabilitative sentence and there is no robust evidence so far to suggest that EM can be a reason for long-term improvements in offenders' lifestyles. However, EM can be a disrupting influence. It can provide offenders with an excuse and reason to change their lifestyle away from activities which are connected with their offending (see Hucklesby, 2008). In this way, EM can be conceived of as habit-breaking (see Hucklesby, 2008). This suggests that the concept of habit and routine should encompass not only creating good or compliant habits but also stopping bad habits which are linked to offending or other anti-social behaviours. An important difference between Bottoms' concept of habit and routine and the notion of habit-breaking is that the former suggests that offenders are passive in this process whereas habit-breaking requires offenders to actively seek to change their lifestyles.

The second area Nellis ignores is the role that significant others might have in compliance. This is particularly important in the case of EM given that it is a sentence which usually confines offenders to their homes, restricting their ability to leave and thus requiring them to spend more time with significant others who share accommodation with them (Hucklesby, 2009). This means that the intensity of involvement of significant others probably demarcates it from other community sentences.

Having introduced the main theoretical contributions which have sought to understand the relationship between community sentences and compliance, the next section reviews the evidence from the research in relation to what offenders said influenced their compliance.

Compliance with EM curfew conditions

This section deals with the influences on compliance articulated by interviewees which are particularly important in the case of EM and which might differentiate the reasons why offenders comply with EM from explanations for compliance with other community sentences. Before doing this, some of the generic factors which shaped offenders' compliance are explored. What is very clear is that decisions about compliance are complex and that a multitude of factors shape offenders' decisions about whether to comply. Questions remain unanswered, however, such as the relative importance of the influences and how they change over time. It is likely that the influences ebb and flow during the duration of the order alongside offenders, commitment to comply (Robinson and McNeill, 2008; McNeill and Robinson, this volume).

Instrumental reasons for compliance relating to the fear of the potential punishment for non-compliance were the most commonly articulated reasons why offenders complied. What interviewees were concerned about was that they did not want to go to prison. This was sometimes linked to fears about having to leave their children and/or partner or losing their job. In reality, the penalty for non-compliance is rarely imprisonment and offenders who had first-hand experience and/or third-party knowledge of the likely outcome of breaches were less likely to comply (Hucklesby, 2009). Offenders were aware that even though they were being electronically monitored, they were able to break their curfew by leaving their house. They articulated reasons for not doing so it terms of their own decisions and motivations to stay in representing attitudes related to Bottoms' conceptualisation of normative compliance and Nellis' trust-based compliance. Related to this was the notion that some offenders simply wanted to do their time and get the curfew 'out of the way', recognising that their situation may get worst (in terms of additional, maybe harsher, punishment) if they were breached.

In terms of normative (Bottoms, 2001) and trust-based (Nellis, 2006a) compliance, offenders seemed to generally abide by the wishes of the court. Most of the offenders had a sense of obligation to the court. They believed that they were sentenced for something they had done, that they deserved to be punished and that the court had the authority to punish them. In this way, courts were viewed as legitimate by offenders. These views appeared to be stronger when offenders felt they had been treated fairly or leniently in terms of the severity of the sentence, suggesting that distributive justice may play a role in offenders' decisions to comply.

Their feelings were also linked to instrumental reasons for complying so offenders demonstrated an awareness that the court's decision was backed up with the threat of punishment if they flouted its authority.

What impact procedural justice had on compliance whilst offenders were actually being monitored was difficult to evaluate because their experiences of monitoring company staff was overwhelmingly positive. Offenders generally reported being treated well by the monitoring officers who visited their homes. They were slightly less positive about staff in the central control room who dealt with the telephone calls between the contractors and the offenders. A few offenders reported isolated instances of when they felt that monitoring officers had not dealt with them professionally. In most instances, offenders reported that their interactions with monitoring officers had impacted upon their thoughts about compliance – positively if they felt they had been treated well and negatively if they felt poorly treated. Those who felt positively often referred to monitoring officers' role in reducing the likelihood that they would not comply. What was less clear was whether being on the receiving end of what was viewed as poor treatment resulted in non-compliance or simply made it more likely. Most offenders suggested that they felt that the way they were treated by staff was particularly important given that the interactions took place in their own homes where there was a general sense that offenders expected a higher level of courteousness than might be the case in a probation office, for example. Together, these findings seem to conform to the procedural justice hypothesis of Tyler and others (see, for example, Tyler, 1990, 1997, 1998; Tyler and Huo, 2002). But perhaps a more intriguing finding was that no offenders questioned the legitimacy of monitoring officers as representatives of a private company or commented upon the fact that they were employed by private sector companies. They accepted and appeared to view EM contractors as legitimate agents of the criminal justice process.

Demographic and situational factors played a role in offenders' compliance. Using the data from the case files, offenders' community ties (residence, employment, family life) were correlated with compliance but not necessarily in the way that might have been expected. Offenders who were not living in their permanent accommodation whilst they were under curfew were less likely to comply than those residing in their usual accommodation. Living alone was correlated with an increased likelihood of non-compliance. By contrast and unexpectedly, offenders who were married or co-habiting were more likely to breach their curfews than single, divorced or separated offenders. Offenders living with children were more likely to be breached probably because of the practicalities of looking after children. A potentially important variable was that the interviews took place over the summer which is particularly relevant because offenders who are electronically monitored are not permitted to use their gardens. Consequently, offenders might breach the requirements by going out in the garden. They might do this to have a cigarette or to assist their children who were playing in the garden. This also raises the possibility that levels of compliance with EM change over the course of the year, which would be an interesting aspect to explore in future research.

Access to the garden is one example of where some of the rules about how electronic monitoring can be used might contribute to increased levels of non-compliance. Such issues might also dent the legitimacy of EM in the view of offenders and therefore impact upon longer-term compliance because they see the rules are particularly unfair or restrictive. Other examples include the ways in which EM is used by the courts. Theoretically, one of the advantages of EM curfews is that they can be used creatively and flexibly to ensure 'adequate' levels of punishment but also to take into account offenders' circumstances, patterns of offending and so on. In reality, they are rarely used in this way. Most curfews are set at between ten and twelve hours per day, overnight and sometime between the hours of 6 pm and 8 am. The rigidity in the way EM is used is likely to contribute to non-compliance because individuals' circumstances are not always taken into consideration. Curfews which started earlier in the evening and finished later in the morning were correlated with an increased number of breaches. Additionally, curfews for a maximum available period (twelve hours in the case of sentences) were also more likely to be breached than those set at ten hours. If offenders view the courts as not taking into consideration their circumstances or their offence, they might view the sentence as less legitimate. An example might be when offenders convicted of shop theft have a curfew imposed overnight. In these circumstances, the link between the offence and the punishment might be lost. These findings suggest that a more flexible and creative use of EM without compromising on the requirement to punish offenders might increase compliance levels. It may also increase the likelihood of long-term benefits in offenders' behaviour, particularly because an area where offenders raised specific concerns about courts' use of curfew hours was in relation to employment (see Hucklesby, 2008). Several offenders suggested that curfew restrictions impeded their ability to work, echoing previous research (Dodgson *et al.*, 2001).

Currently, offenders are not informed about the rules relating to when formal breach action is taken or that leeway is built into the scheme (see CJJI, 2008). According to the regulations governing EM, offenders are able to miss part of their curfew without being breached. However, the lack of transparency in relation to the rules may impact adversely upon offenders' views of the legitimacy of EM and their future compliance. As a result, they receive mixed messages whereby offenders who have missed part of their curfew but remain under the permitted threshold of time which is allowable are told that they will not be breached. Such inaction might lead to offenders (wrongly) believing that enforcement of curfew orders is weak, resulting in further breaches. Similar messages might be received on more than one occasion until suddenly (from the point of view of the offender) they reach the threshold for breach and action is taken without an explanation being given. This is likely to be viewed by offenders as, at best, inconsistent and probably unfair, potentially curtailing their views of the legitimacy of EM. Add to this that rumours and myths abound amongst offenders about how to get around EM and the various rules and practices associated with its use, it is not difficult to see how opaque breach procedures can harm the legitimacy of EM.

Having provided an overview of the findings of the research in the following sections, we turn our attention to three aspects of EM which distinguish it from other community sentences and discuss their role in shaping offenders' compliance decisions.

Technology

The use of technology is the distinguishing feature of EM. The technology facilitates the monitoring of formal compliance and should ensure that any non-compliance is detected. The technology enables consistent information about breaches to be available quickly according to a set of predetermined rules about what is and what is not acceptable. It removes discretion from the process of determining a prima facie case that a breach has occurred. But it does not remove discretion completely. EM monitoring officers and contractors' court teams are required to exercise discretion in relation to any explanations provided for non-compliance by offenders and the action which is subsequently taken. EM might rely on technology but its operation is not devoid of human decision-making. The situation is complicated because two parallel systems of dealing with breaches currently exist in England and Wales (see CJJI, 2008). EM contractors are responsible for breach proceedings where offenders are subject to stand-alone curfew conditions whereas offender managers are responsible for proceedings when a curfew requirement is one of a number of conditions attached to a community order. These parallel processes can result in different and inconsistent outcomes (CJJI, 2008). The regulation of the EM contractors by the Ministry of Justice means that they will always instigate breach proceedings if evidence exists that offenders have not formally complied with their curfew. By contrast, offender managers may use their discretion in deciding whether or not to breach offenders most notably when they may be engaging or making good progress with other requirements, so that offenders are substantively but not always formally complying with their order. The Joint Inspectorate Report (CJJI, 2008) suggested that offender managers were slow to breach offenders when they have been provided with evidence by the EM contractor. In some cases, this might lead to perverse outcomes, given that offenders subject to stand-alone EM requirements are likely to be those convicted of less serious offences and probably pose less risk to the public, yet they are the offenders most likely to face breach proceedings. The limited discretion available to EM contractors means that they must breach offenders when they formally do not comply even if this appears to be an isolated incidence (NAO, 2006). Given the chaotic lives of many offenders and evidence of the 'zigzag' nature of the desistance process (Burnett, 2004; Farrall, 2002; Maruna, 2001), it is almost inevitable that offenders might fail to comply during an order on at least one occasion. Evidence certainly supports this with the National Audit Office (2006) suggesting that most offenders subject to EM curfews will fail to comply at some point during their order even if the violation is not at the level of seriousness to instigate formal breach proceedings. The strict requirements for breaching offenders arises because the contracts between the government and the EM contractors stipulate the action that must be taken by the EM contractors in the event of non-compliance and are more closely monitored than their state employed counterparts. On the one hand, this arguably enhances the credibility of EM and it may prevent potential abuses, particularly when alternative actions may increase the profit margins of private companies (for instance, EM contractors have a financial incentive not to breach offenders because offenders are no longer monitored once they are breached and payments stop). On the other hand, strict adherence to the contracts may result in unnecessary or perverse breach decisions in individual cases and may stifle innovative practices which attempt to increase levels of compliance with EM curfews (see Hucklesby and Sims, 2011).

EM technology must work and be seen to work by offenders whether as an influence on compliance itself or on the likelihood of getting caught. Doubts over the reliability of the technology could have a negative impact on compliance and the legitimacy of EM more broadly. The NAO (2006) was convinced of the reliability of the equipment and there is significant evidence that the technology does work. By contrast, EM technology is surrounded by myths relating to how to prevent it from working (these include putting legs in freezers and wrapping the tag in tinfoil neither of which work). Problems with the technology do sometimes arise in specific circumstances (see CJJI, 2008 for examples). As importantly in terms of the influence of technology on compliance is whether offenders perceive the equipment to work. On this point, the evidence is more mixed. Some offenders in the study believed wholehearted that the technology worked and gave examples of when they had been contacted by the EM contractor having been late in for the start of their curfew or gone out during their curfew. For example, one offender said: 'They rung up when [I was] late so I knew they were watching me. They know what is going on and once you realise then [you] stick to it.' Other offenders were more circumspect. They suggested that the equipment was unreliable on the basis of a range of problems which they had experienced. These included reports that offenders were accused of being out when they reported being in, that equipment made unexplained noises or that monitoring officers had visited them for equipment checks and had replaced faulty equipment. Interviewees generally reported that such problems had made them less likely to comply.

The effectiveness of the technology is only part of the equation in terms of compliance. It was important to offenders that the surveillance was tangible. They reported requiring constant reminders, in the form of telephone calls and visits, to enhance their compliance otherwise it was possible to forget that they were under curfew. Some offenders confessed to testing the system to see if their non-compliance was detected. Consequently, following up non-compliance to alert offenders to the fact that the EM contractor was aware of the breach was a crucial way to enhance future compliance.

Significant others

As already discussed significant others play an enhanced role in EM because the punishment takes place in the domestic sphere. They can have both positive and negative influences on compliance. In some instances, the time spent with family and friends was viewed positively, with offenders reporting improved relationships with partners and children (Hucklesby, 2008). However, if relationships were already strained, the forced confinement resulted in further tensions and sometimes non-compliance. Concerns have also been raised that EM might contribute to domestic violence, potentially increasing the frequency of events (Whitfield, 1997). In terms of non-compliance, most often, arguments and pressure from partners to go out were the catalysts which led to offenders leaving their curfew addresses. A few offenders reported that partners had put pressure on them to go out, threatening to leave them if they did not. More positively and numerously, offenders reported receiving support from their families and friends which assisted them to comply. Much of the support they received was active, which included reminding offenders that curfew periods were about to start either by telephone or text, going to collect offenders to bring them home, family or friends staying in with offenders and/or arranging events at home and individuals going to buy or collect goods during curfew hours. Families and friends were also reported as providing moral support and cajoling offenders into complying. Householders also have to actively give consent to the offenders being electronically monitored in their home. Even if significant others do not actively support offenders, they are passively involved in the operation of EM in that the equipment is in their home and the monitoring company makes visits and telephone calls. In spite of their important role, at the time of the research the EM contractor and their staff paid little attention to the role of the family and did not ensure that they were fully aware of the nature of EM and what it would mean for them.

The working practices of monitoring officers

A defining feature of EM is that it is run by the private sector and it has already been discussed how this shapes the way in which non-compliance is responded to mainly because of the binding contracts which monitoring companies work with. This leaves the question of how monitoring officers might influence offenders' compliance. Monitoring officers differ from probation staff. Their backgrounds, prospects, training and their terms and conditions are very different to statutory sector employees (see Hucklesby, 2011).

The research uncovered some shared values amongst the monitoring officers who were interviewed (see Hucklesby, 2011). They had a sense of mission in that they believed that it was important that offenders were monitored. At the same time, they were very keen to get the job done as quickly as possible. They generally held punitive attitudes towards offenders and were suspicious of them. They were all very conscious of distancing themselves from the police as a way of keeping themselves safe (Hucklesby, 2011). Personal safety was their major preoccupation.

They considered themselves to be vulnerable most of the time they were working because their feelings emanated from their working environment, which involved long periods of time on the road and visiting offender's houses, often alone (for more details see Hucklesby, 2011). Monitoring officers used a number of strategies to deal with these feelings, some of which have the potential to directly impact upon offenders' compliance. The first set of strategies involved not undertaking visits. This might entail refusing to do the visit and letting the company know, leaving visits that they did not want to do until late in the shift in the hope that supervisors would reallocate them to another monitoring officer and reporting that they had visited offenders' properties when they had not. This last practice is likely to have serious ramifications for offenders because they may be reported as absent from their curfew address and therefore non-compliant, resulting in breach proceedings being taken. Instrumental strategies were also used by monitoring officers to improve their safety. These were linked to pragmatic considerations of doing tasks as quickly and safely as possible without confrontation and were linked to conflict avoidance. Using such strategies sometimes resulted in tasks not being completed properly because they were in a rush to get out of properties. This might mean that equipment was not fitted correctly so that it failed to work or gave false alerts of non-compliance and that the requirements of EM were not fully explained to offenders, resulting in them not complying. Another 'safety' strategy of monitoring officers was to avoid confrontations with offenders by saying that visits were to check equipment when their purpose was to investigate possible breaches. They did this because they viewed accusing offenders of breaches as particularly problematic and putting themselves at risk. However, this practice has the potential to impact upon compliance negatively in two ways: by giving the impression that the equipment is faulty and unreliable; and two, by irritating offenders for what they might perceive to be the company's fault. A third range of strategies adopted by monitoring officers to decrease their vulnerability were normative and linked to managing situations and engaging with offenders rather than avoiding contact and possible conflict with them. Normative strategies included treating offenders with respect and in a non-authoritarian manner, not accusing them of non-compliance, talking to them 'normally' and using banter, jokes and humour. Monitoring officers usually dealt with difficult situations by talking offenders down or by 'killing them with kindness' as one interviewee called it. According to procedural justice theory, this final group of strategies is likely to increase rather than decrease offenders' compliance.

Three discernable working credos were evident amongst monitoring officers (Hucklesby, 2011). These were: probation workers, pragmatists and technicians and one can surmise that monitoring officers with different credos might influence offender's compliance in different ways as described in Table 7.1. Seven interviewees could be described as 'Probation workers'. The values displayed by these interviewees included ensuring that they treated offenders with respect, adhering to the ideals of procedural justice (Tyler, 1990). They had a heightened level of trust in offenders compared to the other credos as well as a greater awareness and empathy

TABLE 7.1 Monitoring officers working credos and their influence on compliance

	Probation worker	*Pragmatist*	*Technician*
View of offenders	Some empathy and trust	Non-judgemental	No empathy and heightened suspicion
Time on each visit	As long as it takes to do it thoroughly	As long as it takes to fit the equipment and explain the requirements of EM	As short as possible
Information/advice provided	Yes general advice provided	Only in relation to EM	As little as possible
Compliance influence	Positive plus	Positive	Negative

of offenders' lives and circumstances. They ensured that offenders and their families received all the necessary information about EM and took extra time and care ensuring that they knew everything they needed to know. Half of the monitoring officers interviewed were 'Pragmatists'. Their main concerns were ensuring that they completed tasks efficiently and effectively. They held non-judgemental attitudes towards offenders and their families. They stuck to their job description providing only scant information and advice to offenders and only in relation to EM, mainly because they displayed a lack of trust in offenders. Technicians were the smallest group comprising three interviewees. Their main priority was to fit the equipment and get the job finished as quickly as possible. They had no sympathy or empathy for offenders or their families and had a heightened mistrust of offenders. Consequently, they kept their distance from them with little or no time spent talking to or interacting with offenders or their families.

Two aspects of these credos are likely to impact upon compliance: the way in which offenders were dealt with and the level and depth of information provided about EM to offenders. On these criteria, it is probable that probation workers had the most positive influence on offenders' compliance because they spent time with offenders dealing with them respectfully and providing them with detailed information about the requirements of EM. By contrast, technicians demonstrated little awareness of the importance of procedural justice values and failed to give offenders all the necessary information about how EM operates. The existence of the working credos suggest that offenders experiences of EM may be very different and may result in different levels of compliance. However, offenders are likely to see a range of monitoring officers during the lifetime of their curfew which may neutralise some of the disparities.

Conclusion

EM is a community sentence albeit with elements which distinguish it from other forms of community supervision. In terms of compliance, the features which set it apart from other sentences are: the use of technology; the enhanced involvement of significant others in the sentence; and the involvement of the private sector. Understanding how these factors influence offenders' compliance will improve our knowledge of compliance with criminal justice sanctions more generally.

The use of electronic monitoring technologies has the capacity to strengthen offenders' compliance but the mechanisms by which this occurs are complex. The simple knowledge that someone is watching is likely to be part of the reason why some offenders comply with EM. However, this cannot be divorced, in theory or in practice, from its impact on the likelihood of being caught. Instrumental reasons, that is, the fear of the consequences of non-compliance, were the most widely acknowledged reason for offenders' compliance. Offenders' concerns about going to prison were linked not just to the institution of the prison but also to the consequences for their lives. For this reason, EM is a particularly useful tool to bring about short-term compliance but this leads to criticisms that it is an unconstructive sentence, controlling rather than rehabilitating offenders. In England and Wales, however, the usefulness of EM in supporting other requirements of community orders has been little explored both in practice and in research. More creative use of curfew times linking with other requirements of community sentences (e.g., curfewing offenders the night before they are required to attend drug treatment appointments) and matching peak hours for offending. Using EM in these ways will inevitability make the process of running it more complicated for the EM companies and may increase costs. It also raises issues about whether offenders should always be required to wear tagging equipment if they are monitored for shorter period. This is especially pertinent given that data gleaned from EM is being used increasingly by the police during the investigation of crime.

The role of family and friends in both desistance and compliance has been underplayed and undervalued (Codd, 2007; Mills and Codd, 2007; Hucklesby, 2008, 2009). Whilst it is acknowledged that their role is likely to be enhanced in relation to EM because of the nature of the sentence, they may also play a part in compliance with other community sentences by reminding offenders of appointments and so on. In order to play a positive role in offenders' compliance, significant others need to be aware that offenders have been sentenced and the requirements of the order. The process of electronically monitoring offenders (i.e., the presence of the equipment in the house at the very least) means that household members are more likely to be aware of the sentence, if not its specifics. By contrast, they may be completely unaware of the existence of community orders and/or their specific requirements if offenders choose not to tell them. Attempting to enhance compliance by engaging significant others in the punishment process is controversial, potentially co-opting them as enforcers and agents of the criminal justice process. Recognising that there are boundaries which should not be crossed, increasing their involvement, with both theirs and the offenders' consent, is likely to have benefits for the criminal justice process and significant others.

The working environment of monitoring officers, their practices and their working credos shape how they interact with offenders and how thoroughly they do their work. They have the capacity to impact upon offenders' compliance directly; for example, by not fitting equipment correctly or not fully explaining the requirements of the curfew and, indirectly, by their treatment of offenders. The extent to which such factors are influenced by EM being operated by the private sector is open to debate. On the one hand, profit may be a strong incentive when it comes to policy innovation. For instance, it is in the monitoring companies' interest to minimise non-compliance because they do not get paid once an offender has been breached. On the other hand, working practices are influenced by the need to keep costs to a minimum so, for example, monitoring officers might be encouraged to spend as little time as possible fitting the monitoring equipment. However, at least some, and potentially a substantial part, of how monitoring officers go about their work is not sector specific but is dictated by the working environment and the ways in which EM requirements are used by the courts in England and Wales. Recently, EM contracts between the Ministry of Justice and the EM companies have been more about ensuring value for money than compliance and give little room for manoeuvre in terms of changing practices to improve compliance rates.

This study has highlighted some of the complexities involved in offenders' decisions about whether to comply. It demonstrates that offenders consider many factors in their decisions and that what influences compliance for one individual may not influence it for others or at least to the same extent. It is also evident that non-compliance is not always planned and that offenders' chaotic lives and poor life skills often contributed to non-compliance (see Hucklesby, 2009). Enhancing compliance requires a multi-dimensional approach whereby strategies to increase compliance are tailored to individuals. There is no silver bullet to the problem of non-compliance and it is imperative that we guard against the idea that there is a single solution to this complex issue. It is important not to replicate the mistakes of the past which resulted in a one-dimensional approach to attempts to reduce reoffending (see, for example, Mair, 2004).

References

Bottomley, A.K., Hucklesby, A. and Mair, G. (2004) 'Electronic monitoring of offenders: key developments', *Issues in Community Justice*, Monograph No. 5, London: NAPO.

Bottoms, A.E. (2001) 'Compliance and community penalties', in A. Bottoms, L. Gelsthorpe and S. Rex (eds) *Community Penalties: change or challenges*, Cullompton: Willan Publishing, pp. 87–116.

Burnett, R. (2004) 'To reoffend or not to reoffend? The ambivalence of convicted property offenders', in S. Maruna and R. Immarigeon (eds) *After Crime and Punishment: Ex-offender reintegration and desistance from crime*, Cullompton: Willan Publishing, pp. 152–80.

Cavadino, M. and Dignan, J. (2007) *The Penal System: an introduction*, London: Sage.

Chapman, T. and Hough, M. (1998) *Evidence-Based Practice*, London: Home Office.

Codd, H. (2007) *In the Shadow of the Prison: families, imprisonment and criminal justice*, Cullompton: Willan Publishing.

Criminal Justice Joint Inspection (CJJI) (2008) *A Complicated Business: a joint inspection of electronically monitored curfew requirements, orders and licences*, London: MoJ.

Dodgson, K. *et al.* (2001) *Electronic Monitoring of Released Prisoners: an evaluation of the Home Detention Curfew scheme*, Home Office Research Study 222, London: Home Office.

Farrall, S. (2002) *Rethinking What Works with Offenders*, Cullompton: Willan Publishing.

Harper, G. and Chitty, C. (2005) *The Impact of Corrections on Re-Offending: a review of 'What Works'*, Home Office Research Study 291, London: Home Office.

Hearnden, I. and Millie, A. (2003) *Investigating Links Between Probation Enforcement and Reconviction*, Home Office online report 41/03, London: Home Office.

Hucklesby, A. (2008) 'Vehicles of desistance: the impact of electronically monitored curfew orders', *Criminology and Criminal Justice*, 8(1): 51–71.

—— (2009) 'Understanding offenders' compliance: a case study of electronically monitored curfew orders', *Journal of Law and Society*, 36(2): 248–71.

—— (2010) 'Drug interventions in the remand process' in A. Hucklesby and E. Wincup (eds) *Drug Interventions in Criminal Justice*, Maidenhead: Open University Press, pp. 110–34.

—— (2011) 'The working life of electronic monitoring officers', *Criminology and Criminal Justice*, 11(1): 1–18.

Hucklesby, A. and Sims, C. (2011) 'Compliance with electronic monitoring', paper presented at the VII CEP Conference on Electronic Monitoring, Evora, Portugal, 5–7 May. Available at http://www.cep-probation.org/default.asp?page_id=157&map_id=85.

Liebling, A. (2004) *Prisons and their Moral Performance: a study of values, quality and prison life*, Oxford: Oxford University Press.

Mair, G. (ed.) (2004) *What Matters in Probation*, Cullompton: Willan Publishing.

Mair, G. (2009) 'Community Sentences', in A. Hucklesby and A. Wahidin (eds) *Criminal Justice*, Oxford: Oxford University Press, pp. 165–84.

Maruna, S. (2001) *Making Good: how ex-convicts reform and rebuild their lives*, Washington: American Psychological Association Books.

McGuire, J. (1995) *What Works: Reducing Reoffending*, Chichester: Wiley.

Mills, A. and Codd, H. (2007) 'Prisoners' families', in Y. Yewkes (ed.) *Handbook on Prison*, Devon: Willan Publishing, pp. 672–95.

Ministry of Justice (2010a) *Breaking the Cycle: effective punishment, rehabilitation and sentencing of offenders*, Cm 7972, London: The Stationary Office.

—— (2010b) *Offender Management Caseload Statistics 2009*, England and Wales, London: Ministry of Justice.

—— (2011) *Service Specification for Deliver Curfew Requirement* at http://www.justice.gov.uk/downloads/about/noms/directory-of-services/2011–04–26%20Curfew%20Requirement%20Specification%20P1%200.pdf.

National Audit Office (NAO) (2006) *The Electronic Monitoring of Adult Offenders*, Report by the Comptroller and Auditor General, London: National Audit Office.

Nellis, M. (2003a) 'Electronic monitoring and the future of probation', in W. H. Chui and M. Nellis, *Moving Probation Forward*, Harlow: Pearson Education, pp. 245–57.

—— (2003b) '"They don't even know we're there": the electronic monitoring of offenders in England and Wales', in K. Ball and F. Webster (eds), *The Intensification of Surveillance*, London: Pluto Press, pp. 62–89.

—— (2004) 'Electronic monitoring and the community supervision of offenders', in A. Bottoms, S. Rex and G. Robinson (eds), *Alternatives to Prison*, Cullompton: Willan Publishing, pp. 224–47.

—— (2006a) 'Surveillance, rehabilitation, and electronic monitoring: getting the issues clear', *Criminology and Public Policy*, 5(1): 103–8.

—— (2006b) 'The limitations of electronic monitoring: reflections on the tagging of Peter Williams', *Prison Service Journal*, March. Available at http://www.hmprisonservice.gov.uk/resourcecentre/prisonservicejournal/index.asp?id=5017,3124,11,3148,0,0.

Pratt, J., Brown, D., Hallsworth, S. and Morrison, W. (eds) (2005) *The New Punitiveness: trends, theories and perspectives*, Cullompton: Willan Publishing.

Robinson, G. and McNeill, F. (2008) 'Exploring the dynamics of compliance with community penalties', *Theoretical Criminology*, 12(4): 431–50.

Rogers, P. (2011) 'Specification, benchmarking and costing of EM', paper presented at the VII CEP Conference on Electronic Monitoring, Evora, Portugal, 5–7 May. Available at http://www.cep-probation.org/default.asp?page_id=157&map_id=85.

Shute, S. (2007) *Satellite Tracking of Offenders: a study of the pilots in England and Wales*, Research Study no. 4, London: Ministry of Justice.

Tyler, T. (1990) *Why People Obey the Law*, New Haven: Yale University Press.

—— (1997) 'The psychology of legitimacy: a relational perspective on voluntary defence to authorities', *Personality and Social Psychology Review*, 1: 323–4.

—— (1998) 'Trust and democratic governance', in V. Braithwaite and M. Levi (eds) *Trust and Governance*, New York: Russell Sage Foundation, pp. 269–94.

Tyler, T. and Huo, Y.J. (2002) *Trust in the Law: encouraging public cooperation with the police and the courts*, New York: Russell Sage.

Whitfield, D. (1997) *Tackling the Tag*, Winchester: Waterside Press.

8

IMPLANT TECHNOLOGY AND THE ELECTRONIC MONITORING OF OFFENDERS

Old and new questions about compliance, control and legitimacy[1]

Mike Nellis

The modalities of electronic monitoring

> The idea of placing ICT devices 'under our skin' in order not just to repair but even to enhance human capabilities gives rise to science fiction visions with threat and/or benefit characteristics. However, in some cases, the implantation of microchips with the potential for individual and social forms of control is already taking place.
>
> (European Group on Ethics and Science in New Technologies, 2005)

The advent of remote electronic monitoring (EM) in the 1980s introduced a new modality of compliance into the field of community supervision, based on an individual offender's willingness to abide by more precise spatial and temporal schedules than had ever been possible (or considered desirable) with other non-custodial interventions such as probation and community service. In its most basic form – curfews/house arrest – compliance with EM simply means wearing a small, signal-emitting ankle bracelet and making oneself present in a particular place at a specified time, and in that sense EM is not a disciplinary penalty like probation: internalising norms of law-abidingness is neither required nor intended. It is a form of surveillance which can be used alongside or separately from other, more traditional, means of gaining an offender's compliance – incentives, trust and threats (Nellis, 2004, 2006) – whilst under supervision in the community. Hucklesby's research (2009) indicates that the transcendent threat of imprisonment may well be what compels offenders to take EM seriously, but it is the surveillant modality itself – the precise behavioural commitments required of an offender – that makes the experience of EM formally and subjectively different from other types of offender supervision, and which has raised distinct questions of legitimacy.

EM itself now comes in several different technical forms – house arrest/curfews have been supplemented by the remote monitoring of alcohol use; voice verification, GPS tracking and even inmate tracking systems for use *within* prisons. All are 'individuated monitoring packages', but each entails subtly different patterns of compliance for the offenders subject to them. Mostly in the house arrest form briefly pioneered by Judge Jack Love in Albuquerque, New Mexico in 1982, EM has spread steadily from the USA (where GPS tracking has also become common) to approximately thirty other countries at the time of writing. While never without critics, principled concerns about normative legitimacy (warnings of Big Brother-style overcontrol) gave way over time to more mundane concerns about empirical legitimacy (anxieties about ineffectiveness and undercontrol). EM has not significantly reduced prison-use, as was once anticipated, but various forms of it have come to be seen as 'useful tools' in community supervision.

As spatial forms of regulation (especially exclusion) grow ever more appealing to public protection agencies, new technologies might one day emerge to complement or displace the existing EM repertoire, whereupon questions of compliance and legitimacy will need to be debated anew. Processes of technocorrectional change are little understood, not least in relation to EM. The operation of 'the commercial corrections complex' – the nexus of governmental agencies, corporate organisations, technology manufacturers and professional interest groups that impacts on penal policy-making – has been illuminated, but remains beyond deep and regular academic scrutiny (Lilly, 1992; Nathan, 2003; Nellis, 2009a). The forms a technology takes, the uses to which it is put, the places and pace at which it is introduced and upgraded are always shaped by social, cultural and political forces. There are phases, however, in socio-technical innovation when a new technology's existence (even in prototypical or experimental form) creates new social possibilities and options, and around these new commercial, political and professional groupings emerge to challenge the dominance of 'old ways' and to envisage 'new futures' (Brand, 2005). This, in effect, is what happened with EM in the 1980s. Despite high-profile claims for its potential going back several decades earlier, its advent mostly took criminologists and probation practitioners by surprise, having mostly germinated in intellectual enclaves to which (sociological) criminology had paid little heed, outwith the 'policy communities' from which new penal innovations usually emerged. To avoid further surprises, we should consider potential future forms of EM now, *and also* revisit the prehistory of EM, to better understand the context, and forms, in which it was first imagined, and the legitimacy issues which prevailed then. In doing so, we will need to sharpen conceptual distinctions between 'constraint', 'compliance' and 'control', terms which are rather loosely used in contemporary debate.

The advent of implant technologies

Implanted communication devices (ICDs – which encode, transmit and/or receive information) have been touted as a potentially new means of monitoring offenders, augmenting if not supplanting the wearable equipment which has characterised it to date. No government has yet promoted this, but ongoing developments in the related fields of 'telecare' and 'telehealth', in which computer-based monitoring of both wearable and implanted devices is already being used to improve the lives of the old, the sick, the physically disabled and the mentally disordered, have prompted several commercial organisations, notably Verichip, to consider criminal justice applications. 'Telehealth' technologies monitor lifesigns and movement, and can faciliate locatability in the event of alarms or emergencies. Some commentators see even this as sinister and dehumanising. Paul Virilio (1997: 50), for example, characterises it as 'colonising our organism', and writes scathingly of 'the interactive feats of a biotechnological miniaturisation that will finish off the job of those flourishing large scale mass communication tools that already govern our society'.

Speculation about the significance of implants is sometimes set within a broader 'techno-utopian' debate on the possibility of creating 'post-humans' – technologically enhanced people who may, among other things, utilise brainchips to make them smarter (increasing memory and information capacity), enable them to link to computers and other electronic systems by thought alone, as well as nano-machines which will eradicate diseased cells (Dinello, 2004). In respect of all implant technologies, there are already futurologists extolling their potential, related commercial champions, and activists who either oppose them root and branch or seek merely to regulate and constrain their 'inevitable' development. Science fiction has frequently explored implants (and cognate themes), and both novels and films have helped to shape the symbolic meanings of this technology, often becoming key reference points in public discourse, and, in turn, a part of the 'cultural politics' which affect the technology's subsequent developmental trajectory.[2]

The perceived need for ethical debate on ICDs generally – not merely in relation to offenders – is by no means new to the twenty-first century. It was arguably signalled as far back as 1967 by privacy theorist Alan Westin, who saw 'permanent implacements of "tagging" devices on or in the body' coming (Westin, 1967: 86). By the time attorney Elaine Ramesh (1997) was writing, the 'internal, implanted microchip for identification of humans [was] already a reality' and while recognising its potentially benign uses, she insisted that 'because of the very drastic reduction in personal liberty and privacy that such implantation represents, the legal ramifications need to be explored now'. In the present era – and specifically in respect of offenders – no less a commentator than Michael Tonry, a paragon of liberal level-headedness in international penal debate, takes the prospect of them seriously, and foresees problems:

> In the twenty-first century [the prison] may serve as a humane alternative to biochemical controls on behaviour and electronic controls on movement. The technological gap between drugs that allow deeply mentally disturbed people to function in the community and drugs that offset aggressive impulses or excitement is bridgeable. When that bridge is crossed, there will be those who regard the moral autonomy of offenders as less important than the prevention of harm to victims. Delayed delivery drugs and subcutaneous

computer chips are available now. Some crime controllers will be happy to see them used. In the long term we cannot know how these debates will be resolved but for a time at least imprisonment may serve as a humane alternative to behavioural controls that may be much more deeply violative of human rights and liberties.

(Tonry, 2003: 4–5)

Because techno-utopianism is a largely American phenomenon, these may be distinctively American – as opposed to European – anxieties, at least for now. They may also reflect Tonry's recognition that in the USA, at least, there has been a past willingness to entertain such technocorrectional possibilities, a tendency towards caprice in penal policy (especially at local level), and a perpetual commercial readiness to exploit perceived new opportunities. *The Cincinnati Times* (19 June 2006) reported a law enforcement official talking up the idea of chipping sex offenders, albeit for location monitoring rather than behaviour control: 'people have these GPS chips put in their pets and – in some cases – in their children – in the event of their being lost or kidnapped. I don't see why the same can't be done with probationers.' This actually misunderstands the technology – *RFID chips* have indeed been placed in pets and children, containing information which identifies them if they get lost, but *this type of chip is not in itself linkable to* GPS, which requires a far stronger signal. Nonetheless, allied to a cultural and political willingness to degrade and stigmatise convicted offenders (less evident in Western European penal traditions – Whitman (2003)), it is not difficult *to at least envisage* circumstances in which implants might be used experimentally on offenders in the USA, simply because the statutory ability to invade the human body in this way is a singularly potent expression of the power to punish.

Notwithstanding the extent to which artificial hearts and joints, replacement organs, synthetic skin, corneal and retinal implants, cosmetic enhancements and various sorts of prosthetic limbs have already made 'post-humans' of us, much of what techno-utopians consider desirable still lies in the future, and pose legitimacy problems across the board. Technocorrectional change may never happen in the exact ways being imagined now, which is not to say that there will never be lesser consequences, or unanticipated consequences. To date, several different types of implant, with different purposes, have emerged – medical treatment, behaviour modification, identity verification, locatability and access control – and while some clearly function as one type more than another, there can be overlap. My focus here will be on implanted communication devices (ICDs) because these (may) impinge most directly on existing technologies for monitoring offenders. The distinction I make below, however, between implants for 'mind control' and implants for location monitoring, whilst premised on an undoubted shift of focus in the way EM was first *imagined* (adjusting an individual's attitudes and behaviour) and the way it has *actually developed* (regulating an individual's spatial and temporal routines), cannot be maintained too rigidly. Remote location monitoring of offenders was indeed envisaged (although only practised experimentally) fifty years ago, and as a new 'biosocial criminology' emerges in the twenty-first century (Rose, 2000; Walsh, 2002; Rafter, 2008), neurological and pharmacological means of influencing criminal behaviour may yet return to the agenda, and it is in this context that Tonry's contemporary anxieties should be seen.

Early debates on implants and 'mind control'

To Tonry (and others), implants may seem like the *next* development in EM, but they were in fact part of its prehistory, under consideration even before wearable technology was developed. In the early years of the Cold War, the American government became preoccupied with understanding and countering the threat of Soviet totalitarianism, and, after the Korean war, with the phenomenon of 'brainwashing', during which captured American soldiers had apparently been conditioned to act contrary to their own volition (Seed, 2004; Streatfield, 2006). In the late 1940s, the newly formed Central Intelligence Agency (CIA) initiated a covert, multi-million dollar research project to devise pharmacological, neurological and psychological ways of controlling human behaviour, channelling funds through private medical research foundations and universities (Moran, 1978). Some of the work (arguably an early political expression of techno-utopianism) had a high media profile (although its provenance in the CIA was not exposed until the 1970s), and there were occasional public debates about the ethics of 'mind control', which included references to brain implants. As early as 1956, *Time* magazine quoted electrical engineer Curtis R. Schafer of the Norden Ketay Corporation to the effect that implant-based 'electronics could take over the control of unruly humans' (quoted in Packard, 1957: 196). Such speculation reflected the burgeoning 'cybernetics' movement's emphasis on man–machine interaction, its early optimism about the prospects for automation and its implicit assumption (shared with behaviourists) that all human activities were potentially controllable (Weiner, 1948, 1950). Packard's (1957: 195) own widely read account of the nascent advertising and public relations industries speculated that *merely* psychological means of affecting public attitudes and behaviour might, by the year 2000, segue into 'biocontrol', which he described as a 'new science of controlling mental processes, emotional reactions and sense perceptions by bioelectrical signals'.

Jose Delgado (1915–2011), neuroscience professor at Yale University since 1950, was already working on the 'electrical stimulation of the brain' (ESB) in this period. He famously implanted 'stimoceivers' (electrodes capable of receiving and transmitting radio signals) in cats, monkeys and bulls (and also in some human beings – incarcerated schizophrenics and epileptics) and then showed how transmitted signals could dramatically affect their moods, emotions and behaviour. He also invented implantable 'chemitrodes' that could 'release precise amounts of drugs directly into specific areas of the brain' (Horgan, 2005: 68) and speculated that communication with the brain implants might one day be undertaken by computers rather than human operatives. Delgado mostly envisaged benign medical uses for his technology – he believed ESB superior to the 'barbarism' of lobotomy – but reducing criminal violence (conceived as a neuro-psychological problem) was encompassed within this medical framework. He disavowed the military implications of his work, despite it being funded by the Office of Naval Intelligence, which worked with the CIA on a variety of behaviour control research. His book, *Physical Control of the Mind: towards a psychocivilised society* (Delgado, 1969), received widespread press attention and, whilst not uncontroversial, brought him acclaim as the putative harbinger of a better, less violent world.

Delgado-like ideas about the uses of 'chemitrodes' and the computerised monitoring of personal implants, surfaced in the comments of one D.N. Michael before Congressional Hearings on the future of supervising parolees and mentally ill people in the community in 1966:

> It is not impossible to imagine that parolees will check in and be monitored by transmitters embedded in their flesh, reporting their whereabouts in code and automatically as they pass receiving stations (perhaps like fireboxes) systematically deployed over the country as part of one computer-monitored network. We may reach the point where it will be permissible to allow some emotionally ill people the freedom of the streets, providing they are effectively 'defused' through chemical agents. The task, then for the computer linked sensors would be to telemeter, not their emotional states, but simply the sufficiency of the concentration of the chemical agent to ensure an acceptable emotional state. . . . I am not prepared to speculate whether such a situation would increase or decrease the personal freedom of the emotionally ill person.
> (Michael, 1966: 187, quoted in Schwitzgebel, 1969: 601)

Twins Ralph K. and Robert L. Schwitzgebel (b. 1934) both began their careers in behavioural psychology at Harvard University in the 1950s. Ralph remained there, Robert moved to the Claremont Graduate School in California, and between them they laid the foundation of what later developed as 'electronic monitoring' (although in a punitive, house arrest form with which they never felt wholly comfortable) (Burrell, 2007; Gable and Gable, 2005, 2007).[3] Working within a largely Skinnerian framework, they were committed to rehabilitating offenders, and averse to using punishment. Using a belt-worn 'Behavior-Transmitter Reinforcer' and a 'modifed missile tracking device', they experimented with monitoring individual parolees from a base station in order to give them 'immediate reinforcement' for signs of positive behaviour (using two-way tonal communication), especially in terms of places visited and avoided. Throughout the 1960s they published in prestigious and popular journals (Schwitzgebel R.K., 1963, 1964, 1966, 1968, 1969, 1970, 1971; Schwitzgebel R.L., 1969a, 1969b; Schwitzgebel *et al.*, 1964; Schwitzgebel and Bird, 1970); their work became widely known, and was subject to searching but supportive commentary in the Harvard Law Review (1966). They saw the unobtrusive monitoring of an offender's location as a bonus, but the primary purpose of their technology was the remote reinforcement of positive behaviour. Delgado-like, Ralph Schwitzgebel had in fact once considered using intracranial implants, speculating that if sensors were fitted (on poles) in a designated targeted area, people's physical and neurological states could be monitored, but he realised that ESB was 'primarily . . . a laboratory research technique' and that 'its justification in clinical practice will require considerably more experimentation' (R.L. Schwitzgebel 1973: 17). Nonetheless, in a book that the brothers later edited – designating their and others' field of study as 'psychotechnology' – a chapter by Delgado on brain implants was still included.

In the January 1971 issue of *Transactions on Aerospace and Electronic Systems* (in an article accompanied by a note from the editors testifying to its controversial nature), mathematician and computer specialist Joseph A. Meyer (1971) proposed an elaborate tracking system for the USA's estimated twenty-five million offenders, based on a non-removable wrist-worn transponder and an environment saturated with millions of computer-linked sensors, some public, some privately owned, and some primed to sound an alarm if identifiable individuals or categories of offenders ventured too close. Meyer's emphasis was more akin to (what we now call) 'situational crime prevention' than the Schwitzgebels' behavioural therapy. Simple deterrence – increasing the risks of being caught and punished – was at the heart of his vision: he believed that the comprehensive surveillance of 'curfews and territorial restrictions' would 'make crime pointless' (Meyer, 1971: 2). He grasped that structural disadvantages would need to be ameliorated before deterred offenders would have opportunities to lead fulfilling lives, but he did believe that, meantime, technologically augmented policing alone would drastically reduce crime. He never patented the technology but his vision, as much as the Schwitzgebels', helped attune professional and commercial imaginations (Dobson, 1996) to the punitive and controlling potential of electronic tracking (see also Le Mond and Fry, 1975: 164).

A year after Meyer, criminologists Barton Ingraham and Gerald Smith (1972), at the universities of Maryland and Utah respectively, combined Delgado's and Schwitzgebel's thinking to advocate the insertion of radio receiver-transmitter implants into parolee's brains. This would enable real-time computer monitoring of location and physiological data – heart, pulse, brainwaves, etc., increased activity of which might signify engagement in, or preparation for, transgressive acts. This in turn, depending on how the computer appraised the probabilities, might elicit a disorienting electric shock to pre-empt – 'forget' or 'abandon' are the author's words – the imminent act. Available technology, the authors recognised, was not quite capable of doing this, but they believed that it was only a few years' worth of research and development away.

Constraint, compliance and control

A full understanding of the above developments requires us to delineate precise conceptual distinctions between 'constraint', 'control' and 'compliance'. 'Constraint' is here used as a generic term denoting the entire spectrum of means by which an individual's behaviour might be regulated. The compliance/control distinction reflects (and extends) Max Weber's distinction between power and authority (see Gerth and Mills, 1946). Power imposes submission on or *control over* its subjects; authority, by dint of its perceived legitimacy, elicits *compliance from* its subjects. Compliance in a law enforcement context is agentic, an exercise of volition on the part of the offender, a willing alignment of one's behaviour, however begrudging, with the prohibitions of a penal or civic authority. Non-compliance is always an option. The exercise of control, on the other hand, inhibits action and precludes defiance: it overrules agency rather than enlisting it. Control either presumes that agency is morally irrelevant, or undesirable, or (in the case of Skinnerian behaviourists) that it is a fiction, that all human behaviour is determined by the constant flux of contingent events, and that the only relevant ethical – and political – issue is to find the best way of shaping it.

Compliance, precisely because it is volitional, can be appraised morally, and judged praiseworthy or reprehensible depending on what or whom one aligns one's will to. Control permits no such judgement. A person who is blocked from performing a criminal action by a barred window, a locked door, an electronic checkpoint or (hypothetically) a remotely administered signal to his brain is not *choosing* to be law-abiding in the way that a person placed on probation, after weighing the options, chooses to accept (complies with) the requirements of supervision. Governed by determinist epistemologies, the psychotechnologists erred towards control rather than compliance, although Delgado's use of the term 'mind control' to describe his endeavours was not entirely apposite: 'mind' as such figured little in his calculations. His experiments were performed on brain matter and biochemical systems within the body, and are best characterised as 'organic' interventions. Skinner actually believed that a theory of *mind* ('mentalism', as he called it) was irrelevant to the scientific study and control of behaviour; operant conditioning, he claimed, worked to change behaviour by acting directly on the nervous system in people as well as animals and birds, without the necessity of self-awareness or conscious reflection. All that the psychotechnologists required of their subjects was informed consent, and even that, given their determinist epistemologies, was not always thought indispensable (Schrag, 1978: 180).

Psychotechnology can be understood as an innovative intellectual enclave straddling the border of behaviourism and neuroscience. It was ultimately liberal anxieties about the aspirations towards control in both these fields – the 'illiberal' assumptions underlying them, the dubious practices they spawned, the political dangers they represented – which weakened them in the early to mid-1970s, inevitably weakening psychotechnology as well. Behaviourism had never been fully hegemonic in the academy or in public policy networks, but it had been powerful, and significant individuals in a range of disciplines (including criminology) had come to believe that American society could indeed be redesigned for the better.[4] Humanistic philosophers and psychologists (Krutch, 1954), as well as science fiction writers evoking fears of depersonalisation, brainwashing and roboticisation, had challenged Skinnerian 'operant conditioning' in the 1950s, but it took the civil rights and student protest movements in the 1960s and 1970s, reaction in universities against military-funded research, evidence of the frightening ease with which 'obedience to authority' could be induced (Milgram, 1974) and the ascendancy of liberal-left professionals within the establishment to finally diminish the behaviourists' credibility. There was a certain irony in this for Skinner personally. *Walden Two* (Skinner, 1948), his utopian novel about a community conditioned into peaceable living, chimed well with the 1960s non-violent spirit and sold better then than at any time since publication. Nonetheless, when he restated the same determinist arguments as political philosophy in *Beyond Freedom and Dignity* (Skinner, 1971), explicitly dismissing cherished liberal ideals such as personal autonomy as irrelevant to the making of a better society, support among some erstwhile allies faltered. The harsher forms of behaviour modification – aversion therapy, sometimes using electric shocks (which strict Skinnerians did not support) – and psychiatric excesses more generally were confronted by newly confident legal, political and theoretical critiques. Not the least of these was journalist Jessica Mitford's (1973: 226) which denounced the proposals for electronic tracking put forward by Schwitzgebel, Meyer, and Ingraham and Smith, hinting darkly that government might one day use such technology on the whole population, not just on parolees (see also Sommer, 1976; Ackroyd *et al.*, 1977).

The Schwitgebels' work lost momentum because their equipment still had technical limitations and did not attract commercial sponsorship. Delgado's ESB project (and personal reputation) were tarnished when researchers at the Harvard Medical School suggested that ESB might be used on the 'violent' black people then rioting in America's inner cities (Vernon *et al.*, 1967; see also Mark and Ervin, 1970), and psychiatrist Robert Heath claimed that it should be used to 'cure' male homosexuality.[5] Other psychiatrists and neuroscientists challenged both the therapeutic claims and the ambivalent politics of ESM, some preferring lobotomy! Novelist Michael Crichton (1972), a former student of Frank Ervin's, excoriated Delgado's ideas in *The Terminal Man,* whose concerns echoed and updated those of Anthony Burgess's (1962) *A Clockwork Orange* (and Stanley Kubrick's 1971 film of it). *A Clockwork Orange,* and Ken Kesey's (1962) anti-psychiatry/anti-lobotomy novel *One Flew Over the Cuckoo's Nest* (and Miles Forman's 1975 film) have endured as lasting literary/cinematic legacies of this era: the former is still evoked to both signify and delegitimise the technological manipulation of offenders.

Ultimately, it was not the liberal left, or the counterculture, that finally displaced behaviourism and psychotechnology, but the overwhelming predeliction for punishment over treatment on the part of the New Right, whose influence grew from the mid-1970s on. Harvard Professor of Government James Q. Wilson was the 'criminological' doyen of this movement. His 1975 book *Thinking About Crime* tellingly made no mention of his Harvard contemporaries work on either 'operant conditioning' or 'psychotechnology', although its famous insistence that flawed human nature could not be changed was a thinly veiled rebuke to Skinnerians who had naively proclaimed its infinite plasticity. Critical criminology quickly challenged the New Right, but expressly did not see a return to the problematic theory and practice of behaviourism as a means of doing so. Some such criminologists even feared that the harsher forms of behaviour modification might yet be co-opted into the new punitivism: as late as 1978 Moran still imagined that 'a biomedical model of causality and a biotechnical program of control' (Moran, 1978: 354) could come into being (see also Schrag, 1978). Moran's fears were not entirely groundless, as the 1990s controversy over the use of Norplant (a time-delayed contraceptive implant) with 'welfare-dependent mothers' was later to show (Kapsalis, 1996).

Retributive (and incapacitative)[6] punishment, premised on the idea of a rational, volitional subject, became the norm, and it was in this new neoliberal milieu – in the context of a quest for more viable 'intermediate punishments' – that practical forms of EM were first devised and implemented. Outside criminal justice, advances in microelectronics and mobile information and communication technology had made possible hitherto unprecedented forms of location monitoring: computer salesman Michael Goss was the first to customise these new technologies to create monitoring technology for Judge Love in Albuquerque in 1982, first in his own company NIMCOS and later with BI. Interestingly, 'the largest proportion of the research time was spent in developing a strap that would report tampering but be secure and electronically functional in showers and baths etc' (Timko, 1986). An unremovable strap, of the kind envisaged by Meyer (1971: 13) – his wearable transponder would have been non-removable except by 'special tools, e.g. an abrasive grinding disc or an acetylene torch' – was not considered feasible, but an easily removed (or circumvented) strap would always limit the control potential of wearable devices.

Implants, identity verification and location monitoring

> Existing microminiaturised transmitters the size of a pinhead might be coded with identification data, enclosed in a permanent capsule, and implanted under the skin by a simple surgical operation. Once in place, this tag would do no damage to the body, but when interrogated electronically by an outside beam, it would emit an identifying number.
>
> (Westin, 1967: 86)

Radio frequency identification (RFID) technology, patented in the USA in 1973, uses radio waves to identify or track animate or inanimate objects via tiny chips (containing an integrated circuit for storing and processing alphanumeric information, and an antenna) fastened to or embedded in the object in question. Some emit signals, others require interrogation by an electronic reader. Chip size varies from postage stamp, through long grain-of-rice to dust-particle, while read-range varies from a few inches to several metres, although this can be boosted to facilitate remote location monitoring/telemetry. Initial uses for it were envisaged in mass transit systems, banking, security, hospitals and asset management – anywhere an individual or object, or large numbers thereof, 'needs' to have its identity read and tracked. Privacy and security concerns were raised from the outset: chips can be copied (facilitating identity theft) or wiped by readily available equipment, and how remediable these problems are remains a matter of argument.

To identify people, RFID chips can be carried (ID cards), worn (electronic tags/enmeshed in clothing) or (in principle) implanted. All three, but especially the latter two, can be used for 'somatic surveillance' (Monahan and Wall, 2007), the monitoring of 'lifesigns' and the potential control of bodily functions. They developed quickly in the US as means of tracking pets and livestock, and the idea of implanting chips in people was being mooted in the early 1990s, though technical means had to be found to stop the chip migrating around the body, and health anxieties assuaged. The Hughes aircraft company pioneered a 'syringe implantable transponder' and scanner system which could be used to facilitate staff access to secure areas of their factory (*The Washington Times*, 11 October 1993: 17).

The most ambitious – and unsuccessful – attempt to market an implanted chip involved the Digital Angel, patented in June 1997, and publicly unveiled in October 2000 by Florida-based Applied Digital Solutions Inc. (later called Digital Angel Corporation DIGA). It was portrayed as a genuine medical innovation, the first time a bio-sensor had been linked to web-enabled wireless communication via cell towers and GPS tracking systems. It could be activated remotely, or by the implantee themselves, and could read body temperatures, heartbeats, blood/oxygen levels, pulse rates, insulin levels, and also identify location – enabling medical aid to be dispatched quickly to, say, cardiac patients in the event of an emergency. In addition, it had battlefield uses, enabling commanders to know where soldiers were located, and whether they were alive, wounded or dead, and could also personalise the capacity to use a weapon, thereby increasing firearm safety. Other uses – varieties of asset management – were more conventional, but three specific criminal justice uses were proposed: first, locating people, including children, who had been kidnapped; second, monitoring offenders in the community; and third, monitoring people in witness protection programmes. The overall market was expected to exceed $70 billion, but in June 2001 the Digital Angel was withdrawn amidst rumours of poor performance. In 2008, the company 'divested the human chipping business' in favour of 'animal identification and emergency identification solutions' (personal communication, Joseph J. Grillo, CEO, DIGA, 24 March 2010).

VeriChip Corp was formed in 2001 as a subsidiary of DIGA, to market a somewhat simpler subdermal implant – the verichip – scannable but not remotely monitorable. The US Food and Drug Administration approved it for medical use in humans in October 2004, and the American Medical Association endorsed it in 2007, by which time it was being used experimentally as a form of identification for accessing medical records. This apparently ready acceptance of implants was probably eased by the post-9/11 security climate – in his subsequently notorious 'Privacy is dead. Get over it' speech, a month after the attack on New York, Scott McNealy, CEO of Sun Microsystems, openly anticipated the use of implant chips in new personal identification technologies (Hamblen, 2001: unpaginated). Verichip certainly envisaged the emergence of a law enforcement market for implants, and its CEO also suggested chipping illegal immigrants and guest workers. Tommy Thompson, who was secretary of Health and Human Services when FDA approval was given, subsequently joined Verichip's board, a type of career move also seen in the commercial corrections complex. Other companies arose to service the same market – for example, Microchip Biotechnologies (www.microchipbiotech.com – accessed 14 March 2008).

Monahan and Wall (2007) summarised what little was known about the extent of subdermal implants at their time of writing. Security company CityWatcher.com initially required operatives to be chipped to gain clearance for work on high-security projects but, after a 'media firestorm', ceased making it compulsory. Two hospitals have experimentally chipped volunteer patients with scannable medical records. Some Mexican legal officials were chipped to regulate access to secure offices, and 1,000 Mexican citizens, including children, have been chipped to offset the threat of kidnapping (even though the range over which a kidnap victim can be followed is limited). A Barcelona nightclub famously offered customers the option of an implanted 'credit card', scannable for payment, obviating the need to take cash to the club. Wearable RFID has been used to track some children in Japan, where schools have chipped students clothing, school bags and ID cards; the civil liberty implications of this seem scarcely less pertinent than if the chips had been implanted.

All of these uses are on people who have strong incentives not to sabotage the chips: many offenders may not be so motivated. In terms of tracking and tracing, implants have no obvious advantages over existing wearable EM technology, not least their limited battery power and geographical range compared to GPS, and while it is less easy for an offender to 'surgically' remove an implant than an ankle bracelet (though not impossible), it far easier to block the signal. In principle, it would now be possible to build something akin to Joseph Meyer's 'transponder surveillance system', using localised scanning systems – the existing inmate tracking systems are already microcosms of it – but in public space quite what the advantage of localised scanning systems using implant technology would be over GPS-based systems using wearable technology is unclear. It could presumably be used to restrict access (or exit) at checkpoints, which is a means of enforcing control rather than eliciting compliance. Ramesh (1997) has further suggested that just as chips could contain medical records, so they could also contain criminal records, scannable by prospective employees and police in routine stop and searches, which, whilst not an insignificant way of 'marking' an offender, is a pretty mundane use compared to what had been envisaged by, say, Ingraham and Smith.

In respect of electronically monitoring offenders, at least as currently practised, there are many things that RFID chips cannot do well – although that may reflect underinvestment in research and development rather than insurmountable technical limitations:

> they do not measure bodily functions, but augmentations are already in the works for them to detect body temperature, heart rate and other vital signs and then communicate that information to computer systems outside the body. As well, RFID implants do not currently allow for modulations of

body systems or human behaviour, such as the release of medication or electrical impulses, but these types of complementary medical devices do exist and are already being used to treat 'diseases' such as severe depression.

(Monahan and Wall 2007: 168)

Critical responses to implant tagging

Both Schwitzgebel (1971) and Ingraham and Smith (1972) argued that desirable technological advances in crime control might well be held back by archaic laws based on an unscientific, even pre-scientific, understanding of human behaviour. Most lawyers saw the law–science relationship the other way round. Over two decades ago, and with stimoceivers and the Schwitzgebel experiments in mind, legal academic Christopher Weeramantry (1983) characterised the law as a 'slumbering sentinel' in respect of technological advance. In respect of the uses to which contemporary implant technology might be put, anticipatory legislation is under consideration, and in some US jurisdictions already enacted. A number of broadly based human rights organisations are aware of developments in implant technology, and outside specific medical uses have largely sought to cast it as a violation of rights, which should be outlawed in advance. Even medical uses without informed consent – and sometimes even with – are suspect, because consent is not a form of 'moral magic' which makes the intrinsically unacceptable acceptable, especially when it is the powerless who are asked to consent. To convey the gravity of what they believe is at stake, opponents of chipping have evoked the well-known history of unethical medical experimentation – thalidomide babies, Willowbrook and Tuskegee – and invoked the Nuremberg Code itself as the ground on which chipping should be restricted.[7]

In the US, however, the provenance of this anti-chipping legislation is not always as straightforward as might be imagined. One of the more curious responses to subdermal implants in the US has come from evangelical Christian groups, who are interpreting the advent of chipping human beings as 'the mark of the beast' referred to in the Book of Revelation, an eschatological sign that the tyranny of the Antichrist is underway (Albrecht and McIntyre, 2006). Revelation 13:16–17 says 'He also forced everyone, small and great, to receive a mark on his right hand or on his forehead, so that no one could buy or sell unless he had the mark. Which is the name of the beast or the number of his name.' This is part of a wider Christian propaganda industry which markets modernised versions of apocalyptic thinking to converts and interested non-believers, in essence 'Christian science fiction', notably the *Left Behind* series of novels by right-wing Baptist pastor Tim LaHaye and Jerry B. Jenkins (2002, for example) and the (straight-to-DVD) film *Six: the mark unleashed* (dir. Kevin Downes, 2004) (O'Donnell, 2007). Not all conservative Baptists share this outlook but Monahan and Wall (2007: 166) suggest that it may be 'more of an impetus than privacy concerns for US legislation proscribing mandatory implants in employees, immigrants or others'.

Privacy activists Katherine Albrecht and Liz McIntyre (2005, 2006) have made both secular and Christian arguments against what they call 'spychips'. They founded CASPIAN (Consumers Against Supermarket Privacy Invasion and Numbering) in 1999 to campaign against retail surveillance (the use and tracking of RFID chips in consumer goods) and added the irresponsible use of RFID more generally (including implant chipping of people) to its mandate in 2002. In this latter regard, CASPIAN has developed a prototype 'Bodily Integrity Act' – arguing from a human dignity premise, with added data on health risks – and encouraged states to adopt it. The Act focuses on both implanted and wearable tracking devices, and specifically prohibits the chipping of under 18s, even with their guardians' consent. It further prohibits the chipping of corpses in morgues, and discrimination against people who refuse to be chipped. By 2008, California, Wisconsin and North Dakota had enacted such legislation, and Colorado, Ohio, Georgia, Oklahoma and Florida had it pending.

In Europe, the use of implant technology is taken seriously enough to have attracted the attention of the European Group on Ethics in Science and New Technology (EGE), a twelve member advisory group which advises the European Union on the ethical values that might be brought to bear on scientific and technological developments.[8] On 16 March 2005 the EGE adopted Opinion No. 20 on 'Ethical Aspects of ICT implants in the Human Body'. It accepts that implant technology is already in use, and that there will be momentum towards using it further. The Opinion covers information and communication technology (ICT) implants generally, not just RFID, and, like CASPIAN, grounds itself in a concern with human dignity, not just data protection. It distinguishes between the use of such implants for medical repair, health enhancement and behaviour control (especially of employees). Thus, cardiac pacemakers and brain implants to alleviate Parkinson's tremors are 'ethically unproblematic' as are 'ICT implants [which] enhance physical and mental characteristics' so long as they merely align children or adults who are in some way deficient with the normal range of the population, rather than creating super-humans. Nothing specific is said about the use of implants in criminal justice, but they explicitly oppose the use of implants becoming part of 'systems of untenable restriction and or even negation of basic rights'. In particular, 'the use of ICT implants in order to obtain remote control over the will of the people should be strictly prohibited'. Their insistence that implants should never be used where a 'less intrusive method' of achieving the same purpose can be found makes it unlikely that implants could *ever* be adopted as an electronic monitoring technology – visibility apart, wearable technology is by definition less intrusive, although as the EGE also recognise, it poses ethical problems of its own. They conclude:

> A broad social and political debate is needed as to what kind of applications should be accepted and legally approved, particularly concerning surveillance and enhancement. A precautionary approach is recommended by the EGE. The Member States and their national ethics councils have a

responsibility to create conditions for education and constructive, well informed debates in this area.

(EGE, 2005, unpaginated)

Conclusion

Between its inception in the intellectual enclave of psychotechnology and its subsequent actualisation in a broader political culture of neoliberalism (which formally accentuated notions of rational choice and personal responsibility), the assumed potential of electronic monitoring shifted from direct attempts at mental and behavioural control (however misconceived) to compliance with imposed regulations. Even as a means of eliciting compliance, however, EM was championed as more demanding, and more tightly calibrated than the softer, humanistic forms of gaining compliance traditionally required by community-based offender supervisors – the showing of trust in the context of a supportive professional relationship, the offering of incentives, even the issuing of threats and warnings (Nellis, 2009b). Wearable technology made possible degrees of real-time surveillance (all or part of the day), or at least approximations to it; it did not remove an offender's capacity for agency, but it made violations of imposed regulations more easily detectable. The techno-utopian dream of control that was inscribed in the earliest conceptions of EM remains latent in its contemporary manifestations, evidenced by occasional debates about the desirability of developing an unremovable strap, 'zapping' technologies (Nellis, 2010) and, to a lesser extent, implants.[9]

It is, however, improbable, in the foreseeable future – largely for technical reasons – that implant technology will become part of the electronic monitoring of offenders as that penal practice is currently configured, that is, in terms of an 'individuated monitoring package'. Unless they are required, Norplant-style, to affect bodily processes (as Michael Tonry imagines they might be), ICD implants currently have no practical advantages for offender location monitoring over wearable technology, which is already versatile and sophisticated, and becoming ever more so. The putative 'choice' between implants and wearables, however, is never *simply* a question of technical efficacy – their legitimacy, grounded in moral and (as importantly) emotional reactions to them, matters too. Implants can be construed as violations (or augmentations) of 'bodily integrity', thereby raising legitimacy issues that wearables do not – at least, not to the same degree. Even the merely subdermal implanting of RFID chips, let alone brain implants, creates deeper ethical anxieties than the issues of stigma and locational privacy raised by wearables. In a criminal justice (if not necessarily a medical) context, implants pose basic questions about the reach of state power, but above and beyond that they can be conjured into harbingers of 'cyborgisation' and 'posthumanity' which may have sinister (or enlivening) implications for us all (Gray, 1995; Kurzweil, 2005). The spectre of eugenically based politics is more easily mobilised in relation to implants, and while foreseeable future debates about legitimate interventions in medicine and criminal justice will remain anchored in questions about what it means to be 'moral', they may eventually be supplemented by harder questions about what it means to be 'human' (as, in respect of reproductive technologies and some forms of 'telehealth', and repeatedly in science fiction, they already have (see Chorost's (2005) account of how a computer-augmented hearing aid, implanted in his skull, altered his sense of self)).

If debate about implanting offenders occurs, it will take place against a background of socio-technical developments in body modification (for health or cosmetic reasons), general advances in biosocial criminology and the increasing surveillance of mobility (Geary, 2002; Rafter, 2008; Ross and Hilborn, 2008; Urry, 2007) – and, one hopes, the complex legitimacy issues to which each gives rise. Nicholas Rose (2000: 6) noted the emergence of 'a new biology of control' a decade ago, centred on experimental developments in molecular genetics, neurochemistry and neurobiology, and 'focused not on "crime" in general, but on violent, aggressive and antisocial behaviour', particularly sexual violence. He portrayed this not as a 'new eugenics', but more as a refinement of actuarial justice, the identification, treatment and control of individuals 'whose very [biological] make-up renders them dangerous to others' (ibid.: 21). Given the prevailing neoliberal milieu, and the notions of personal responsibility and moral culpability entrenched in Western judicial traditions, Rose did not anticipate the emergence of a new biological determinism in criminal justice: attempts to introduce it in court, for example, legal defences based on the chromosomal disposition to violence of the defendant, had largely failed. Future psychopharmacological interventions, he anticipated, would (like antabuse for alcoholism, and lithium for manic depression) actually enable subjects 'to build the capacities and competences necessary for them to monitor and control their own risk', (ibid.: 21). However, even if the writ of neoliberalism continues to run, it is not impossible, given commercial and political investment in 'the new biology of control' (including neuroscience), that intellectual enclaves and policy communities will emerge – perhaps military-related (Moreno, 2006) – in which brains/minds (especially those of offenders) are conceived of as amenable to rewiring and re-programming, and in which the *inhibition* of certain thoughts and actions takes precedence over the mere *prohibition* of activities (and its corollary, willed compliance). Neuroscience historian Stephen Mentor (2008: 21) has suggested 'that the rhetoric of social control and state interest in minding the minds of its citizens is a virus that, active or dormant, has haunted brain research from the start, as it has haunted the development of the state' – and is in play again.

Any actual experimental use of implants on offenders may well be a merely localised development – one county, one state, one clinic – outside mainstream criminal justice. It may also be a purely capricious development (based on faulty, or incomplete science and an opportunist conjunction of commercial and political interests) rather than a rational, evidence-based one, but capricious developments haunt the American criminal justice scene. Crude lobotomies, for example, harmed thousands of patients before the practice was delegitimised (Mentor, 2008). Lie detection technologies based on imperfectly understood brain imaging technologies are already in intermittent use (Greely and Illes, 2007). Even the reasonably widespread GPS tracking, given the absence of a tenable theoretical rationale for its use on released sex offenders, might itself be regarded as a capricious development (Button *et al.*, 2009) – and in that sense Michael Tonry's anxieties about the coming of implants are not groundless. Sex offenders, precisely because of the 'forms of abjection' that can 'legitimately' be visited on them in the name of punishment or treatment, would be likely targets for experiments with anti-libidinal implants (Spencer, 2009). Some offenders may even demand them, as some have demanded chemical castration in the past, in order to be free of 'urges' they believe they cannot control (Harrison, 2010).

Even if 'the new biology of (mind and behaviour) control' falters, or simply proceeds without recourse to implants, RFID tracking technology may develop for reasons entirely disconnected from concerns about 'pathological' aggression and violence, albeit still with implications for crime control. Wearable and portable transponders may well play a larger part in facilitating the future surveillance of mobility, facilitating 'checkpoint' access to public, private or personal spaces, mass transit systems, security zones, communication networks, as well as shaping and monitoring consumer behaviour (Jones, 2005, 2008). Cresswell (2010: 28) notes that 'a global network of RFID receivers placed in key mobility nodes such as airports, seaports, highways, distribution centres and warehouses' has already been predicted, 'all of which will be constantly reading, processing and evaluating people's behaviors and purchases'. Whether the emergent architecture of mobility monitoring will ever prompt the widespread use of implants, as depicted in the BBC's dystopian drama *The Last Enemy* (dir. Iain B. MacDonald, 2008) seems unlikely, but as Renzema (2009) has pointed out, any form of embedded environmental surveillance – 'uberveillance', as Clarke (2007) calls it – would by its very ubiquity reduce the need to single out offenders for 'individuated monitoring packages' of the kind that contemporary EM exemplifies – offenders will be trackable and traceable by the same means as ordinary citizens. We are, of course straying into the realms of science fiction here, but as this article has shown, much of what has come to pass in EM has been prefigured in science fiction, and it would surely be unwise to think we have reached the endpoint of its trajectory, whether implants are used or not.

References

Ackroyd, C., Margolis, K., Rosenhead, J. and Shallice, T. (1977) *The Technology of Political Control*. Harmondsworth: Penguin.

Albrecht, K. and McIntyre, L. (2005) *Spychips: how major corporations and governments plan to track your every move with RFID*. Nashville, TN: Nelson Current.

—— (2006) *The Spychips Threat: why Christians should resist RFID and electronic surveillance*. Nashville, TN: Nelson Current.

Ben-Tov, S. (1995) *The Artificial Paradise: science fiction and American reality*. Anne Arbour: University of Michigan Press.

Brand, R. (2005) *Synchronising Science and Technology with Human Behaviour*. London: Earthscan.

Brooks, D. (2002) *On Paradise Drive: How we live now (and always have) in the future tense.* New York: Simon and Schuster.

Burgess, A. (1962) *A Clockwork Orange.* Oxford: Heinemann.

Burrell, W. (2007) 'Editorial Introduction', *Perspectives: the Journal of the American Probation and Parole Association,* 31(1): 23.

Button, D.M., deMichelle, M. and Payne, B.K. (2009) 'Using electronic monitoring to supervise sex offenders: legislative patterns and implications for community corrections officers', *Criminal Justice Policy Review* Online first.

Chorost, M. (2005) *Rebuilt: how becoming part computer made me more human.* Boston: Houghton Mifflin Company.

Clarke, R. (1970) *Crime in America: observations on its nature, causes, prevention and control.* New York: Pocket Books.

—— (2007) 'What "uberveillance" is and what to do about it', in K. Michael and M.G. Michael (eds) *From Dataveillance to Uberveillance and the Realpolitik of the Transparent Society,* the second workshop on the social implications of national security. University of Wollongong, Australia. Research Network Secure Australia.

Cresswell, T. (2010) 'Towards a politics of mobility', *Environment and Planning D: Space and Society,* 28: 17–31.

Crichton, M. (1972) *The Terminal Man.* London: Jonathan Cape.

Delgado, J.M.R. (1969) *Physical Control of the Mind: Towards a psychocivilised society.* New York: Harper and Row.

Dinello, D. (2004) *Technophobia: Science Fiction Visions of Posthuman Technology.* Austin: University of Texas Press.

Dobson, D. (1996) 'Reality today was fantasy yesterday', *IEEE Aerospace and Electronic Systems,* 11(7): 1–4.

European Group on Ethics and Science in New Technologies (2005) *Ethical Aspects of ICT Implants in the Human Body.* Opinion No 20 presented to the European Commission.

Gable, R.K. and Gable, R.S. (2005) 'Electronic monitoring: positive intervention strategies', *Federal Probation,* 69(1), www.uscourts.gov/fedprob.

—— (2007) 'Increasing the effectiveness of electronic monitoring', *Perspectives: the Journal of the American Probation and Parole Association,* 31(1): 24–9.

Geary, J. (2002) *The Body Electric: an anatomy of the new bionic senses.* London: Phoenix.

Gerth, H. and Mills, C.W. (1946) *From Max Weber. Essays in Sociology.* New York: Oxford University Press.

Gray, C.H. (ed.) (1995) *The Cyborg Handbook.* London: Routledge.

Greely, H.T. and Illes, J. (2007) 'Neuroscience-based lie detection: the urgent need for regulation', *American Journal of Law and Medicine,* 33: 377–431.

Hamblen, M. (2001) *McNealy calls for smart cards to help security.* www.computerworld.com.

Harrison, K. (2010) 'The use of pharmacotherapy with high risk sex offenders', in K. Harrison (ed.) *Managing High Risk Sex Offenders in The Community: risk management, treatment and social responsibility.* Cullompton: Willan, pp. 105–32.

Harvard Law Review (1966) 'Notes: Anthropotelemetry – Dr Schwitzgebel's machine', *Harvard Law Review,* 80: 403–18.

Horgan, J. (2005) *The Forgotten Era of Brain Chips.* Scientific American at www.sciam.com, 66–73.

House, D. (2009) 'Shadow tagging systems'. Paper presented at the Conference Permanente Europeene de la Probation conference New Developments in Electronic Monitoring: media, myths and managing expectations, 7–9 May.

Hucklesby, A. (2009) 'understanding offender's compliance: a case study of electronically monitored curfew orders', *Journal of Law and Society,* 36(2): 248–71.

Ingraham, B.L. and Smith, G.S. (1972) 'The use of electronics in the observation and control of human behaviour and its possible use in rehabilitation and parole', *Issues in Criminology*, 7(2).

Jones, R. (2005) 'Surveillance', in C. Hale, K. Hayward, A. Wahidin and E. Wincup (eds) *Criminology*. Oxford: Oxford University Press.

—— (2008) 'Checkpoint security: gateways, airports and the architecture of security', in K.F. Aas, H.O. Grundus and H.M. Lomell (eds) *Technologies of Insecurity: the surveillance of everyday life*. London: Routledge, pp. 81–102.

Kapsalis, T. (1996) 'Norplant 2, the next generation: contraceptive technology and science fiction', *New Formations: a journal of culture/theory/politics*, special issue on Technoscience, 29: 46–58.

Kesey, K. (1962) *One Flew Over the Cuckoo's Nest*. New York: The Viking Press.

Krutch, J.W. (1954) *The Measure of Man: on freedom, human values, survival and the modern temper:* New York: Grosset and Dunlap.

Kurzweil, R. (2005) *The Singularity is Near: when humans transcend biology*. London: Duckworth.

LaHaye, T. and Jenkins, J.B. (2002) *The Remnant: on the brink of Armageddon*. Carol Stream, IL: Tyndale House Publishing.

Le Mond, A. and Fry, R. (1975) *No Place to Hide: a guide bugs, wire taps, surveillance and privacy invasions*. New York: St Martins Press.

Lilly, J.R. (1992) 'Selling justice: electronic monitoring and the security industry', *Justice Quarterly*, 9: 493–503.

Mark, V.H. and Ervin, F.R. (1970) *Violence and the Brain*. New York: Harper and Row.

Mentor, S. (2008) 'The machinery of consciousness: a cautionary tale', *Anthropology of Consciousness*, 18(1): 20–50.

Meyer, J.A. (1971) 'Crime deterrent transponder system', *Transactions on Aerospace and Electronic Systems*, vol. AES-7(1): 1–22.

Michael, D.N. (1966) 'Speculations on the relation of the computer to individual freedom and the right to privacy. The computer and invasion of privacy' – hearings before a Subcommittee on Government Operations. 89th Congress, 184–93, July 16–28 1966.

Milgram, S. (1974) *Obedience to Authority: an experimental view*. New York: Harper and Row.

Miller, J.G. (1991) *The Last One Over the Wall: the Massachusetts experiment in closing reform Schools*. Ohio: Ohio University Press.

Mitford, J. (1973) *Kind and Unusual Punishment: the prison business*. New York: Knopf (published in England under the title *The American Prison Business* (1974) London: George Allen and Unwin).

Monahan, T. and Wall, T. (2007) 'Somatic surveillance: corporeal control through information networks', *Surveillance and Society*, 4(3): 154–73.

Moran, R. (1978) 'Biomedical research and the politics of crime control: a historical perspective', *Contemporary Crises*, 2: 335–57.

Moreno, J.D. (2001) *Undue Risk: secret state experiments on humans*. London: Routledge.

—— (2006) *Mind Wars: Brain Research and National Defence*. Chicago: University of Chicago Press.

Nathan, S. (2003) 'Private prisons: emerging and transformative economies', in A. Coyle, A. Campbell and R. Neufeld (eds) *Capitalist Punishment. Prison privatization and human rights*. London: Zed Books, pp. 189–201.

Nellis, M. (2004) 'Electronic monitoring and community supervision of offenders', in A.E. Bottoms, S. Rex and G. Robinson (eds) *Alternatives to Prison: options for an insecure society*. Cullompton: Willan, pp. 224–47.

—— (2006) 'Surveillance, rehabilitation and electronic monitoring: getting the issues clear', *Criminology and Public Policy*, 5(1): 401–7.

—— (2009a) 'Electronically monitoring offenders and penal innovation in a telematic society', in P. Knepper, J. Doak and J. Shapland (eds) *Urban Crime Prevention, Surveillance and Restorative Justice: effects of social technologies*. Boca Raton: CRC Press/Taylor and Francis, pp. 101–22.

—— (2009b) 'Surveillance and confinement: explaining and understanding the experience of electronically monitored curfews', *European Journal of Probation*, 1(1): 41–65.

—— (2010) 'Eternal vigilance inc.: satellite tracking of offenders in real-time', *Journal of Technology and Human Services*, 28(1–2): 23–43.

O'Donnell, M. (2007) 'Something smart going on: the apocalyptic aesthetics of surveillance', in K. Michael and M.G. Michael (eds) *From Dataveillance to Uberveillance and the Realpolitik of the Transparent Society:* the second workshop on the social implications of national security. University of Wollongong, Australia. Research Network Secure Australia.

Packard, V. (1957) *The Hidden Persuaders*. New York: Pocket Books.

Rafter, N. (2008) *The Criminal Brain: understanding biological theories of crime*. New York: New York University Press.

Ramesh, E.M. (1997) 'Time Enough? consequences of implant microchip implantation'. www.piercelaw.edu/risk/vol8/fall/ramesh.htm (accessed March 2010).

Renzema, M. (2009) 'Rationalising the use of electronic monitoring', *Journal of Offender Monitoring*, 22(1): 12–15.

Rose, N. (2000) 'The biology of culpability: pathological identity and crime control in a biological culture', *Theoretical Criminology*, 4(1): 5–34.

Ross, R. and Hilborn, J. (2008) *Rehabilitating Rehabilitation: neurocriminology for the treatment of anti-social behaviour*. Ottawa: Cognitive Centre of Canada.

Schrag, P. (1978) *Mind Control*. New York: Dell Publishing.

Schwitzgebel, R.K. (1963) 'Delinquents with tape recorders', *New Society*, 31 January.

—— (1964) *Streetcorner Research: an experimental approach to the juvenile delinquent*. Cambridge, MA: Harvard University Press.

—— (1966) 'Electronic Innovation in the Behavioural Sciences: a call to responsibility', *American Psychologist*, 22(5): 364–70.

—— (1968) 'Electronic alternatives to imprisonment', *Lex et Scientia*, 5: 99–104.

—— (1969) 'Issues in the use of an electronic rehabilitation system with chronic recidivists', *Law and Society Review*, 3(4): 597–611.

—— (1970) 'Behavioural electronics could empty the worlds prisons', *The Fururist*, April, 59–60.

—— (1971) *Development and Legal Regulation of Coercive Behavior Modification Techniques with Offenders*. Rockville, MD: National Institute of Mental Health.

Schwitzgebel, R.K., Schwitzgebel, R.L., Panke, W.N. and Hurd, W.S. (1964) 'A programme of research in behavioural electronics', *Behavioral Science*, 9: 233–8.

Schwitzgebel, R.L. (1969a) 'A belt from big brother', *Psychology Today*, 2(11): 45–7.

—— (1969b) 'A remote instrumentation system for behavior modification', in C. Franks and R.D. Rubin (eds) *Advances in Behaviour Therapy*. New York: Academic Books, pp. 181–203.

—— (1973) 'Emotions and machines: a commentary on the context and strategy psychotechnology', in R.L. Schwitzgebel and R.K. Schwitzgebel (eds) *Psychotechnology: electronic control of mind and behaviour*. New York: Holt, Rheinhart and Wilson, pp. 1–33.

Schwitzgebel, R.L. and Bird, R.M. (1970) 'Sociotechnical design factors in remote instrumentation with humans in natural environments', *Behaviour Research Methods and Instrumentation*, 2: 212–31.

Schwitzgebel, R.L. and Schwitzgebel, R.K. (eds) (1973) *Psychotechnology: electronic control of mind and behavior*. New York: Holt, Rheinhart and Wilson.

Seed, D. (1999) *American Science Fiction and the Cold War: literature and film*. Edinburgh: Edinburgh University Press.

—— (2004) *Brainwashing: the fictions of mind control*. London: The Kent State University Press.

Skinner, B.F. (1948) *Walden Two*. New York: Macmillan.

—— (1971) *Beyond Freedom and Dignity*. London: Jonathan Cape.

Sommer, R. (1976) *The End of Imprisonment*. New York: Oxford University Press.

Spencer, D. (2009) 'Sex Offender as Homo Sacer', *Punishment and Society*, 11(2): 219–40.

Spufford, F. and Uglow, J. (1996) *Cultural Babbage: Technology, Time and Invention*. London: Faber.

Streatfield, D. (2006) *Brainwash: the secret history of mind control*. London: Hodder and Stoughton.

Timko, F. (1986) 'Electronic Monitoring – How it all began: conversations with Love and Goss', *Journal of Probation and Parole*, 17: 2–16.

Tonry, M. (ed.) (2003) *The Future of Imprisonment*. Oxford: Oxford University Press.

Urry J. (2007) *Mobilities*. Cambridge: Polity Press.

Vernon, M.H., Sweet, H.W. and Ervin, F.R. (1967) 'Role of brain disease in urban riots and violence', *Journal of the American Medical Association*, 201(11) September.

Virilio P. (1997) *Open Sky*. London: Verso.

Walsh, A. (2002) *Biosocial Criminology*. Cincinnati, OH: Andersen.

Weeramantry, C.G. (1983) *The Slumbering Sentinels: law and human rights in the wake of technology*. Harmondsworth: Penguin.

Weiner, N. (1948) *Cybernetics: or control and communication in the animal and the machine*. Cambridge, MA: MIT Press.

—— (1950) *The Human Use of Human Beings: cybernetics and society*. Boston: Houghton Miflin.

Westin, A. (1967) *Privacy and Freedom*. New York: Atheneum.

Wheeler, H. (ed.) (1973) *Beyond the Punitive Society: a critique of B F Skinner's 'Beyond Freedom and Dignity'*. London: Wildwood House.

Whitman, J.Q. (2003) *Harsh Justice: criminal punishment and the widening divide between American and Europe*. Oxford: Oxford University Press.

Wilson, J.Q. (1975) *Thinking about Crime*. New York: Basic Books.

Winkler, M. (1991) 'Walking prisons: the developing technology of electronic controls', *The Futurist*, July–August: 34–6.

Notes

1   I am indebted to Richard Jones, Marc Renzema, Raymond Bell, Adrian Beck, Bob Lilly and Jason Ditton for various sorts of help with this chapter.

2   A range of post-war American cultural and literary studies attest to the idea that the USA, more so than Europe, has been particularly prone to believing that technology could and should contribute to the creation of a modern utopia, albeit one once tinged with Puritan values (Ben-Tov, 1995; Spufford and Uglow, 1996; Brooks, 2002). Much post-war thinking in futurology, science fiction – and psychotechnology – gave expression to this embedded utopian sensibility, although in science fiction the extrapolations were as often dystopian as utopian. The extent to which EM technologies were prefigured in American science fiction has been recognised, but remains underexplored, although Seed (1999, 2004) makes a good start.

3   Ralph and Robert Schwitzgebel changed their surname to Gable in 1982, and subsequently published under that latter name. Although, like other psychotechnologists, they

were naive in not fully recognising the political dangers inherent in their work, they were ahead of their time in realising that technology would have to be reckoned with in the crime control field, and their writings are immensely insightful and erudite.

4 There is an irony here, because some commentators had seen in operant conditioning the prospect of going 'beyond the punitive society' (Wheeler, 1973). Renowned criminologist Donald Cressey, for example, a convert to Skinnerism, had once said 'I dream of writing a criminal code for the US . . . that doesn't have any punishment in it . . . Skinner has provided the frame' (quoted in Miller, 1991: 247). Former attorney general Ramsay Clarke (1970: 245) took seriously the view that 'behavioral scientists can tell us how to condition violence from our personal capacity'.

5 Delgado left Yale for a prestigious academic post in Madrid in 1974, switching his interest to less invasive means of influencing the brain, including electromagnetism. At the time of writing, Delgado is looked back upon as an important pioneer in neuroscientific research (Horgan, 2005).

6 Incapacitation as a rationale for incarceration can – like the term 'incorrigible' – encompass both volitional and determinist understandings of offender behaviour. Preventive detention, a precursor of incapacitation, was often justified by reference to pathological behaviour over which offenders had no control but – as in the rhetoric surrounding contemporary American supermax prisons – prolonged custodial sentences can just as easily be used to contain those deemed wilfully evil.

7 Thalidomide was marketed as a sedative drug in 1957, but without being properly tested: it caused severe deformities in the babies of expectant mothers to whom it was prescribed. In the Tuskegee (Alabama) syphillis study, the US Public Health Department studied the progress of the deliberately untreated disease in 400 poor Black people; it was exposed in 1972, after forty years. The Willowbrook scandal involved a hospital for mentally retarded children in New York where, between 1963 and 1966, doctors intentionally inoculated some of them with the hepatitis virus in order to study its effects (see Moreno, 2001). The Nuremburg Code was devised at the end of World War II to ensure that the kinds of medical experiments performed on prisoners by the Nazis would never occur again, and set rigorous standards of informed consent for all subsequent medical research.

8 The European Group on Ethics and Science in New Technologies (2005) is an 'independent, multidisciplinary and pluralist advisory group', with twelve members (biology, genetics, medicine, philosophy, theology, information sciences, law), chaired by Swedish philosopher Goran Hermeren.

9 The trope of remotely preventing a monitored offender from doing something aggressive, by remotely 'zapping' him or her with some kind of electrical impulse to the brain, found in Delgado (1969) and Ingraham and Smith (1972) resurfaced in somewhat cruder form in the second wave of debate about offending tracking in the USA. Colorado probation officer Max Winkler (1991) suggested that offenders who strayed into designated exclusion zones should be temporarily incapacitated, taser-like, by an electric shock administered through their ankle bracelet. Such technology was never developed in the USA, but a South African company went as far as to make satellite tracking equipment which could do this, although it has never been used there either (House, 2009).

9

'STICKS AND CARROTS . . . AND SERMONS'

Some thoughts on compliance and legitimacy in the regulation of youth anti-social behaviour

Adam Crawford

This chapter explores some of the issues of legitimacy and compliance at the peripheries of criminal justice in the context of anti-social behaviour related interventions. Governmental concerns regarding 'anti-social behaviour', incivility and disorder have become a major political preoccupation in the last decade or so. Whilst this has found expression in various Western societies (van Swaaningen, 2008; Levi, 2009; Beckett and Herbert, 2010), nowhere has this been more evident than in the UK, England in particular,[1] where it has provided the fertile terrain out of which considerable regulatory innovations have spawned. Above all else, the British anti-social behaviour agenda and many of the new powers to which it has given rise are targeted at, and concerned with, the question of governing 'troublesome youth'. The panoply of new laws, powers and technologies has been considerable. Novel regulatory tools include, inter alia, anti-social behaviour orders (ASBO), housing injunctions, acceptable behaviour contracts, parenting orders, parenting contracts, tenancy demotion orders, 'crack-house' and premise closure orders, designated public places orders, dispersal orders, (alcohol-related) directions to leave an area, as well as a variety of penalty notices for disorder.

In this chapter, it will be argued that such novel technologies of control fashioned in the name of regulating anti-social behaviour present acute legitimacy challenges and embody mixed assumptions about behavioural motivation and agency with significant implications for compliance, especially for young people. They do so, not only because they straddle and blur distinctions between criminal and civil legal processes, as well as fuse informal and formal interventions, but also because they constitute a cluster of civil preventative orders, prohibitions and conditional support interventions whereby non-compliance is rendered an offence and thus punishable. Failure to fulfil the terms of an initial order, 'contract' or 'agreement' provides the grounds for subsequent criminalisation. Hence, many of these tools constitute, what Simester and von Hirsch (2006) have termed, 'two-step prohibitions'. These are civil orders backed up by criminal penalties, whereby the possibility of criminal sanctions arises in respect of future conduct, not in relation to the initial conduct that gave rise to the order in the first place.[2] Significantly, the behaviour that breaches the conditions or agreed terms may under all other circumstances constitute permissible legal activities.[3] Prohibitions often include terms relating to non-association – not to meet with named individuals or be in groups in public – exclusion from designated places, not participating in certain activities and/or 'catch-all' requirements not to engage in future (often undefined) 'anti-social behaviour'. Such conditions, imposed at the first step, thus create something tantamount to what the European Commissioner for Human Rights, Gil-Robles described (in relation to ASBOs) as 'personalised penal codes, where noncriminal behaviour becomes criminal for individuals who have incurred the wrath of the community' (2005: 34). Allied regulatory innovations include a growing range of police powers to direct individuals or groups to leave specified areas, breach of which is grounds for an offence,[4] and an array of quasi-voluntary agreements and contracts where the take-up of forms of 'support' or counselling, potentially alongside prohibitions, is conditional and non-criminal sanctions are attached to the failure to comply.[5] What these have in common is that they deploy conditionality to influence behaviour and, in some instances, the conditions are a prerequisite for accessing certain benefits of citizenship, notably access to welfare provisions and services (White, 2003). Here, crime control is enmeshed with wider social, family, housing and urban policy goals; blurring and (con)fusing what were hitherto more distinct policy domains with their own regimes of social regulation and levers of control.

The legal definition of anti-social behaviour, as behaviour that 'causes or is likely to cause harassment, alarm or distress',[6] introduces the perceptions of others as central criteria. It reflects a future-regarding, preventative orientation, whereby early intervention is triggered in order to forestall the (possible or potential) escalation of 'problematic' behaviour. In this, the new powers illustrate a broader trend in crime control that fosters precaution, prevention and pre-emption through more intensive, more extensive and earlier interventions (Crawford, 2010). Here, a precautionary approach to prevention implies a governmental responsibility to intervene and protect the public and wider community from exposure to harm where knowledge about the probability of future harmful acts (if there is no intervention) is uncertain, insufficient or inconclusive but where there are indications of possible adverse effects or plausible risks. As a result, precaution refigures the burden of proof and the grounds for falsification, to the extent that protections are deemed appropriate to be relaxed only if further evidence emerges that supports an alternative explanation. Such a precautionary approach has increasingly leaked into other fields of public policy where the scientific evidence is contested or uncertain; for example, the regulation of illegal drug use (Nutt, 2009). It implies circumstances in which there are reasonable grounds for concern that an activity is causing, or could cause, harm but where there is uncertainty about the probability of the risk and the degree of harm. Here, the precautionary logic of early intervention is justified in consequentialist (communitarian) terms – so as to 'nip it in the bud' or in response to the question 'what if?' Such governmental thinking is informed frequently by fear of potentially catastrophic outcomes or 'worst-case scenarios' (Sunstein, 2007).

As forms of pre-emptive governance, these new modes of regulation have significant implications for traditional criminal justice values and civil liberties – notably they raise questions for the presumption of innocence, the evidentiary burden of proof, due process protections and principles of proportionality. More generally, they provoke a radical re-thinking of the legitimate grounds for early interventions and the appropriate boundaries between civil and criminal procedures and responses. Should the state intervene only on the basis of known past incidents or probable grounds to suspect future misbehaviour and an identified threshold of seriousness? Is intervention justifiable by reference to future risks, likely or possible eventualities, or uncertain outcomes? What are the limits that ought to constrain both the preventive scope of legal interventions and the use of civil procedures and remedies for crime control purposes? Hence, to what extent are these hybrid powers legitimate?

Legitimacy

With regard to the latter question, all modes of intervention by which governmental authorities seek to change behaviour whether by compulsion, command, influence, inducement or architecture, raise questions about their legitimacy. Following Beetham, we can understand legitimacy in terms of the extent to which new powers 'conform to established rules'; the 'rules can be justified by reference to beliefs shared by both dominant and subordinate'; and 'there is evidence of consent by the subordinate to the particular power relations' (1991: 16). In relation to the first dimension of legitimacy, there have been significant debates about the extent to which specific new regulatory powers may contravene 'established legal rules', most notably human rights protections via the European Convention on Human Rights (ECHR) (Ashworth, 2004; Bakalis, 2007).[7] This has been reflected in the various legal challenges to specific powers, including the ASBO. Notable was the House of Lords' judgement in the case of *McCann and others* ([2003] 1 AC 787), where it held that, contrary to the initial intentions of the government, whilst the proceedings were indeed civil in nature, both domestically and for the purposes of the ECHR, a higher standard of proof than the 'balance of probabilities' should apply given the severity of the allegations and possible sanctions.[8] There was also the damning judgement in the case of *AF and other* ([2009] UKHL 28) in relation to the counter-terrorism 'control order' (introduced by the Prevention of Terrorism Act 2005), an analogous civil preventive order, in large part modelled on the ASBO (Macdonald, 2007). There have be allied challenges to the dispersal order – where the authorisation process has been deemed by the courts as pivotal in legitimising the extensive powers available to the police in designated dispersal zones (*Sierny v. Director of Public Prosecutions* [2006] EWHC 716). Moreover, searching questions have been raised about the compatibility of 'acceptable behaviour contracts' (ABCs) with Article 6 of the ECHR (see Cosgrove and Cosgrove, 2011).

In many senses, the new powers were designed, elaborated and embraced precisely because they afford speedier and more flexible solutions that are unencumbered by the rigours of civil liberties protections associated with traditional criminal justice principles. Many anti-social behaviour powers, thus, conform with (and confirm) Ericson's depiction of 'counter-law', whereby: 'New laws are enacted and new uses of existing law are invented to erode or eliminate traditional principles, standards, and procedures of criminal law that get in the way of pre-empting imagined sources of harm' (2007: 27). This latent rationale was explicitly recognised by senior New Labour politicians whilst in office. Tony Blair, for example, in a speech in September 2005 acknowledged: '[T]he whole purpose of the antisocial behaviour legislation is to change the terms of trade if you like, change the rules of the game, make sure that when we need to act quickly, we are able to act quickly' (cited in Crawford, 2009a: 810). In interview, Charles Clarke (the Home Secretary from 2004 to 2006) made this point in slightly more colloquial language:

> the truth is, the reason for a lot of these things [new powers] . . . is a lack of confidence in the court procedure. So, the problem was that going through the regular court procedures . . . was actually happening seven or eight months later. So there was actually no impact, the court system was having zero impact on the actual social conditions which it was supposed to regulate. And that was a reinforcing model, so people gave up referring things to the courts, the police themselves gave up, everyone said 'well fuck there's nothing we can do, so just let it go' . . . But [now] the courts can solve this by taking their decisions quickly. But actually, as you know, the legalistic crap that goes on from all kinds of people just to stop a proper decision being taken, means that we felt, and I feel very strongly, that we have to take decisive action to show communities that this is going to be addressed.
>
> (Personal interview, 2 November 2006)

This was reflected in the New Labour government's call to 'rebalance criminal justice in favour of the law-abiding majority' (Home Office, 2006), in the sense of shifting the emphasis away from a rights-based discourse to one that emphasises social responsibilities and conditionality. David Blunkett, Charles Clarke's predecessor as Home Secretary (2001–04), encapsulated this ethos in his call for a 'something for something society' in his introduction to the *Respect and Responsibility* White Paper (Home Office, 2003: 3) which preceded the Anti-Social Behaviour Act 2003. In interview, he located the perceived need for novel regulatory tools in the collapse of informal community controls, as well as failings in the criminal justice system:

There was a response to that which said; 'well hang on, is there a step in between doing nothing?' which a lot of the policing and local government services were doing, literally nothing, but just letting things rip. Albeit a civil order that actually has quite substantial consequences and can in the breach, then become part of criminal law and you can be sent to jail . . . ASBOs were supposed to be something other than straight into the criminal law. Although actually I think they were seen as a fast-track to being able to do something . . . I think the perceived problem was that the norm was the checks and balances, the positive pressures of society, were breaking down. Families were becoming less stable, communities were becoming less functional . . . As that broke down, all of that went and the criminal law couldn't possibly cope with it. Policing services were unable to cope with it.

(Personal interview, 12 January 2007)

From this perspective, rather than being part of the solution, criminal justice is conceived as part of the problem. In this vein, Blair (2006) concluded:

it is the culture of political and legal decision-making that has to change, to take account of the way the world has changed . . . It is a complete change of mindset, an avowed, articulated determination to make protection of the law-abiding public the priority and to measure that not by the theory of the textbook but by the reality of the street and community in which real people live real lives.

In seeking new modes of regulation that responded to a perceived desire to do, and to be seen to be doing, something about low-level but cumulative uncivil behaviour, the new hybrid tools represented a direct challenge to, and assault upon, traditional conceptions of criminal justice, undermining established legal principles of due process, proportionality and special protections afforded to young people. For instance, given the capacious definition of 'anti-social behaviour' and the wide-ranging nature of the grounds that may trigger an ASBO, ABC, parenting or dispersal order, it is not clear that the application of the law is entirely know-able in advance. As commentators have noted, in many senses the new 'anti-social behaviour' powers affront the 'principle of maximum certainty' and the require-ments of 'predictability' and 'fair warning' (Ashworth, 2006: 74). The lack of 'fair warning' evident in much anti-social behaviour legislation may mean: 'it is ultimately impossible to be sure that you have acted cautiously enough in the face of the uncertainties involved and that the problem of insecurity is therefore created by the law rather than solved by it' (Ramsay, 2009: 135–6). This undoubtedly offends certain jurisprudential principles regarding the nature and scope of legitimate criminal laws and effective legal constraint on the operation of the state's power to punish. In Ericson's terms, 'vagueness is precisely the feature that is crucial to the success of anti-social behaviour legislation as counter-law' (2007: 167). As Ashworth warns, 'there comes a point when the legislative devices being used or proposed are so disrespectful of fundamental principles that questions have to be asked about their legitimacy in a country committed to the protection of human rights' (2004: 265).

Whether or not the new anti-social behaviour tools conform to Beetham's other dimensions of legitimacy is also questionable. Certainly, the high breach rates of ASBOs – over two-thirds (68 per cent) in the case of juveniles – raises questions about their effectiveness and the extent to which those 'subordinate groups' consent to the particular power relations established by them. The empirical evidence into the use and impact of ASBOs suggests that those subject to them often see them as ineffective and in some instances illegitimate, notably in the breach of the conditions attached to them (Youth Justice Board, 2006; Matthews *et al.*, 2007; Wain and Burney, 2007). The benefits of ASBOs are more unambiguously political and derive 'not in any real hope that it alone will change an individual's behaviour, but by virtue of the tariff leaping custodial sanction that breach of the order can bring' (Squires, 2006: 12) and in its capacity (in parallel with other powers) to send a signal that something is being done by those in authority in response to local anxieties about neighbourhood decline (Crawford, 2008).

In the face of these and allied objections, in February 2011, the Coalition government announced proposals to abolish the ASBO (Home Office, 2011). However, it intends to replace this with two new powers – the Criminal Behaviour Order and the Crime Prevention Injunction (the former is a criminal and the latter a civil power). Both share many similarities with variants of the ASBO (in its civil and criminal guises). The proposed new Crime Prevention Injunction is intended to 'bring together restrictions on future behaviour and support to address underlying problems . . . that can quickly stop anti-social behaviour before it escalates' (Home Office, 2011: 5), echoing its pre-emptive logic. In many senses, the new orders represent little more than a 'rebranding' of the pre-existing tools rather than a change in principle, purpose or substance. Elsewhere in the same consultation paper the government also spelt out its plans to extend and 'normalise' the erstwhile 'exceptional' dispersal order powers and further promote the use of ABCs.

More generally, early intervention with young people and families has secured a prominent place in the current government's agenda (Allen and Duncan Smith, 2009; Field 2010). In support of this, an influential government-commissioned report championed an 'early intervention culture' and 'proper co-ordination of the machinery of government to put Early Intervention at the heart of departmental strategies, including those seeking to . . . reduce crime' (Allen, 2011: xviii). In common with the legacy of anti-social behaviour interventions, scant regard has been afforded to the ethical problems and legal issues raised by early intervention programmes with young people. Furthermore, insufficient recognition has been given to the statistical barriers and uncertain scientific evidence of effectiveness that suggest substantial flows *out of* as well as *in to* the pool of children who develop chronic conduct problems (Utting, 2004). By contrast, Gatti highlights the right of children not to be classified as future delinquents, whether they go on to become delinquents or not, as presenting 'one of the greatest ethical problems raised by early prevention programmes' (1998: 120). The history of youth crime prevention reminds us that well-intentioned programmes can cause problems rather than resolve or ameliorate them.[9]

Evaluating effectiveness or counting numbers?

Yet, hitherto, little attention has been accorded to the effectiveness of anti-social behaviour powers and their capacity to induce behavioural compliance per se. Under the New Labour administration, government energies were largely restricted to extolling the virtues of interventions and encouraging their greater use – via the institutions of the central Anti-Social Behaviour Unit and subsequent Respect Taskforce – with little reference to any robust evidence base.[10] Monitoring implementation and impact was largely restricted to measuring, counting and comparing the uptake of powers via the collection of limited data on their use from court returns, annual surveys of local community safety partnerships and public perceptions elicited via the British Crime Survey. This wilful neglect of evaluation and assessment of social impact of the panoply of new powers was roundly condemned by the House of Common's Committee of Public Accounts (2007).

Nevertheless, the available data show that the reality of local implementation often belied the rhetorical pronouncements of central government (Cooper *et al.*, 2009; Crawford *et al.*, forthcoming). Both within and between parts of the UK, there has been considerable local variation in the take-up and use of formal tools and powers. This has not been linked directly to differences in the extent or type of local problems, but often appears to be due, in large part, to local preferences for particular approaches to enforcement and support, the willingness of key individuals to experiment with new tools and the capacity of local interests to organise and promote an enforcement-led or alternative responses (Burney, 2009; Clarke *et al.*, 2011). There is abundant evidence that national anti-social behaviour policies are often resisted and refashioned through implementation (Youth Justice Board, 2006; Crawford, 2008), as a result of which the expectations of Whitehall are frequently modified and adapted. The complex inter-organisational nature of local partnership arrangements, implicated in the delivery of anti-social behaviour interventions, renders this process of policy translation simultaneously more unexceptional and more nuanced. Inevitably, it is most evident in the context of devolved government, notably Scotland and to a lesser degree Wales, but also exists within and between local community safety partnerships, producing divergent local cultures of control. In practice, the governance of anti-social behaviour comprises an opaque and ill-defined policy domain in which diverse organisational interests, working assumptions, priorities and multi-disciplinary approaches coalesce, often in awkward combinations (Crawford, 2009a; Burney, 2009).

What follows, however, focuses on the assumptions about compliance that inform such technologies of control – notably with regard to young people – and their implications. The discussion will explore the different forms of compliance deployed in new civil preventive orders and allied forms of behavioural regulation, the theories about motivations and agency, as well as the interactions and balance between different levers of control that they imply. The chapter will conclude by questioning the implications of 'thinking about compliance' in relation to young people and the interactional effects of diverse forms of regulation. It begins with consideration of conceptions of regulation and compliance that inform our understandings of the manner in which new technologies of control might be assessed.

Regulation and compliance

At the heart of all forms of regulation and governance lies the problem of control. Broadly defined, regulation encompasses intentional activities that seek to direct, influence or manipulate behaviour and the flow of events (Black, 2001). According to Hood *et al.* (2001: 23), it entails three constituent elements: a *goal component* – the rule, standard or set of values against which behaviour or action is to be compared and contrasted; a *monitoring component* – some mechanism or process of feedback for monitoring or evaluating what happens in pursuance of the goal; and a *realignment component* – some form of corrective action or response that is designed or at least attempts to realign the subjects of control where deviation from the goal is perceived; namely, a mechanism for enforcing rules. The traditional lens of regulation over the last two centuries has focused upon the role of state authorities in setting goals, monitoring compliance and realigning divergences. In relation to behaviour, command-and-control based mechanisms – of which the criminal law is the archetypical form – are believed to have been the principal regulatory tools at the state's disposal. Like Ayres' (2006: 4) 'linguistically challenged parrots' the dominant legal tools tended to rely on ritualistically commanding 'prohibit it' or 'mandate it'.

In contrast to command-and-control, regulation is said to become 'responsive' where regulators recognise and respond to the conduct of those they seek to regulate in ways that are sensitive to the capacity of the regulated to regulate themselves and the conditions in which regulation occurs (Ayres and Braithwaite, 1992; Braithwaite, 2002a). Here, the task of regulation is redefined; the aim becomes one of regulated 'self-regulation'. It is assumed that the traditional methods of command-and-control, backed up with the threat of coercive sanctions, are not only inefficient and ineffective, but also inappropriate under current conditions of 'governance'. The new logic of regulation is that: first, 'governments can't do it alone' (Halpern *et al.*, 2004: 3), as the influences on behaviour lie far from the reach of governments and the state, thus necessitating greater engagement with and involvement of non-state actors and individual citizens; second, prevention is better (financially as well as socially) than 'late intervention' in most fields of public policy (Allen, 2011); and third, giving people greater responsibility and 'choice' is in itself a good thing. It also assumes that ultimately voluntary compliance and self-regulation are both preferable and more effective with regard to compliance with social and legal norms.

More recent analyses of regulation have highlighted the pluralistic nature of regulation freed from its (conceptual) chains to the sovereign state and a recognition that regulation operates through complex forms of parochial and private government. As Black notes, this process of 'decentring' entails both a re-articulation of regulatory authority and capacities beyond the state (narrowly defined) and a recognition of the limitations of the state alone to induce compliance: 'Essentially, decentred regulation involves a shift (and recognition of such a shift) in the locus of the activity of "regulating" from the state to other, multiple, locations, and the adoption on the part of the state of particular strategies of regulation' (2001: 112).

As I will seek to show, this process of decentring (in both its guises – as a change in the way of seeing things and a changed order of things) is particularly evident with regard to behavioural regulation of youth crime and anti-social behaviour. Not only has it become more evidently acknowledged that the state has limited capacity to effect change but it also has become clear that other institutions of civil society are more effective sources of regulatory authority, behavioural control and powers of persuasion. In contrast to command-and-control style approaches, the new regulatory responses have sought to persuade, organise, steer, align and 'nudge' (Thaler and Sunstein, 2008) multiple actors in seeking to change personal behaviour. In so doing, they straddle conventional distinctions between civil and criminal law and formal and informal responses, as well as operating across and through the boundaries of the public and private spheres. In this shift, the capacity to induce compliance is a key touchstone of success. Furthermore, it has sharpened the conceptual debate about what we mean by compliance and how it might be understood in different fields of social life. In this context, compliance can be understood as a purposive and wilful response to a request, order or direction made by a (legal) regulatory authority with power(s) to enforce in some form or other (i.e., through a sanction, punishment or corrective act) the initial direction. As such, compliance is largely concerned with the effectiveness of systems of regulation and their capacity to induce changed behaviour among targeted populations. In this, compliance as a lens through which to examine regulatory systems has a largely instrumental logic; it is concerned with getting things done (or changed). However, effectiveness may depend on other dimensions of regulation; namely, the responsiveness and coherence of regulatory regimes. Here, responsiveness refers to the manner in which regulatory regimes fit with, and relate to, other forms of regulation. This prompts descriptive questions about the resonance or dissonance between different systems of control, as well as normative questions about how better systems of regulation can work with and through existing systems of regulation rooted in social, economic and cultural life. By contrast, coherence is concerned with the logic and consistency of the norms and values within a system of regulation: the extent to which the norms interact with each other to produce an integrated whole.

Compliance may be understood as expressed through behavioural change or shifts in attitudes in line with a rule or direction. These need not necessarily proceed in tandem. Likewise, the rule or direction may itself be founded in law or stem from some other (non-legal or quasi-legal) normative expectation. Bottoms (2001: 88–9) differentiates between two principal types of compliance: 'short-term requirement compliance' and 'longer-term legal compliance'. Allied to this, Robinson and McNeill go on to distinguish between two ideal types of 'short-term requirement compliance' (2008: 434; this volume). *Formal* compliance constitutes behaviour that technically fulfils the requirement but does not necessarily result in a change in values, views or norms – it amounts to a type of 'work to rule', whereby compliance is the minimum to get by. By contrast, *substantive* compliance implies an active engagement with the normative dimensions of the order or direction and the responsibilities that it evokes – it amount to an acceptance of the 'spirit of the rule'. There are parallels here with Tyler's (2011) differentiation between 'rule adherence' (following rules) and 'performance' (being productive) in understanding why people cooperate. He associates compliance with narrow rule adherence, whereas wider forms of cooperation encompass perform-ance. Implicit in Robinson and McNeill's distinction is not simply the temporal issue – of short/long-term duration – alluded to by Bottoms, but also an attitudinal and motivational shift whereby the values implicated in, and associated with, a rule are accepted and commitment to them embraced. Because of its motivational and normative anchoring, this form of compliance is seen as more enduring and sustainable, and, therefore, is preferable as an outcome of regulation.

Exploring this further, Valerie Braithwaite (2003; this volume) identifies five motivational postures along a continuum of compliance: commitment, capitulation, resistance, disengagement and game-playing. Only the first two comprise forms of deference whilst the latter three are all forms of defiance. Once again, it is the values that adhere to commitment that differentiate it from forms of capitulation, which come close to Robinson and McNeill's formal compliance. There are close parallels with Doreen McBarnet's (2003; this volume) differentiation between *committed compliance, capitulative compliance, non-compliance and creative compliance*. She highlights the latter type or compliance in order to explore the creative strategies used in tax avoidance that comply with the law but defy the spirit of the law – a form of 'work to rule'. As McBarnet contends: 'Creative compliance will be found in any area of law in which those subject to it have the motivation and the resources (in terms of money and/or know-how) to resist legal control legally' (2003: 230).

In both McBarnet's and Braithwaite's typologies, modes of compliance that derive from, and evoke, commitments in terms of social norms constitute richer forms of 'substantive compliance'. Consequently, much of the compliance literature is preoccupied with how best to foster 'committed compliance' and therefore calls attention to questions about its measurement. Yet, measuring compliance is intrinsically difficult. In the context of community penalties and criminal sanctions, compliance tends to be conflated with known re-offending and reconviction; a highly unreliable indicator in itself not least because reconviction does not simply equate with failure nor does non-reconviction equal success (Mair *et al.*, 1997). Measuring compliance depends in large part on the nature and quality of the monitoring component of regulation: How well are breaches detected or deviations from the rule ascertained? What factors influence the propensity to record breaches or act upon deviations? What is the will on the part of regulators to record or pursue breaches where they are minor and/or do not constitute an escalation of behaviour? Furthermore, some modes of compliant behaviour are more amenable to measurement than others, whilst measuring attitudes and motivational shifts present acute problems of social desirability prompting concerns about reliability and sincerity. Attitudes and 'motivational postures' cannot be read as reflecting behaviour. After all, people do not always do what they say they do.

Valerie Braithwaite (2003) shows how regulators often make the mistake of expecting consistency between attitudes and behaviour. By contrast, in the context of tax regulation, she shows how those who 'resist most vocally', 'challenge tax authority decisions' and are 'openly critical of the institution' are 'not discernibly more non-compliant as a group than taxpayers who choose other ways of engaging with the system' (ibid.: 15). There is a long history of criminological research that highlights a dissonance between what people say and what they do. People often fail to obey laws that they say they believe in. Interesting for the purpose of this chapter are examples that Braithwaite provides with regard to situations in which people voice defiance or resistance but end up complying nevertheless. She shows how motivational postures reflect the social distance that individuals wish to place between themselves and regulators, whereby increasing social distance indicates increasing dislike for the authority and a lowering of the status ascribed to that authority. However, it does not, necessarily, signal disobedience. Motivational postures are the social signals that individuals send to authority, to others and to themselves to communicate preferred social distance from that authority. This is especially important for compliance in the 'shadow of criminalisation', precisely because regulators often interpret defiance as an indicator of, or proxy for, non-compliance.

Such defiance is frequently evident where youths, individually or (more frequently) in groups, challenge or question police directions – with particular salience for thinking about the motivational postures adopted by young people in relation to authority. For example, perceptions of unfairness may provoke active motivational postures that suggest defiance. This is especially likely where young people wish to reinforce their social distance from authority, notably in peer group situations. Moreover, the manner in which legal authorities respond to postures of defiance may structure subsequent encounters and interactions in a way that reinforces the likelihood of non-compliance. This was illustrated in the policing of dispersal orders which provide the police with powers to disperse groups of two or more people in designated zones where anti-social behaviour has been perceived to be a problem. Police issued directions to disperse, research suggests, can prompt some young people to question the justifications for the order drawing them into adversarial relations with police, such that: 'How someone responds to authority, whether with deference or defiance, becomes a, if not *the*, salient factor in subsequent authoritative assessments and decisions, more important potentially than the initial behaviour itself' (Crawford and Lister, 2007: 66, emphasis in original).

Consequently, there are dangers that directions to disperse become an 'attitude test', whereby individuals who fail are met with an escalation of response. Analogous interactions have been found in police/youth encounters in relation to stop and search powers (Bowling and Phillips, 2007: 952), and similar issues pertain to the use of ASBOs (Ramsay, 2004: 919).

In sum, compliance as a measurement of behaviour is conceptually rather limited and limiting as a lens of analysis. It approximates more closely to an output indicator rather than a social outcome, as it is defined more by the exigencies of the regulatory regime rather than by the activities, conduct or values of the subjects of regulation. As such, compliance tends to be seen in pathological terms as a deviation from the norm: as a problem, rather than a solution. This is alluded to by McBarnet in her identification of the issue of commitment in compliance and Tyler's preference for the more positive (and actively performative) concept of cooperation. Much of the criminological debate, however, focuses on tackling the attitude to non-compliance – on asking why someone does not comply with a particular direction or norm – rather than on how and why people comply and conform or, as Tyler (in this volume; 2011) argues, why people cooperate. Most especially, this results in a relative neglect for questions about people's normative commitments to the values that underlie orders in relation to which their conformity or deviance is evaluated or judged.

Finally, much of the compliance literature assumes – rather than questions – the agency and capacity of the regulated to comply. It assumes an active choice to comply or defy without questioning the competencies or capabilities of the subjects of regulation to do so. It often fails to ask the question: what are the conditions conducive to foster compliance for different individuals? Or what resources are necessary for compliance (especially the variety of 'committed compliance') to occur? The general absence from policy in much of the anti-social behaviour agenda of sufficient consideration given to the supportive conditions conducive to foster compliance with the new tools and powers was acknowledged by one of its principal architects, David Blunkett, in interview:

> I think there was a desire to see building blocks which would entitle you to be able to dig your way out of a problem and to require that society also recognised that there might be something it needed to do as well. And we haven't been as good on that latter bit as we have on the others. My regret is we didn't ever really get properly engaged . . . in saying what do we do on the positive side of helping people themselves to get out of this, rather than merely the threat that if you don't comply, you'll be in trouble.
>
> (Personal interview, 12 January 2007)

To illustrate this point, ASBOs, for example, only allow for negative prohibitions with no explicit attention given to questions about institutionalised support programmes to assist people who are the subject of them to overcome personal difficulties which might impede their compliance. It was five years after ASBOs were first introduced that individual support orders (ISOs) finally became available to the courts, to provide support and 'positive obligations' to address the causes of behaviour and assist compliance alongside an ASBO given to a young person.[11] Despite the fact that now, when a juvenile receives an ASBO, the court is required to consider making an ISO, nevertheless, in the period from 2004 to the end 2010 only 8.4 per cent of all juveniles given an ASBO were also issued with an ISO. This rises only moderately to 11.5 per cent for those minors aged 10–14.

Consequently, the rational choice individual implied in much policy debate concerning the regulation of personal behaviour and reflected in the compliance literature tends to be assumed to be an (almost muscularly) agentic and competent actor. Little recognition is accorded not only to the biases and blunders, the fallibility of choice and the irrationality of decisions that behavioural economists have shown to influence (adult) behaviour and decision-making (Kahneman *et al.*, 1982; Jolls *et al.*, 1998), but also to the cognitive limitations of some people, notably youths.[12] As Sunstein and Thaler highlight: 'in many domains people lack clear, stable or well-ordered preferences . . . contextual influences render the very meaning of the term "preferences" unclear' (2003: 1161). They go on to assert that: 'in some cases individuals make inferior decisions in terms of their own welfare-decisions that they would change if they had complete information, unlimited cognitive abilities and no lack of self-control' (ibid.: 1162). As they have more recently argued, this fallibility can be used for public purposes by 'choice architects', through planned architecture and design as a form of 'libertarian paternalism', whereby default positions and rules, and subtle 'nudges' are deployed to steer choices to public goals and to improve individual well-being (Thaler and Sunstein, 2008), essentially by protecting individuals from their own bad choices.

Young people, rights and responsibilities

The exposure of limitations on rational choice models of human decision-making have particular implications for the study of regulation and compliance in relation to young people. For, where the prevailing assumption has been that adults behave in their own best interests, this logic has tended to be inverted with regard to children and young people. We have assumed, at least for the last century or so, that children and young people do not necessarily behave in their own best interests. Rather, it is presumed that young people need to be protected from their own 'bad choices' and that in this adults know better what is in a child's or young person's 'best interests'.

Yet, there is something of a paradox in public policy regarding the status of youth, especially with regard to their behaviour. On the one hand, we have witnessed the relatively recent (in historic terms) stretching of youth beyond the teenage years both de facto and *de jure*. Examples include: delayed entry into the workplace; extended periods of further and higher education; and the raising of the age at which young people can engage in harmful activities, such as buying tobacco and alcohol. On the other hand, we have seen the 'adulteration of young people' in relation to criminal wrong-doing and anti-social behaviour. Children and young people are increasingly treated like adults for the purpose of rendering them responsible (and hence, accountable) for their conduct. This is particularly marked in the jurisdictions of the UK, as compared to other European countries (Muncie and Goldson, 2006). This countervailing logic of adulteration in the context of criminal justice is evidenced not only by the abolition of *doli incapax* and the concomitant lowering of criminal responsibility to children as young as 10 (under the Crime and Disorder Act 1998), but also the more general erosion of 'special procedural protections' once deemed essential to safeguard young people from the stigma and formality of the criminal justice process. Changes to the youth court, youth sentences and custodial regimes have eroded the distinctiveness of the youth justice system. The significant use of ASBOs in relation to juveniles has hastened an erosion of the right to anonymity in civil and criminal proceedings (Cobb, 2007).[13] Furthermore, because they are informal, ABCs can be, and are, used with children under 10 – sometimes as young as seven!

Despite successive governments' insistence on the correlativity of responsibility and rights, this appears to be singularly lacking when seen from the perspective of children and young people, who are blessed with responsibility for personal behaviour but limited rights. Whilst criminal responsibility attaches to children as young as 10, it is less clear what rights accrue to them from this age.[14] Just as there are dangers of under as well as over protection, there are pitfalls of too much as well as too little responsibility. One of the protections of childhood has traditionally taken the form of young people not being burdened with inappropriate responsibilities or compelled to take decisions that they are not or may not be competent to take. Children may be doubly vulnerable: first, by being denied participation rights they may be unable to control the experiences which they are subject to because of their status as child; and second, they may be burdened with excessive responsibility beyond their capabilities. In many instances, the claim that young people are given a voice and choice in informal proceedings and in determining outcomes is likely to be a 'sham' due to evident power imbalances (Wonnacott, 1999). The reality is more probably that choices are presented as varieties of 'take it or leave it' arrangements, in which young people are given limited information upon which to base their preferences and their participation in a room full of adults is severely restricted or minimal. Moreover, in the context of accusations about anti-social behaviour, the presence of 'coercive sticks' – even whether these are held in the background or as a last resort (Braithwaite, 1997) – is likely to undermine any sense of voluntariness or unconstrained choice.

Even in genuinely deliberative proceedings in which young people feel free to express themselves unconstrained, there are clear and present dangers of inappropriately over-burdening young people through forms of 'responsive' regulation which presuppose the capacity to formulate and articulate preferences, weigh risks, compare opportunities and costs, choose from options presented and comply with decisions made. Exercising 'voice' in deliberative negotiations and 'restorative' forums demands certain attributes and competencies which may not be available to all youths. Some young people may be better capable of exercising their voice than others. Voice is inherently unequal, especially amongst young people, such that for many it constitutes nothing more than an 'obstructed ideal'. One only needs to conjure up the image of an eight year old presented with an acceptable behaviour contract to sign against a background of threats over the possible eviction from social housing of his parents to confront the force of such an anachronism.

Models of compliance

Implicit in the foregoing arguments is the contention that the various new technologies of anti-social behaviour regulation rest upon and embody theories of compliance. Yet, these are rarely rendered explicit either in general policy debates or individual instances of decision-making. These models of compliance, outlined thus far, vary in their emphasis upon the formal or substantive quality of compliance, the extent to which it reflects commitment and/or the extent to which it is grounded in long-term normative attachments as opposed to short-term situational contingencies. Developing upon this literature prompts an interrogation of assumptions about human motivations, values and personal capacities implicit in differing forms of compliance. All attempts to influence behaviour are founded, to some extent or other, on assumptions about the likely preferences that incite human behaviour and the capacity of people to realise their desires or preferences. Hence, regulatory strategies, policies and interventions that seek to change or manipulate human behaviour will embody theories about personal *motivation* and individual *capacity*. In essence, motivation relates to the internal forces that provoke action, whilst capacity refers to the ability of a person to carry out the desired action; sometimes defined as 'agency'. The term 'capacity' is preferred here as it speaks to the different competencies that young people (in particular) may or may not have at a given time/place, as well as those capabilities that they develop or acquire across the life-course. It incorporates both external structural and social constraints upon, and resources available to, individuals, as well as personal abilities and situational dynamics.

Motivation

If we focus on the question of motivation first, we can identify two types of reasoning that influence motivations. These are: first, instrumental or prudential; and second, normative, moral or social.

Instrumental motivation

Instrumental motivation is understood in terms of the furtherance of self-interest. Individuals are treated as 'rational choice actors' who know their preferences and make prudent self-regarding decisions. Self-interest, here, may extend beyond the acquisition of material wealth – attributed to the classical *'homo economicus'* –

to wider considerations such as status, regard, power and authority. From this perspective, compliance can be fostered by altering the costs and benefits that accrue to any given activity. Much of the criminological literature on compliance has focused narrowly on instrumental dynamics, specifically the risks and costs associated with non-compliance that arise from the threat of sanction. Compliance, here, is associated with deterrence – measured through a combination of the certainty and severity of punishments and sanctions.

Like much criminology, policies informed by theories of instrumental compliance have focused predominantly on increasing the *costs* of criminal behaviour rather than augmenting the relative *benefits* of alternative lawful activity. Less attention, therefore, has been given to the question of rewards or incentives for compliance. This largely reflects the criminological preoccupation with making sense of pathology rather than normalcy. The question usually asked is 'why do people deviate from legal norms?' rather than the more prevalent issues 'why do most people, most of the time conform?' Nevertheless, interrogating compliance should encourage us to consider the sources of social order and conformity.

In this vein, there has been a revival of interest in incentive-based 'reward' schemes that seek to foster compliance through self-interested calculation, but by altering the incentives to non-deviant ('pro-social' in the fashionable phraseology) behaviour. Incentive projects have developed particularly in relation to young people, both those at risk of offending and those already identified as (persistent) offenders. The research evidence appears to suggest that reward schemes work less well with older youths and more persistent offenders (Home Office, 2004). Additionally, reward as a lever of compliance presents a number of difficulties. First, there are moral hazards associated with rewards. The truly rational actor may exploit the offer of reward. Reward can cloud nobler motives of virtuous behaviour, as moral judgements are eclipsed by baser instincts of personal gain and individual benefit. Consequently, rewards can induce the wrong kind of cultural disposition within the regime of regulation. In addition, rewards can provoke 'reactance' on the part of the regulated (Braithwaite, 2002b: 16–19), as can punishments even more significantly. Perceptions of rewards as controlling may reduce feelings of self-determination and undermine personal motivation. They can send negative messages about self-worth and identity. If rewards are interpreted as an attempt to manipulate behaviour, the regulated may react to this blatant attempt at control in ways that undermine voluntary compliance.

An over-application of reward may produce a more general disassociation or dissonance effect whereby internal self-motivation is overtaken by extrinsic rewards. In a classic study in the context of pre-school education, Lepper *et al.* (1973) showed how children's intrinsic interests can be undermined by the use of extrinsic rewards. In their study, children who were rewarded for engaging in drawing activities in the classroom were less likely to engage in these activities once the reward was removed compared to those children who were simply given the opportunity to engage in the activity without the benefit of rewards or given the same reward unexpectedly. The study seemed to show that once the extrinsic benefit or incentive was removed, the activity appeared less attractive to the children, suggesting that the extrinsic reward had served to undermine the interest by inducing the child to engage in the activity as an explicit means to some ulterior end (Greene and Lepper, 1974). The authors attribute this to an 'over-justification effect', whereby young people make post-behavioural attributions about the causes of their own behaviour based upon the conditions within which it occurred. Hence, when someone is rewarded for doing some task they attribute their behaviour to the reward rather than their initial interest in doing the activity. Consequently, this can have a negative impact upon their intrinsic interest in the activity which is reduced compared to what it initially may have been. A child may reason that: 'if someone is going to reward me for doing something it must be so boring and dull that I would not otherwise want to do it'. Lepper (1981) subsequently argued that the more salient the instrumentality between an activity and a reward, the more likely the reward will undermine intrinsic motivations. By contrast, where the reward conveys non-instrumental information about positive competency or normative cues about values and self-worth, this may compensate some of the detrimental effects on intrinsic motivation.

From the perspective of cognitive evaluation theory, the effects of a reward will depend on how it affects perceived self-determination and perceived competence (i.e., interactional effects with perceptions of agency and competency, to which we return below). Rewards may be interpreted by their recipients in two potentially contradictory ways: either as external controllers of their behaviour – thus eroding their need for autonomy – or as informational indicators of their competence. In many cases, rewards will have contradictory effects, simultaneously experienced as controlling and informational. However, unexpected rewards (such as praise) are more likely to enhance feelings of competence without undermining autonomy.

Deci and colleagues (1999) conclude their meta-analysis of the available psychological research (drawn from 128 experiments) with a number of important observations. Crucially, they found a significantly differential impact of tangible and verbal rewards on recipients. Verbal rewards, as a form of positive feedback can have an enhancing effect on intrinsic motivation. This is largely explained by the fact that verbal rewards are typically unexpected. With regard to tangible rewards they assert:

> Our findings raise deeply important questions about when and how to use rewards in real-world settings . . . The findings indicate that tangible rewards offered for engaging in completing or doing well at a task were deleterious to intrinsic motivation . . . Thus if people use tangible rewards, it is necessary that they be extremely careful if they are concerned about the intrinsic motivation and task persistence of the people they are rewarding.
>
> (Deci *et al.*, 1999: 656)

In parallel with Bottoms' (2001: 88–9) differentiation between 'short-term requirement compliance' and 'longer-term legal compliance' it may be that rewards are more likely to stimulate the former and may actually serve to undermine the latter. Deci and colleagues explain how this operates:

> the primary negative effect of rewards is that they tend to forestall self-regulation. In other words, reward contingencies undermine people's taking responsibility for motivating or regulating themselves. When institutions – families, schools, businesses and athletics teams, for example – focus on the short term and opt for controlling people's behaviour, they may be having a substantially negative long-term effect.
>
> (Deci *et al.*, 1999: 659)

In the context of 'anti-social behaviour', the presence of rewards gives rise to an additional normative problem of 'less eligibility'. Why should people who behave badly in the first place be rewarded? Should those individuals who err be given opportunities otherwise not available to their peers who remain law-abiding? If so, what kind of message does this send out to honest, non-troublesome youths who do not engage in anti-social behaviour? This last question becomes even more poignant if we believe all people to be rational choice actors, as the easiest way to access goods, opportunities and assistance may be to turn to unsociable or disruptive acts. Yet, if we reinterpret 'reward' in a non-instrumentally reductionist way, we may begin to move beyond a self-interested calculation of compliance. Reward schemes, particularly where the benefits are more tangential, may speak less to self-interest and more to norms of reciprocity. Here, looser notions of reward may incorporate a normative dimension, in which reciprocation is couched in a relationship of broad equivalence: the normative equivalence of *Mrs Doasyouwouldbedoneby*.[15] Reward may also be linked with self-identity in so far as it can serve to build esteem and a positive self-image, both of which may be important where individuals suffer from perceptions of low self-esteem or self-worth.

Normative motivation

Normative compliance operates whereby motivation is triggered by commitments, beliefs, attachments and perceptions of legitimacy. It constructs the young person as a 'moral agent' capable of virtuous acts. Bottoms (2001) sub-divides normative compliance into three component types: (i) acceptance of, or belief in, a norm; (ii) attachment leading to compliance; and (iii) the role of legitimacy. The first of these concerns the conscious internalisation and favourable reception of a set of norms or rules of conduct which lead people to behave in particular ways. It acknowledges the type of moral commitment that McBarnet (2003) alludes to in her notion of 'committed compliance'. Here, the norms that inform the regime of regulation and underlie the rules are consistent and in accord with the accepted beliefs of the person concerned. The second type relates to attachments to others, whereby norms are conveyed by and implicated in interpersonal relationships, social bonds and networks of trust. As such it is relational. Bottoms' final type of normative compliance deriving from legitimacy, returns us to the themes raised earlier concerning the manner in which the proper exercise of formal authority informs compliance. It alludes to perceptions of the legitimacy of the regulatory institutions and individuals in positions of authority, as well as perceptions of legitimacy fostered by experiences of procedural justice (Tyler, 2006; Tyler and Fagan, 2008). From this perspective, legitimate social arrangements that involve fair procedures, treat people with respect and dignity, and provide them with participation in informed decision-making processes, it is assumed will generate normative commitments to compliance.

In exploring why people cooperate, Tyler (2011) identifies five types of social motivations which include: attitudes, values, identity, procedural justice and motive-based trust. These dovetail quite closely with those normative types of motivation/compliance discussed above. Tyler (this volume) rightly highlights the detrimental over-reliance on instrumental motivations – the 'myth of self-interest' – in public policies concerning the management of behaviour (notably criminality) which have tended to dominate at the expense of considerations of normative and social motivations.

There are certain parallels here with Le Grand's (2003) four ideal types of knights, knaves, pawns and queens. However, Le Grand's differentiation between motivation that is self-interested and altruistic is somewhat different to that of instrumental and normative motivation used here. His focus concerns the interests served (self or others) rather than the nature of the forces (instrumental or normative) that stimulate behaviour. Whilst there are important similarities, Le Grand's differentiation between *knightly* (altruistic) and *knavely* (self-interested) motivation tends to bifurcate motivation as either/or, whereas the distinction between instrumental and normative allows more readily for the coexistence and interaction between different forms of motivation. It is harder to be both altruistic and self-interested, at least in the way Le Grand defines the terms, than it is to be motivated simultaneously by both instrumental and normative concerns. In line with earlier arguments, Le Grand acknowledges that treating people as knaves, particularly where governments do so may undermine their knightly motivations – those motivated predominantly by public-spirited sentiments and altruism – and, as a consequence, foster knavish (self-interested) behaviour.

Le Grand's analysis is concerned with the motivations of professional public servants, service providers and public policy-makers as well as service users/ recipients. Whilst our focus, here, is principally on the motivations of service recipients (young people especially), Le Grand raises some interesting and important issues about the impact of the motivations of professional service workers on public services and the manner in which their motivations can be influenced (reinforced or undermined) by government policy designs. For example, he argues that government programmes using hierarchical 'command-and-control' style decision-making practices reduce altruism ('knightly' motivations) because workers are disempowered and become de-motivated or attempt to avoid the system. In a similar vein, he highlights how systems of monitoring of service workers and performance measurement to ensure that policy goals are being met often reduce trust which, in turn, negatively impacts worker motivation. Moreover, Le Grand's focus is in relation to a variety of what we might call social welfare and 'caring' services. His analysis has less to say about more coercive contexts of social control policies. The notion of altruism as a motivation to 'help others' has greater resonance in the context of 'care' than it does in relation to 'control' measures. Those who are the subjects of control are less likely to be motivated by 'other-directed' activities than by factors that appeal to their normative instincts.

The reality is that people often have mixed motivations that inform their behaviour and interactions with others. Some will be stimulated by pursuit of personal self-interest (instrumental factors). Others will be inspired by altruistic or normative reasons. However, our understanding of both motivations and compliance will be better served by a more extensive exploration of the normative dimensions and the manner in which they interact with – either in mutually supportive or conflictual ways – instrumental considerations.

Agency and capacity

Agency involves the power individuals have to make their own choices, both in terms of the power they are granted within public systems and the capacities they have to exploit and maximise the range of choices and scope for action afforded to them. On the question of agency, Le Grand asks: how much control should be given to consumers or recipients of government services? Le Grand argues that citizens have traditionally been conceived as *pawns*, the passive and disempowered subjects of public services (be it education, health, housing or welfare systems), rather than as *queens*, the active users, endowed with the freedom to choose between competing options and differing service providers. Whilst Le Grand's primary focus of concern is welfare services, his conceptual models provide insights for wider public policies that combine elements of welfare and control. Le Grand argues that individuals should be treated as 'queens' with agency to make decisions rather than 'pawns' where public service professionals make decisions on behalf of recipients. For, implicit (and explicit) in his arguments is the thesis that high-quality, legitimate, effective, efficient, responsive and equitable public services are those that empower service recipients and users in ways that foster and work with the grain of the motivations of users and professional providers. Above all else, these issues have implications for compliance.

Le Grand suggests that the nature of decision-making power differs in regards to 'the nature of the type of service offered, the quantity of the service used, and the provider of the service' (2003: 74). He outlines three approaches regarding how much power recipients should have to make decisions. The 'liberal approach' asserts that the most important element of policy design is to allow for individuals' freedom of action. This approach advocates for recipients to be actively engaged in decisions and therefore always treated as queens rather than passive pawns. Moreover, there is some evidence to suggest that there are motivational benefits for self-identity that accrue to treating people as active decision-makers (Halpern *et al.*, 2004). By contrast, the 'welfarist approach' recognises that whilst, in general, individuals know best what will contribute most to their welfare, nevertheless there are many instances in which public service professionals should have decision-making power on behalf of recipients. Although this paternalistic removal of decision-making power from users diminishes their agency, this is justified in situations in which: (i) users prefer to delegate authority to others (i.e., they choose to be pawns); (ii) users have little knowledge or expertise in comparison to professionals; (iii) individuals suffer particular weakness of will (such as alcohol/drug addictions); (iv) the decision-making is particularly emotionally charged; or (v) users could make self-interested decisions on behalf of others (i.e., parents for children). In these situations, Le Grand argues that policies should empower users with the knowledge and choice to make their own decisions. Here, he connects the issue of individual agency with public service motivation. He contends that if agency is removed from recipients and given to professionals, there are no guarantees that professionals can or will make the best choice for the recipient. Lastly, the 'communitarian approach' is primarily concerned with the impact of individual decision-making on the wider community or society as a whole. The communitarian approach is wary of treating users as queens to make their own decisions because of the potential for negative externalities from users' self-interested decisions, such as overuse of services or adverse effects on well-being. If public service professionals make these decisions, negative externalities could be reduced because professionals could ensure the greater good for society. However, Le Grand is aptly sceptical of government's ability to reduce negative externalities and wary of the limited ability of public service professionals to assess a rigours cost-benefit analysis on the implications of specific decisions for society as a whole.

Le Grand's distinction regarding agency between queens and pawns provides a valuable conceptual continuum along which to think about not only the ways in which citizen's agency is conceived by service providers and embedded within public systems or regulatory regimes, but also the differential capacities and capabilities that service recipients have to make choices and exploit the scope for manoeuvre and control afforded to them by public service providers and regulatory systems. However, the notion of 'capacity', with its references to physical, emotional, cognitive, rational and contractual competencies, offers more nuanced ways of thinking about agency and notions of power. The question of capacities is particularly salient in any discussions about the manner in which young people are conceived and the agency accorded to them by public services.

There is not an extensive literature that attempts to analyse the decision-making performance of adolescents and/or how adolescents differ from adults in this regard. However, what research there is (much of it in the context of healthcare decisions) shows similarities in the mistakes people of all ages make: 'Errors associated in the common imagination with one's youth are often made throughout life, and bad decisions attributed to youth may not be as strongly associated with age as is often claimed' (O'Donoghue and Rabin, 2001: 31). Many common conceptions of how youths differ from adults do not seem to be borne out by the research evidence (Furby and Beyth-Marom, 1992). Weithorn and Campbell (1982) presented adolescents with hypothetical medical- and psychological-treatment decisions, finding that 14 year olds scored as well as 18 and 21 year olds in competency. The evidence suggests that adolescents are similar to adults in terms of their ability to perform decision-making processes.

Young people seem to differ more from adults in how they value the consequences of decisions. In fact, research in developmental psychology that studies adolescent behaviour focuses not on the decision-making process, but rather on what considerations matter most to adolescents. Youths differ from adults in the emphasis they accord to their concern for identity formation, establishing autonomy and maintaining the regard of peers. One implication is that the things that matter most for young people have a tendency to increase short-term benefits (over long-term costs). This means that errors common to both adults and young people are magnified and become more problematic for youths, even if youths and adults do not differ in their inherent propensity for these errors. The different preferences that inform youths' decisions are also affected by projection bias which predicts that youths will underestimate how much their preferences will change as they age. Hence the (limited) value accorded to long-term costs may change as young people progress along the life-course. The high level of risk-taking activities undertaken by young people suggests that they suffer what appear like excessive myopia expressed in trading off present versus future consequences but, in essence, may be a product of projection bias – projecting their present preferences into the future.

Mixed models

Drawing together the above discussion and to highlight the complex mix of both motivations and capacities among young people, it is useful to specify five broad ideal types that revolve around two axes informing compliance (see Crawford, 2007): the first (points 1 and 2, below) relates to questions of motivation and the second concerns different levels of capacity or agency along a continuum (points 3–5, below):

1. Normative compliance: whereby motivation is triggered by normative commitments, beliefs, attachments and perceptions of legitimacy – a *moral agent* capable of virtuous acts.
2. Instrumental compliance: whereby motivation is premised on maximising self-interest and stimulated by sanctions and rewards – a *prudential rational choice actor*.
3. Unassisted compliance: whereby the individual is deemed fully competent and able to exercise self-determination and personal agency – an *active agent* ('queen'-like) capable of independent action – reflecting a 'liberal approach'.
4. Enabled compliance: whereby the individual is deemed not fully competent, but dependent and with limited capacity for independent action, self-

determination and personal agency – a needy individual requiring empowerment and assistance – or where the wider society needs protection from the decisions of individuals; in accordance with a 'communitarian approach'.

5. Imposed compliance: whereby the individual is a passive victim of circumstance, unable or unwilling to assert sufficient agency due to his or her limited scope of action – an incompetent, weak, dependent or vulnerable individual – where public professionals are deemed to be in a better position to make choices on behalf of recipients, reflecting a 'welfarist approach'.

These can be represented diagrammatically as in Figure 9.1. This typology prompts a number of questions about the assumptions that inform systems of behavioural regulation in specific ways: To what extent are motivations understood as either instrumental or moral? To what extent are young people conceived as capable of knowing their interests and articulating their preferences? And to what extent, are they in reality capable of so doing?

A further point of note is that the assumptions that inform policies, interventions and mechanisms of control are just that; they are *assumptions*. As such, they must interact with the actual motivations and capacities of real people in authentic situations. It is in the possible conjuncture or disjuncture between assumptions about motivation and capacity and the actual motivations and capacities of specific individuals or groups that the effectiveness or otherwise of interventions lies. The relationship between these assumptions and the realities of human motivation and agency are fundamental to understanding public policies, their implementation and implications. Hence, debates about compliance with technologies of control must engage with individuals' subjectivity and the manner in which regulation is

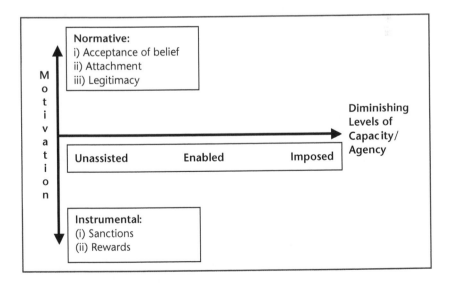

FIGURE 9.1 Types of compliance

interpreted and experienced by those who are subject to it. This provokes questions regarding the ways in which people respond and react to attempts to influence their behaviour. As Le Grand shows, those who design policies that seek to induce compliance in others may have very different motivations and capacities to those who are on the receiving end of regulatory measures. It may be difficult for policy designers and those charged with implementation (despite pretensions to the contrary) to know what it is like to be the subject of control measures. The dangers of misjudging the audience are particularly evident with regard to adult designers of control policies targeted at young people. Technologies of control that assume those to whom they are aimed at are motivated by normative orientations will have very different effects if those people are in fact motivated by instrumental concerns. Correspondingly, measures that assume people to be instrumentally self-interested will have distorted effects if the policies serve to erode virtuous or moral motivations. Likewise, interventions that treat people as passive, incompetent or lacking capacity may de-motivate and demoralise those people to whom they are targeted. Finally, where interventions treat people as active and competent agents, they may give them too much responsibility or scope for control such that they may make mistakes that damage their own or other's welfare.

However, reality is more fluid than such bald typologies might suggest. Nevertheless, such typologies usefully accentuate the different, and potentially competing, assumptions that underlie and inform specific regimes of regulation. They highlight how technologies of control that assume those to whom they are targeted are moral agents will have very different effects if most are in fact self-interested actors. Likewise, regimes of control that assume people to be self-interested actors will have distorted effects if they serve to erode normative commitments and motivations. Similarly, policies that treat people as lacking in agency may patronise and de-motivate. Finally, where policies treat people as wholly active agents, they may give them too much scope such that they may make mistakes that damage their own or other's welfare. With regard to young people in particular, the typologies prompt consideration of the extent to which and how young people are to be assisted and enabled to make agreements and comply with them.

Sticks and carrots . . . and sermons

As I have argued elsewhere, many anti-social behaviour interventions have (or at least appeal to) a contract-like quality. They constitute forms of 'contractual governance' (Crawford, 2003, 2009b). This aping of the contractual agreement implies notions of exchange and instrumental reasoning. Contract as the archetypical neo-classical instrument of regulation – which mimics forms of control derived from modes of consumption and commerce – communicate a language of self-determination and choice that engages people as active and free citizens and as informed and responsible consumers. Such an approach holds out coercive 'sticks' and supportive 'carrots' as levers of motivation and behavioural change.

Interestingly, 'sticks and carrots' was the apt title of the Scottish guidance issued by the Scottish Executive (2005) on the use of ABCs. Moreover, contracts constitute a particular way of thinking about relations between state and citizen, establishing what Collins describes as 'a discrete communication system between individuals in which the contract "thinks" about the relation between people in a particular way' (1999: 15). They transform diffuse expectations about the future into more specific and concrete obligations and in so doing bestow a quality of 'explicitness' but also confine expectations and separate them from wider social commitments, pressures, norms or practices that are indeterminate and extensive. As such, contracts are delimited and exhibit a quality of 'boundedness'. They encircle particular facets of a relationship, sheltering wider aspects of human interactions from view, thus reducing the complexity of human relations to specified essentials and pathways that have significance within the contractual arrangement.

A youth worker engaged in implementing anti-social behaviour interventions with young people in Yorkshire articulated, in interview, prevalent concerns about the deficiencies of such an instrumental logic:

> So we have the wider social policy narrative now which is about sanctions and rewards. I mean if you do a psychological analysis, this is really thin . . . When that's the only strategy that we've got for working with [adolescents], sanction and reward, sanction and reward . . . There's no hope in hell of any kind of profound moral education, as a result of which young people say to themselves, 'maybe I shouldn't do this'.
>
> (Youth worker, May 2006)

Yet despite the fact that contract-like arrangements embody an instrumental discourse, it would be wrong to suggest that the anti-social behaviour agenda solely asserts a prudential, self-interested reasoning. The anti-social behaviour agenda and contractualism as a mode of regulation also embody values and virtues (Freedland and King, 2003). Frequently, 'sticks and carrots' are accompanied and supplemented by 'sermons' in which notions of responsible agency are conceived in highly moralistic tones that accord privilege not only to individual autonomy and choice but also to moral responsibility. As Jayasuriya contends, the new contractualism embodies a 'rather distinctive moral sociology which seeks to lay out proper modes of social conduct' (2002: 312). This gives rise to a paradox of liberal intent producing illiberal outcomes; a neo-liberal instrument (the contract) hosting a neo-conservative moral content. This clash and confusion of values has additional distinctive implications for compliance.

Furthermore, the anti-social behaviour agenda by combining and straddling the work of diverse (public, private and voluntary) organisations has revealed both the manner in which different regulatory systems (with diverse assumptions about compliance) can co-exist (sometimes in antagonistic or tense relations) with regard to the same problems and targeted at the same people and the ways in which they might be combined, such that different levers of control supplement and reinforce each other. Much criminology tends to operate under the rather naive fallacy that criminal justice sanctions have the greatest instrumental sway over recipients due to their overt punitiveness. What practitioners – police officers in particular – quickly came to learn whilst implementing novel anti-social behaviour tools was that criminal justice sanctions are not always perceived as the most significant levers of control when effecting behaviour. This is especially evident in the context of social housing where the civil levers of control – associated with demotion and eviction – are often perceived as far more dramatic in their impact than the threat of punishment through the police and courts. Furthermore, the experience of partnership working between police and housing highlights the capacity to combine control systems in a form of 'regulatory pluralism' whereby 'complementary instrument mixes' are preferred over 'single instrument approaches' (Gunningham and Sinclair, 1998). Sergeant Paul Dunn, the police officer credited with the introduction of 'acceptable behaviour contacts' in Islington in late 1999 (see Bullock and Jones, 2004), in interview explained this dual realisation:

> Talking to the housing staff, I actually realised that we were slightly tunnel-visioned . . . I was unaware of what housing was doing with their tenants, holding interviews with them which they did on a day to day basis. So, the particular individual that we were starting to look at from the perspective of an ASBO application was already being invited in for a tenancy interview and he was already being arrested by the local police. What surprised me when I sat in on the tenancy meeting was the responsibility and the concern taken by the parents – who were both seasoned criminals – in relation to the housing interview which was non-existent with the police interview. So, the criminal justice system wasn't a threat to that particular family because they'd all been involved in it for many years. What was hugely concerning to the family was the possibility that their son's behaviour could take away the family home and affect the parents. Furthermore, the young person was also deeply concerned that his behaviour could actually bring about this problem for his parents.
>
> (Paul Dunn, Personal Interview, August 2005)

This highlights, first, the prevailing fragmented approach to behavioural problems and, second, the fact that for some people in certain circumstances, criminal justice sanctions are not necessarily the most powerful administrative tools with which to effect change or induce discipline through the threat of sanctions. Nor are they necessarily the most punitive. The fear of eviction, as in this instance, or exclusion from school in the context of education, may be far more potent sanctions than a conviction, fine or criminal punishment. Similar analogies can be drawn with threats of losing certain state benefits, denial of access to key resources or loss of employment.

The additional insight alluded to above pertains to the combined effects of joint or multiple systems of regulation. Consequently, joint visits from police and housing became the preferred means of delivering ABCs as this facilitated a hybrid space in which the combined weight of criminal and housing sanctions could be deployed to encourage engagement on the part of young people and their parents. Paul Dunn explains:

> Now what that created was every time I started an ABCs, I was the good guy for families because all I could do was arrest them . . . Actually, to them I had no clout whatsoever, the housing had all the influence and they would very rarely talk to one of these families. But we sort of swapped responsibilities and I would talk about tenancies as a police officer and the housing officer would talk about criminal justice and ASBOs. But that in itself created a sort of strange local partnership in action but also to prove to the families that we were actually wanting to work with them but we now had the tools and the support and the strategies in place that if we needed to take action, either through housing or through the criminal justice system, we'd both work together to do that. So it was very much in their interest actually to work with us.
>
> (Personal Interview, August 2005)

However, this combination of regulatory approaches, tools, sanctions and levers of control raises important ethical, legal and social questions concerning the interactional effects of different regulatory approaches and technologies and the complementary or ambiguous relations between them. It also prompts concerns about 'regulatory overload', 'net-widening' and 'mess-thinning' (Cohen, 1985; Brown, 2004). In a precautionary organisational culture, there are evident dangers of professional assumptions that all instruments (or as many as possible) should be used rather than the minimum number necessary to achieve the desired result – offending notions of parsimony or proportionality. The result may be young people overburdened by regulation.

Conclusions

In reality, young people are liable to be motivated by diverse levers, dependent upon particular situational contingencies, in which decisions are made, wider social constraints, personal identity and capacities. The crucial question, then, is whether different assumptions about motivation can co-exist without adverse implications for compliance. This raises issues regarding possible interaction effects, both between the various types of compliance and between compliance mechanisms and different groups or individuals (Bottoms, 2001: 104). These may serve to reinforce pressures towards compliance, pull in different directions potentially undermining each other, or compound pressures against compliance. As a result of interactional effects and confused assumptions about motivation and agency/capacity, the concern is that young people may be being set up to fail within these novel systems of regulation.

Bottoms sagely notes:

> Those who seek to induce compliance in others very often think they know what it will be like to be on the receiving end of the measures that they administer. But . . . people in power frequently misjudge their audiences.
>
> (2001: 99)

The implications of this insight are likely to be particularly apposite with regard to regulatory systems designed by adults and imposed on young people. Yet we know very little about the manner in which young people interpret and react to attempts to alter their behaviour through diverse forms of normative and instrumental inducements. We also have insufficient knowledge about how the interaction of competing logics is understood and experienced by young people. What are the implications of treating a young person as capable one moment and incompetent the next, as a rational actor one day and a moral agent the next? This chapter has sought to shed some light on the issues that pertain to a more rigorous discussion and analysis of how we might understand and think about compliance in the context of anti-social behaviour interventions with young people. Fleshing out the implications of some of these insights will demand empirical enquiries that test and explore assumptions about motivation and capacity that implicitly or explicitly inform regulatory interventions (see Crawford *et al.*, forthcoming).

As we have seen, young people are subject to diverse, ambiguous and inconsistent messages as to their competencies as they proceed through their transition to adulthood. More profoundly, young people may experience being treated as fully competent – as rational adult actors – as liberating or constraining, or even perhaps both simultaneously. Denying their youthful status, their dependencies and limitations may impose obligations and responsibilities upon young people that they are not well equipped to deal with. But there are also broader dangers that in the language of choice, the structural challenges that confront young people in their transition to adulthood are seen through the lens of behaviour and reduced to personal decisions. From such a perspective, failure to comply too easily becomes seen as symptomatic of poor choices made by uninformed, unmotivated, incompetent or irresponsible individuals. To avoid this, the study of compliance needs to (re)connect with not only the normative and non-instrumental dimensions of motivation, but also with the wider social forces and resources that enable individuals – young people in particular – to be capable of exercising responsibility and addressing the social inequalities and differential personal capabilities that constrain their capacity to determine and shape their own futures.

References

Allen, G. (2011) *Early Intervention: The Next Steps*, London: Cabinet Office.

Allen, G. and Duncan Smith, I. (2009) *Early Intervention: Good Parents, Great Kids, Better Citizens*, London: Centre for Social Justice and Smith Institute.

Ashworth, A. (2004) 'Social control and anti-social behaviour: the subversion of human rights' *Law Quarterly Review*, 120: 263–91.

—— (2006) 'Four threats to the presumption of innocence', *South African Law Journal*, 123: 62–96.

Ayres, I. (2006) 'Menus matter', *University of Chicago Law Review*, 73(3): 3–15.

Ayres, I. and Braithwaite, J. (1992) *Responsive Regulation: Transcending the Deregulation Debate*, Oxford: Oxford University Press.

Bakalis, C. (2007) 'Asbos, "Preventative Orders" and the European Court of Human Rights', *European Human Rights Law Review*, 4: 427–40.

Beckett, K. and Herbert, S. (2010) *Banished: The New Social Control in Urban America*, Oxford: Oxford University Press.

Beetham, D. (1991) *The Legitimation of Power*, London: Macmillan.

Black, J. (2001) 'Decentring regulation: the role of regulation and self-regulation in a "post-regulatory" world', *Current Legal Problems*, 54: 103–46.

Blair, T. (2006) 'Our nation's future – criminal justice system', speech 23 June. http://www.number-10.gov.uk/output/Page9737.asp.

Bottoms, A.E. (2001) 'Compliance and community penalties', in A.E. Bottoms, L. Gelsthorpe and S. Rex (eds) *Community Penalties: Change and Challenge*, Cullompton: Willan, pp. 87–116.

Bowling, B. and Phillips, C. (2007) 'Disproportionate and discriminatory: reviewing the evidence on police stop and search', *Modern Law Review*, 70(6): 936–61.

Braithwaite, J. (1997) 'On Speaking softly and carrying sticks: neglected dimensions of republican separation of powers', *University of Toronto Law Journal*, 47: 1–57.

—— (2002a) *Restorative Justice and Responsive Regulation*, Oxford: Oxford University Press.

—— (2002b) 'Rewards and regulation', *Journal of Law and Society*, 29(1): 12–26.

Braithwaite, V. (2003) 'Dancing with tax authorities: motivational postures and non-compliant actors', in V. Braithwaite (ed.) *Taxing Democracy: Understanding Tax Avoidance and Evasion*, Aldershot: Ashgate, pp. 15–39.

Brown, A. (2004) 'Anti-social behaviour, crime control and social control', *Howard Journal*, 43(2): 203–11.

Bullock, K. and Jones, B. (2004) *Acceptable Behaviour Contracts Addressing Anti Social Behaviour in the London Borough of Islington*, online Report 02/04, London: Home Office.

Burney, E. (2009) *Making People Behave: Anti-social behaviour, politics and policy*, Cullompton: Willan.

Cave, E. (2010) 'Seen but not heard? Children in clinical trials', *Medical Law Review*, 18: 1–27.

Clarke, A., Williams, K., Wydall, S., Gray, P., Liddle, M. and Smith, A. (2011) *Describing and Assessing Interventions to Address Anti-Social Behaviour*, Research Report 51, London: Home Office.

Cobb, N. (2007) 'Governance through publicity: ASBOs, young people, and the problematization of the right to anonymity', *Journal of Law and Society*, 34(3): 342–73.

Cohen, S. (1985) *Visions of Social Control*, Cambridge: Polity.

Collins, H. (1999) *Regulating Contracts*, Oxford: Oxford University Press.

Cooper, C., Brown, G., Powell, H. and Sapsed, E. (2009) *Exploration of Local Variations in the Use of Anti-Social Behaviour Tools and Powers*, Research Report 21, London: Home Office.

Cosgrove, J. and Cosgrove, M. (2011) *The Compatibility of Acceptable Behaviour Contracts with Article 6.1 of the European Convention on Human Rights*, Fair Play for Children. Available at: http://www.fairplayforchildren.org/pdf/1318907062.pdf.

Crawford, A. (2003) 'Contractual governance of deviant behaviour', *Journal of Law and Society*, 30(4): 479–505.

—— (2007) 'Situating restorative youth justice in crime control and prevention', *Acta Juridica*, 1–21.

—— (2008) 'Dispersal powers and the symbolic role of anti-social behaviour legislation', *Modern Law Review*, 71(5): 753–84.

—— (2009a) 'Governing through anti-social behaviour: regulatory challenges to criminal justice', *British Journal of Criminology*, 49(6): 810–31.

—— (2009b) 'Restorative justice and anti-social behaviour interventions as contractual governance', in P. Knepper, J. Shapland and J. Doak (eds) *Urban Crime Prevention, Surveillance, and Restorative Justice: Effects of Social Technologies*, London: Taylor & Francis, pp. 167–94.

—— (2010) 'Regulating civility, governing security and policing (dis)order under conditions of uncertainty', in J. Blad, M. Hildebrandt, K. Rozemond, M. Schuilenburg and P. Van Calster (eds) *Governing Security under the Rule of Law*, The Hague: Eleven International Publishing, pp. 9–35.

Crawford, A., Lewis, S. and Traynor, P. (forthcoming) *Anti-Social Behaviour Interventions with Young People*, Bristol: Policy Press.

Crawford, A. and Lister, S. (2007) *The Use and Impact of Dispersal Orders: Sticking Plasters and Wake Up Calls*, Bristol: Policy Press.

Deci, E.L., Koestner, R. and Ryan, R.M. (1999) 'A meta-analytic review of experiments examining the effects of extrinsic rewards on intrinsic motivation', *Psychological Bulletin*, 125: 627–68.

Ericson, R. (2007) *Crime in an Insecure World*, Cambridge: Polity.

Field, F. (2010) *The Foundation Years: preventing poor children becoming poor adults*, London: The Stationery Office.

Freedland, M. and King, D. (2003) 'Contractual governance and illiberal contracts: Some problems of contractualism as an instrument of behaviour management by agencies of government', *Cambridge Journal of Economics*, 27: 465–77.

Furby, L. and Beyth-Marom, R. (1992) 'Risk taking in adolescence: A decisionmaking perspective', *Developmental Review* 12: 1–44.

Gatti, U. (1998) 'Ethical issues raised when early intervention is used to prevent crime', *European Journal on Criminal Policy and Research*, 6: 113–32.

Gil-Robles, A. (2005) *Report by the Commissioner for Human Rights on his Visit to the United Kingdom, 4–12 November 2004*, Strasburg: Council of Europe.

Greene, D. and Lepper, M.R. (1974) 'Effects of extrinsic rewards on children's subsequent intrinsic interest', *Child Development*, 45(4): 1141–5.

Gunningham, N. and Sinclair, D. (1998) 'Designing smart regulation', in N. Gunningham and P. Grabosky (eds) *Smart Regulation: Designing Environmental Policy*, Oxford: Oxford University Press.

Halpern, D., Bates, C., Mulgan, G. and Aldridge, S., with Beales, G. and Heathfield, A. (2004) *Personal Responsibility and Changing Behaviour: the state of knowledge and its implications for policy*, Prime Minister's Strategy Unit, London: Cabinet Office.

Home Office (2003) *Respect and Responsibility – Taking a Stand Against Anti-Social Behaviour*, London: Home Office.

——— (2004) *Preventative Approaches Targeting Young People in Local Authority Residential Care*, Development and Practice Report 14, London: Home Office.

——— (2006) *Rebalancing the Criminal Justice System in Favour of the Law-abiding Majority*, London: Home Office.

——— (2011) *More Effective Responses to Anti-Social Behaviour*, London: Home Office.

Hood, C., Rothstein, H. and Baldwin, R. (2001) *The Government of Risk: Understanding Risk Regulation Regimes*, Oxford: Oxford University Press.

House of Common's Committee of Public Accounts (2007) *Tackling Anti-Social Behaviour, Forty-fourth report of Session 2006–7*, London: Stationery Office.

Jayasuriya, K. (2002) 'The new contractualism: neo-liberal or democratic?' *Political Quarterly*, 309–20.

Jolls, C., Sunstein, C.R. and Thaler, R. (1998) 'A behavioral approach to law and economics', *Stanford Law Review*, 50: 1471–550.

Kahneman, D., Slovic, P., and Tversky, A. (1982) *Judgment Under Uncertainty: Heuristics and Biases*, New York: Cambridge University Press.

Le Grand, J. (2003) *Motivation, Agency and Public Policy*, Oxford: Oxford University Press.

Lepper, M.R. (1981) 'Intrinsic and extrinsic motivation in children: Detrimental effects of superfluous social controls', in W.A. Collins (ed.) *Aspects of the Development of Competence: The Minnesota Symposium on Child Psychology, Volume 4*, Hillsdale, NJ: Erlbaum, pp. 155–214.

Lepper, M.R., Greene, D. and Nisbett, R.E. (1973) 'Undermining children's intrinsic interest with extrinsic rewards: a test of the overjustification hypothesis', *Journal of Personality and Social Psychology*, 28: 129–37.

Levi, R. (2009) 'Making counter-law: on having no apparent purpose in Chicago', *British Journal of Criminology*, 49(2): 131–49.

Macdonald, S. (2007) 'ASBOs and control orders: two recurring themes, two apparent contradictions', *Parliamentary Affairs*, 60: 601–24.

Mair, G., Lloyd, C. and Hough, M. (1997) 'The limitations of reconviction rates', in G. Mair (ed.) *Evaluating the Effectiveness of Community Penalties*, Aldershot: Ashgate, pp. 34–46.

Matthews, R., Easton, H., Briggs, D. and Pease, K. (2007) *Assessing the Use and Impact of Anti-Social Behaviour Orders*, Bristol: The Policy Press.

McBarnet, D. (2003) 'When compliance is not the solution but the problem: from changes in law to changes in attitude', in V. Braithwaite (ed.) *Taxing Democracy: Understanding Tax Avoidance and Evasion*, Aldershot: Ashgate, pp. 229–44.

McCord, J. (1978) 'A thirty-year follow-up of treatment effects', *American Psychologist*, 33(3): 284–89.

Moran, M. (2003) *The British Regulatory State: High Modernism and Hyper Innovation*, Oxford: Oxford University Press.

Muncie, J. and Goldson, B. (2006) 'States of transition: convergence and diversity in international youth justice', in J. Muncie and B. Goldson (eds) *Comparative Youth Justice*, London: Sage, pp. 196–218.

Nutt, D. (2009) 'Estimating drug harms: A risky business', *Briefing 10*, London: Centre for Crime and Justice Studies.

O'Donoghue, T. and Rabin, M. (2001) 'Risky behavior among youths some issues from behavioral economics' in J. Gruber (ed.) *Risky Behavior Among Youths: An Economic Analysis*, Chicago: University of Chicago Press, pp. 29–67.

Ramsay, P. (2004) 'What is anti-social behaviour?', *Criminal Law Review*, 908–25.

—— (2009) 'The theory of vulnerable autonomy and the legitimacy of the civil preventive order', in B. McSherry, A. Norrie and S. Bronitt (eds) *Regulating Deviance: The Redirection of Criminalisation and the Futures of Criminal Law*, Oxford: Hart Publishing, pp. 109–39.

Robinson, G. and McNeill, F. (2008) 'Exploring the dynamics of compliance with community penalties', *Theoretical Criminology*, 12(4): 431–49.

Scottish Executive (2005) *'Sticks and Carrots': Guidance on Acceptable Behaviour Contracts*, Edinburgh: Scottish Executive.

Shute, S. (2004) 'New civil preventative orders', *Criminal Law Review*, 417–44.

Simester, A.P. and von Hirsch, A. (2006) 'Regulating offensive conduct through two-step prohibitions', in A. von Hirsch and A.P. Simester (eds) *Incivilities: Regulating Offensive Behaviour*, Oxford: Hart Publishing, pp. 173–94.

Squires, P. (2006) 'New labour and the politics of anti-social behaviour', *Critical Social Policy*, 26(1): 144–68.

Sunstein, C.R. (2007) *Worst-Case Scenarios*, Cambridge, MA: Harvard University Press.

Sunstein, C.R. and Thaler, R.H. (2003) 'Libertarian paternalism is not an oxymoron', *University of Chicago Law Review*, 70(4): 1159–202.

Thaler, R.H. and Sunstein, C.R. (2008) *Nudge: Improving Decisions About Health, Wealth, and Happiness*, New Haven: Yale University Press.

Tversky, A. and Kahneman, D. (1974) 'Judgment under uncertainty: Heuristics and biases', *Science*, 185(4157): 1124–31.

Tyler, T.R. (2006) *Why People Obey the Law*, Princeton: Princeton University Press.

—— (2011) *Why People Cooperate: The Role of Social Motivations*, Princeton: Princeton University Press.

Tyler, T.R. and Fagan, J. (2008) 'Why do people cooperate with the police?', *Ohio Journal of Criminal Law*, 6: 231–75.

Utting, D. (2004) 'Overview and conclusion', in C. Sutton, D. Utting and D. Farrington (eds) *Support from the Start: Working with Young Children and their Families to Reduce the Risks of Crime and Anti-Social Behaviour*, London: Department for Education and Skills.

van Swaaningen, R. (2008) 'Sweeping the street: civil society and community safety in Rotterdam', in J. Shapland (ed.) *Justice, Community and Civil Society: A Contested Terrain*, Cullompton: Willan, pp. 87–106.

Wain, N. with Burney, E. (2007) *The ASBO Wrong Turning – Dead End*, London: Howard League for Penal Reform.

Weithorn, L.A. and Campbell, S.B. (1982) 'The competency of children and adolescents to make informed treatment decisions', *Child Development*, 53(6): 1589–98.

White, S. (2003) *The Civic Minimum: On the Rights and Obligations of Economic Citizenship*, Oxford: Oxford University Press.

Wonnacott, C. (1999) 'The counterfeit contract – reform, pretence and muddled principles in the new referral order', *Child and Family Law Quarterly*, 11(3): 271–87.

Youth Justice Board (2006) *Anti-Social Behaviour Orders*, London: YJB.

Notes

1 Many of the specific powers referred to in this chapter are different in their legal status and implementation in Scotland and to a lesser extent Northern Ireland, as compared to England and Wales. Nevertheless, the broader trends and developments that they express are abundantly evident across the UK (see, for example, Crawford, 2008).

2 In addition to ASBOs, other examples of civil preventative orders include: the controversial (counter-terrorism related) control orders (which were replace in early 2011 with

terrorism prevention and investigation measures); football banning orders; foreign travel orders; sexual offences prevention orders; risk of sexual harm orders; drinking banning orders; and serious crime prevention orders (see Shute, 2004; Ramsay, 2009).

3 Although their basic legal structure is similar both to the long-standing application that a person be 'bound over to keep the peace' and to applications under various provisions relating to health and safety at work that originate in the nineteenth century, the immediate roots of the new civil preventive orders lie in legislative developments in the 1990s. The most closely related legal instrument in form is the Statutory Nuisance Abatement Notice, s.79 of the Environmental Protection Act 1990.

4 For example, police powers to disperse people from a designated dispersal zone under the Anti-Social Behaviour Act (s. 30) and designated public place under the Criminal Justice and Police Act 2001 (s. 13) or to avoid a risk of future drink-related disorder as provided by the Violent Crime Reduction Act 2006 (s. 27).

5 Such as the requirement under the Drugs Act 2005 (ss. 9 and 10) for those testing positive for specified Class A drugs whether or not charged with an offence to attend 'assessment' and family intervention tenancies, as well as acceptable behaviour contracts and parenting contracts.

6 Crime and Disorder Act 1998, s 1.

7 As enshrined under the Human Rights Act 1998.

8 As a consequence, a burden of proof almost indistinguishable from the criminal 'beyond reasonable doubt' applies in civil ASBO application hearings. This judicial compromise further clouds the civil/criminal distinction and institutionalises the use of civil hearings for crime control purposes.

9 For instance, the Cambridge-Somerville project of the 1930s (McCord, 1978).

10 Vociferously led and championed by its head and chief spokesperson, Louise Casey who, in 2011, was appointed by the Coalition Government as head of the new 'Troubled Families' Unit, in the Department of Communities and Local Government. The Unit is charged with targeting the 120,000 most troubled families through early intervention programmes.

11 An ISO is solely available for juveniles subject to an ASBO. The only analogous support order for adults is the drug intervention order, which is available where misuse of controlled drugs is associated with the anti-social behaviour.

12 Tversky and Kahneman's (1974) paper in *Science* highlighting the impact of heuristics and biases opened the way for much subsequent research which exposed the flawed nature of 'rational choice' and the assumption that people have well-defined preferences (or goals) and make decisions to maximise those preferences. Subsequent research has exposed the systemic errors in people's actual choices that fly in the face of what neo-classical economic theory predicts.

13 Up to the end of 2010, some 7,785 ASBOs were issued to young people aged 10–17 in England and Wales, over 38 per cent of the total (20,335).

14 Important steps have been made in this regard but more often by the courts rather than the legislature. For instance, it was left to the House of Lords in the landmark ruling of *Gillick v. West Norfolk and Wisbech Area Health Authority* ([1985] 3 All ER 402, HL) to empower minors to consent to medical treatment when they reach an age and maturity sufficient to judge what the treatment entails and to assess its benefits and disadvantages. This ruling was confirmed post Human Rights Act 1998 in *R. (Axon) v. Secretary of State for Health* ([1006] EWHC 37 (Admin)). But even here, the child's autonomy rights are not omnipotent. They must be balanced with her welfare rights or her 'developmental interests' (Cave, 2010: 5).

15 The name of a character in *The Water Babies* by Charles Kingsley.

INDEX